ᴅᴠᴏ

The New World of UN Peace Operations

The New World of UN Peace Operations

Learning to Build Peace?

Thorsten Benner, Stephan Mergenthaler,
and Philipp Rotmann

OXFORD
UNIVERSITY PRESS

OXFORD
UNIVERSITY PRESS

Great Clarendon Street, Oxford ox2 6DP

Oxford University Press is a department of the University of Oxford.
It furthers the University's objective of excellence in research, scholarship,
and education by publishing worldwide in

Oxford New York

Auckland Cape Town Dar es Salaam Hong Kong Karachi
Kuala Lumpur Madrid Melbourne Mexico City Nairobi
New Delhi Shanghai Taipei Toronto

With offices in

Argentina Austria Brazil Chile Czech Republic France Greece
Guatemala Hungary Italy Japan Poland Portugal Singapore
South Korea Switzerland Thailand Turkey Ukraine Vietnam

Oxford is a registered trade mark of Oxford University Press
in the UK and in certain other countries

Published in the United States
by Oxford University Press Inc., New York

British Library Cataloguing in Publication Data
Data available

Library of Congress Cataloging in Publication Data
Data available

Typeset by SPI Publisher Services, Pondicherry, India
Printed in Great Britain
on acid-free paper by
MPG Books Group, Bodmin and King's Lynn

ISBN 978-0-19-959488-7

3 5 7 9 10 8 6 4 2

Dedication

Hédi Annabi
Kai Buchholz
Renée Carrier
Luiz Carlos da Costa
Jan Olaf Hausotter
Simone Trudo
Nicole Valenta
Fred Wooldridge

Victims of the earthquake on January 12, 2010, in Haiti

Acknowledgments

This book would not exist if it were not for the large number of officials, colleagues, and friends who generously facilitated our journey into the world of peace operations.

The research for this book was funded by two grants from the German Foundation for Peace Research (Deutsche Stiftung Friedensforschung (DSF)), without whose support it would not have been possible for a young research institute to venture into a new field. We are very grateful to Volker Rittberger (the foundation's long-standing president) and Thomas Held (its managing director) for taking an early interest in the project, helping to sharpen its focus and providing wise counsel.

During the course of our research, we have benefited from the continuous exchange of ideas with a number of core partners. Ricardo Soares de Oliveira, now at Oxford University, brought us into a joint project with James Mayall at Cambridge University. He invited us to two stimulating workshops in Bellagio and Cambridge and helped shape some of the central themes of the project. Richard Caplan, also at Oxford University, provided indispensable suggestions for sharpening and placing the book manuscript. At the University of Konstanz, Wolfgang Seibel, Till Blume, Rainer Breul, and Julian Junk guided us through the world of public administration research. Colleagues at the Social Science Research Center (WZB), Berlin, in particular Ariane Berthoin Antal, Michael Zürn, Martin Binder, Kathrin Böhling, Marthias Ecker-Erhardt, and Monika Heupel, provided critical feedback in workshops and colloquiums. At the Center for Peace Operations (ZIF), Berlin, Winrich Kühne, Almut Wieland-Karimi, Wibke Hansen, Tobias Pietz, and Leopold von Carlowitz offered critical contacts and insights. At New York University, Richard Gowan, Bruce Jones, and Simon Chesterman generously shared their detailed knowledge of the UN apparatus. Scott Gilmore at the Peace Dividend Trust provided support and inspiration as a model to strive for in terms of promoting innovation in peace operations. Bill Durch at the Stimson Center went far beyond the call of duty to provide feedback on crucial aspects of the book. The late Ernst Haas provided part of the inspiration for this book.

Closer to home, we would like to thank our colleagues at the Global Public Policy Institute (GPPi) in Berlin, in particular Björn Conrad, Steffen Eckhard,

Wade Hoxtell, Kai Koddenbrock, Claudia Meier, Joel Sandhu, Julia Steets, Jan Martin Witte, and Wolfgang Reinicke, the institute's director, for providing a stimulating work environment and a constant source of support. Our GPPi colleague Andrea Binder helped build the intellectual foundations for the book during a pilot project. Hannes Ebert provided outstanding research assistance on the chapter on reintegration during a crucial phase of the project. Throughout the five years of research, we relied on the support of a number of dedicated research assistants: Ramsey Ben-Achour, Sarah Brockmeier, Hauke Broecker, Julian Detzel, Eric Edwards, James Eley, Leo Ghione, Jakob Hensing, James Hollway, Jihae Kim, Oliver Krentz, Mitja Müller, Alex Odlum, Jan Ortgies, Dan Pasternak, Laura Peitz, Justin Sosne, Joshua Tartakovsky, and Clara Weinhardt.

Our understanding of peace operations relies on the time and insights offered by a large number of officials who despite their gruelling schedules made time for research interviews in person in New York, in the field (Haiti, Liberia, Timor-Leste), and on the phone. Due to the confidential nature of the interviews, we cannot list all interviewees. We would like to thank Jean-Marie Guéhenno, former Under-Secretary-General in the UN Department of Peacekeeping Operations (DPKO), for agreeing to share reflections on his tenure and reform agenda. Key members of his dedicated team also generously shared their time, insights, and enthusiasm for improving peace operations with us: Salman Ahmed, David Haeri, David Harland, Eiko Ikegaya, Paul Keating, Sébastien Lapierre, Kyoko Ono, Ed Rees, Ugo Solinas, and Fatemeh Ziai. Also in New York, Dominik Bartsch, Meg Carey, Andrew Hughes, Robert Pulver, Hansjörg Strohmeyer, Dmitry Titov, and Margareta Wahlström generously gave their time and experience to support our research.

Suzanne Granfar, Radhika Padayachi, and Alex Rose were wonderful hosts in Timor-Leste, where Wolfgang Weisbrod-Weber shared his insights as a longtime insider of peacekeeping and José Caetano Guterres, Agio Pereira, Casimiro Dos Santos, Sophia Cason, and Ed Rees helped us better understand local perspectives. Asith Bhattacharjee, Ekkehard Griep, Dionne Maxwell, Uli Schiefelbein, and Yang Wang opened doors in Liberia. Chris Stone, Christine Cole, and Brian Welch at the Harvard Kennedy School's Program in Criminal Justice Policy and Management provided the opportunity for Philipp Rotmann's research trip to Haiti. In Port-au-Prince, Kai Buchholz, Ann Frotscher, Jan Olaf Hausotter, Eric Mouillefarine, Fred Wooldridge, and Nicole Valenta were very generous with their time and hospitality, as were Hédi Annabi and Luiz Carlos da Costa in sharing their accumulated wisdom spanning several decades in the service of the United Nations. Eight months later, many of them lost their lives in the line of duty during the catastrophic earthquake of January 12, 2010. We dedicate this book to their memory and that of the other victims of this tragedy.

At various stages of the project, the following individuals provided important feedback and support: René Aubry, Séverine Autesserre, Michael Barnett, Michael W. Bauer, Mats Berdal, Raphael Bossong, Fabian Breuer, Susanna Campbell, Andrew Carpenter, Scott N. Carlson, Sven Chojnacki, Christopher Daase, Michael Doyle, Klaus Dingwerth, Sebastian von Einsiedel, Stefan Feller, Kai Fischbach, Annika Hansen, Anna Herrhausen, Dietmar Herz, Markus Jachtenfuchs, Kathleen Jennings, Ian Johnstone, Anja Kaspersen, Dieter Kerwer, Mark Kroeker, Dan Large, Sergey Lagodinsky, Andrea Liese, Michael Lipson, Ed Luck, Tim Maurer, Heiko Nitzschke, Timo Noetzel, Richard Monk, Robert Muggah, Thant Myint-U, Gordon Peake, Susanne Pihs, Ian Quick, Thomas Rid, Thomas Risse, Maria Elisabeth Rotter, John Ruggie, Henriette Sachse, Monika Schlicher, Ulrich Schneckener, Bernd Siebenhüner, Anne-Marie Slaughter, Johannes Varwick, Richard Warren, Silke Weinlich, Peter Wittig, Bernhard Zangl, and Dominik Zaum.

We very much profited from the detailed comments and suggestions provided by the anonymous reviewers of the research proposal and the book manuscript. Jenny Lunsford, Sarah Parker, and Elizabeth Suffling at Oxford University Press supported by Abhirami Ravikumar skilfully guided the production of the book. Dominic Byatt, chief editor at OUP, took on our project with great enthusiasm and patiently shepherded a trio of novice authors through the vagaries of turning a proposal into a book. We could not have wished for a better publishing partner.

Table of Contents

List of Figures and Table

Abbreviations

ACABQ	Advisory Committee on Administrative and Budgetary Questions (UN)
ASG	Assistant Secretary-General
AU	African Union
BCPR	Bureau for Crisis Prevention and Recovery (UNDP)
CEB	Chief Executives Board (of the UN agencies and programs)
CIVPOL	Civilian police
CLJAU	Criminal Law and Judicial Advisory Unit (UN DPKO)
COESPU	Center of Excellence for Stability Police Units
DDR	Disarmament, Demobilization, and Reintegration
DFS	Department of Field Support (UN)
DPA	Department of Political Affairs (UN)
DPI	Department of Public Information (UN)
DPKO	Department of Peacekeeping Operations (UN)
DRC	Democratic Republic of Congo
DSF	Deutsche Stiftung Friedensforschung
DSRSG	Deputy Special Representative of the Secretary-General
ECHA	Executive Committee on Humanitarian Affairs (UN)
ECPS	Executive Committee on Peace and Security (UN)
ERC	Emergency Relief Coordinator
EU	European Union
FC	Force Commander
FPU	Formed Police Unit
GA	General Assembly (UN)
HC	Humanitarian Coordinator (OCHA)
IDDRS	Integrated Disarmament, Demobilization, and Reintegration Standards
ILO	International Labor Organization
IMPP	Integrated Mission Planning Process
IMTF	Integrated Mission Task Force
IO	International organization
IPAC	International Policing Advisory Council
IPTF	International Police Task Force (UN)
IR	International Relations as a discipline
ITS	Integrated Training Service (UN DPKO)

JMAC	Joint Mission Analysis Centre
KFOR	Kosovo Force (NATO)
MINUSTAH	Mission des Nations Unies pour la Stabilisation en Haïti
NATO	North Atlantic Treaty Organization
NGO	Non-governmental organization
OCHA	Office for the Coordination of Humanitarian Affairs (UN)
OHCHR	Office of the High Commissioner for Human Rights (UN)
OL	Organizational learning
ONUC	Opération des Nations Unies au Congo
ONUSAL	Misión de Observadores de las Naciones Unidas en El Salvador
OROLSI	Office of Rule of Law and Security Institutions (UN DPKO)
OSCE	Organisation for Security and Co-operation in Europe
PBPS	Peacekeeping Best Practices Section (UN DPKO)
PBSO	Peacebuilding Support Office (UN)
PC	Police Commander
QIP	Quick Impact Project
RBB	Results-Based Budgeting (UN)
RC	Resident Coordinator (UNDP)
RUF	Revolutionary United Front
SC	Security Council (UN)
SFOR	Stabilization Force (NATO)
SG	Secretary-General (UN)
SOP	Standard Operating Procedure
SPC	Standing Police Capacity (UN DPKO)
SRSG	Special Representative of the Secretary-General
UK	United Kingdom
UN	United Nations
UNAMSIL	United Nations Assistance Mission in Sierra Leone
UNDP	United Nations Development Programme
UNEF	United Nations Emergency Force
UNHCR	United Nations High Commissioner for Refugees
UNICEF	United Nations Children's Fund
UNIFEM	United Nations Development Fund for Women
UNITAR	United Nations Institute for Training and Research
UNMIK	United Nations Interim Administration Mission in Kosovo
UNMIL	United Nations Mission in Liberia
UNMIS	United Nations Mission in Sudan
UNMISET	United Nations Mission of Support in Timor-Leste
UNMIT	United Nations Mission in Timor-Leste
UNODC	United Nations Office on Drugs and Crime
UNPOL	United Nations Police
UNPROFOR	United Nations Protection Force
UNSAS	United Nations Stand-by Arrangements System

UNTAET	United Nations Transitional Administration in East Timor
UNTSO	United Nations Truce Supervision Organization
US	United States of America
USG	Under-Secretary-General
USIP	United States Institute for Peace
WFP	World Food Programme

1

Introduction

In May 2003, Sergio Vieira de Mello was tasked to establish a new UN peace operation in Iraq. In his view, the UN would be most useful in postwar Iraq as a 'knowledge mission,' offering advice to the US-led occupation based on its rich institutional experience in post-conflict reconstruction. He asked UN headquarters in New York to send him the key lessons from the organization's decade-long experience in building police forces in post-conflict settings from Haiti to Bosnia. To his dismay, the UN had nothing on hand to respond to his request. All existing experience on policing, like most other peacebuilding activities, was confined to a few dozen key practitioners many of whom had left the UN after a few years. The organization as a whole had failed to invest in gathering lessons and developing doctrine and guidance; hence, Vieira de Mello returned to Baghdad empty-handed.[1]

Three years earlier, in the spring of 2000, Vieira de Mello had sat down to write a paper on his experience as the United Nations transitional administrator in Kosovo and East Timor, heading the organization's most ambitious peace operations to date. Under the title 'How Not To Run A Country: Lessons for the UN from Kosovo and East Timor,' he points to the many shortcomings of the organization's efforts: the lack of preparedness, the dilemmas of executive authority and local ownership, the lack of focus on the maintenance of law and order, and the turf wars between agencies. He concluded that: 'To date the UN, like many other large bureaucracies, has proven more adept at repeating mistakes, than at learning lessons. Time to change' (Vieira de Mello 2000: 21). His superiors in New York thought otherwise and denied him permission to publish his lessons (Power 2008: 342).

De Mello's experience with the institutional weakness of learning in the UN is far from unique. Alvaro de Soto, another senior UN diplomat, quipped that 'no wheel shall go un-reinvented' (Chesterman 2004: 256). This unwritten

---

[1] Interview with senior UN official, New York, May 2008.

rule was only broken in the wake of catastrophic events such as the UN's failures in preventing genocide and mass atrocities in Rwanda and Srebrenica that prompted organization-wide soul-searching and reflection on the highest order questions of intervention (Jones 2007). If not prompted by catastrophe, there were few, if any, efforts at organization-wide learning on the key tasks of peace operations. Learning did occur within individual missions but the lessons did not feed into the organization at large (Howard 2008). If experience traveled between missions, then it did so in an unsystematic and dangerous way: peacekeepers took the template from the last mission they served in and used it in their next assignment. Often against their own better judgment, born from the pressure to get a new mission running in the absence of adequate capacity for analysis, planning, and learning, they followed the logic that 'what served us well in Sierra Leone also has to work in Haiti.' Unsurprisingly, reality often proved this 'copy & paste' logic wrong. For a long time, the organization did not have procedures in place to reflect on these outright failures in a systematic way.

This was a direct consequence of the United Nations' failure to invest in the learning capacity of the peace operations bureaucracy. This was also the diagnosis offered by the landmark 'Report of the Panel on UN Peace Operations,' issued in August 2000 and widely known as the 'Brahimi report' after the panel's chairman, former Algerian foreign minister Lakhdar Brahimi. The panel stressed that 'not enough has been done to improve the system's ability to tap that (field) experience or to feed it back into the development of operational doctrine, plans, procedures or mandates' (United Nations 2000: 39). While the Brahimi report was being prepared, Secretary-General Kofi Annan appointed Jean-Marie Guéhenno, a French scholar-diplomat, to be the world's top peacekeeper and lead the Department of Peacekeeping Operations (DPKO). As he prepared for the new assignment, Guéhenno quickly came to share the Brahimi report's diagnosis on the weakness of doctrine, planning, and knowledge management at the bureaucratic heart of a sprawling UN peace operations apparatus.

For Guéhenno, trained as a French administrator, it was striking that DPKO was neither a fully developed bureaucracy nor a modern institution that valued the importance of knowledge. In a number of ways, DPKO in 2000 reminded him more of a feudal system than a rational bureaucracy. Personal allegiances and networks ruled and there was a lack of standard operating procedures covering even the most central tasks such as starting a new mission. These glaring institutional gaps were the legacy of the early decades of peacekeeping during the Cold War in which a small number of peacekeepers had been deployed as neutral observers to a peace settlement or armistice line. In their time, as Brian Urquhart (1998 [1993]: 268) fondly recalls in his biography of Ralph Bunche, the old boys' club of officials running peacekeeping all conveniently fitted around a single conference table in the UN's New York headquarters. For decades thereafter, the old boys were the living institutional memory of peacekeeping.

When Guéhenno went on a series of field visits to Sierra Leone, Bosnia, and Kosovo in the summer of 2000 prior to assuming his post in New York the reality of peace operations had changed dramatically. The visits gave Guéhenno a taste of what the situation felt like on the ground when the UN Security Council mandated ever more missions in ever more difficult environments with ever more complex mandates. After the failed attempt of the 1990s, it was the world powers' second try to realize the original promise of an active and effective UN role in building peace – and the second chance for the world organization to rise to the challenge after the end of the Cold War. This trend of expansion in every dimension came to define the first decade of the twenty-first century – not just in number but also in scope. Between June 1999 and 2010, UN peace operations grew by a factor of eight in terms of personnel and by a factor of ten in terms of budget, reaching 125,000 troops, police, and civilians deployed in July 2010. A far cry from the 'thin blue line' separating opposing armies and reporting armistice violations in the Middle East, their tasks have come to include 'to support political transitions, humanitarian response, security sector reform, economic recovery, human rights reform, the build-up of rule of law institutions' (Roy 2009: 17). In the words of leading scholar Michael Barnett, today's ambitious post-conflict peace-building efforts 'imagine transforming political, economic, social, and cultural structures to promote what is broadly understood to be a more progressive, peaceful, and prosperous country' (Barnett 2011: 126).

For Guéhenno, it was clear that with their sprawling growth and increasing complexity, modern peace operations are an inherently knowledge-based venture. But all too often, the UN blue helmets, policemen, and other civilian officials were not attuned to this new world of peace operations. They were 'flying blind' in their efforts to stabilize countries ravaged by war. With peace operations having become the UN's multibillion-dollar flagship activity and millions in otherwise forgotten places from Timor-Leste to the Democratic Republic of the Congo pinning their hopes for peace and stability on the blue flag of the United Nations, it was downright irresponsible to have officials effectively flying blind when going about their tasks and where achieving even moderate success in the face of adverse conditions on the ground requires exceptional individual leadership. If UN missions stood any chance of succeeding with their ambitious mandates of helping to transform war-ravaged societies and build institutions, the organization needed to shape up. The UN peace operations bureaucracy, Guéhenno argued, needed to become an organization that works for and can be made to work by the average staff member. As part of professionalizing its operations, it needed to put

3

knowledge, doctrine development, and systematic reflection on failures and successes at the center of the organization. In other words: the UN peace operations apparatus had to transform itself into a 'learning organization' – a goal that the entire system of UN agencies set for itself not much later (UN CEB 2003).

Guéhenno's rationale was straightforward: UN officials in the field find themselves in a fragile and fluid organization set up on the fly. Staff turnover is high and planning horizons for new deployments are very short. Officials on the ground come from very different professional and cultural backgrounds to work together on very complex challenges that many see as mission impossible. To have a fighting chance to achieve the goals set by the Security Council in New York officials on the ground at the very least need a common frame of reference, a common understanding, and vision of how to go about their task. They need to have fora for exchanging experience with their peers from other missions. And they need to be enabled and encouraged to help the organization as a whole to reflect on successes and failures and build up a common knowledge base.

With his leadership and support, a new generation of younger UN officials who joined headquarters after having gained first-hand field experience in the 1990s developed an ambitious reform agenda to remake the peace operations bureaucracy as a more professional learning organization. Starting in late 2003, months after the tragic death of Sergio Vieira de Mello in Iraq, they designed new systems for guidance development and knowledge management, taking their cues as much from the private sector as from effective public sector organizations as varied as the World Bank and the Indian Army.

This is when the real work began: the reformers needed to convince their own fellow officials and their powerful principals, the UN's member states, of the virtues of their reform agenda. While they could build on the arguments and momentum generated by the Brahimi report, they faced an uphill battle with both their own bureaucracy and member states. After all, building up a learning organization is costly: significant investment in terms of money and in terms of time would be needed. Time is a particularly precious resource in an organization in a constant emergency mode where there is always an urgent crisis here and now that requires attention. The reform agenda also challenged the established organizational culture. Many seasoned peacekeeping officials thought of 'knowledge management' and the 'learning organization' as business school fads utterly inappropriate to pursue for an international bureaucracy priding itself on political judgment rather than management speak.

More fundamentally, the reformer's quest to professionalize the peace operations bureaucracy ran counter to a traditionally skeptical body of scholarship about learning in large organizations, particularly in political bureaucracies (Crozier 1964). The literature argues that because bureaucracies are insulated from the competitive pressures of the market place they are unlikely to learn unless confronted with major catastrophes threatening organizational survival.

Against these odds, the evolution of the peace operations bureaucracy during the past decade of expansion presents an intriguing laboratory to explore a fundamental question that affects our understanding not just of peace operations but of international organizations more generally: how exactly does the UN learn in peace operations and what are the factors enabling and hindering learning? Academic research has thus far neglected this pressing question – missing out on an opportunity to advance research on international organizations in a critically important field. Our book seeks to close this gap through a conceptually innovative and empirically rich analysis of learning in UN peace operations. It provides a critical 'organizational biography' of the UN peace operations bureaucracy and its attempt to turn itself into a learning organization.

Empirical Focus and Case Selection

While there are about as many definitions of peacebuilding as there are actors using it (Barnett et al. 2007), the practice of UN peace operations has mostly followed the canonical definition of Secretary-General Boutros-Ghali's Agenda for Peace: 'rebuilding the institutions and infrastructures of nations torn by civil war … which will tend to strengthen and solidify peace in order to avoid a relapse into conflict' (Boutros-Ghali 1992: para. 15, 21). In this sense, peacebuilding describes an expansive set of activities distinct from either traditional or robust peacekeeping, that is, the deployment of a neutral military-diplomatic mission to observe and potentially enforce the terms of an armistice agreement and/or a mandate handed down by the UN Security Council. The mandates of modern peace operations essentially fused peace-keeping and peacebuilding tasks in a way that also blurred the line between the responsibilities of DPKO and those of the roughly three dozen other Secretariat departments, funds, programs, and agencies that have come to engage in some aspect of civilian peacebuilding.

This multidimensional nature of modern peace operations features prominently in our case studies, several of which transcend organizational boundaries. At the same time, our analytical focus lies squarely with DPKO, the political and administrative center of the peace operations bureaucracy and the only UN organization whose core business is peace operations. To select DPKO as the 'focal organization' is also a conscious choice in favor of going deep rather than broad in this ambitious first cut at analyzing organizational learning in UN peace operations as a whole. Given the sheer size and diversity of the sprawling network of organizations in the UN family, a single study was not going to be able to do equal justice to the knowledge management and learning efforts at the Department of Political Affairs (DPA)'s Policy Planning and Mediation Support Unit, the Office for the Coordination of Humanitarian Affairs (OCHA)'s Policy Development and Studies Branch, the Bureau for Crisis Prevention and Recovery at the UN Development Programme (UNDP), the Conflict Cluster at the UN Development Organizations Coordination Office, and the Peacebuilding Support Office's Policy Analysis Branch. They will hopefully be at the center of future research to trace learning.

For the decade following the publication of the Brahimi report in August 2000, we zoom into a dozen cases of attempted learning across four policy domains in peacebuilding: police assistance (within the area of security), judicial reform (institution-building), reintegration of former combatants (social and economic rehabilitation), and mission integration (as a crosscutting challenge). For three cases per domain, we trace in detail how a particular group within the bureaucracy, based on new knowledge or experience, framed some part of existing practice as a problem and their proposal as its solution, advocated for 'learning the lesson,' and either failed or succeeded in getting their proposal officially adopted and implemented. The approach of analyzing learning within issue areas rather than within missions allows us to track organization-wide rather than mission-specific processes over a longer period of time.[2] For learning to be of lasting consequence for the organization at large the process needs to go beyond individual missions.

Our case studies have been selected in order to maximize variation along three dimensions: the subject of proposed lessons, the organizational context, and different outcomes along the learning cycle. *First* and foremost, we chose our cases so that they represent a broad cross section of the core activities of modern peace operations, especially the expansion of civilian and political institution-building. We picked three cases each from the following four thematic clusters: police assistance (security), judicial reform (governance), reintegration of former combatants (welfare), and mission integration within the UN system (as a crosscutting challenge). Spreading our cases out in this way covers a number of potential sources of variation, such as the extent of organizational experience, differences in the structural setup and resource endowment, diverging organizational subcultures, as well as qualitative differences in the political climate of UN action in each field. In line with the scope of this

---

[2] The only other study on learning in UN peace operations on the global academic market, Lise Morjé Howard's *UN Peacekeeping in Civil Wars*, chooses to limit itself to analyzing learning *within* particular UN missions. Howard briefly touches on organization-wide learning ('second-order learning'), but given that she focuses on the UN missions of the 1990s, when there was very little organization-wide capacity for learning, this remains an afterthought in her analysis (Howard 2008).

book and the use of the term at the UN, the chapter on 'mission integration' limits its focus on integration among the different components of UN peace operations (military, police, diplomatic, human rights, etc., formally delimited by the scope of the mission budget) and the various humanitarian and development agencies within the UN family. They include, among others, OCHA, UNDP, the UN High Commissioner for Refugees (UNHCR), the World Food Programme (WFP), UNICEF, and the World Bank. To include other international organizations such as NATO, EU, or AU, bilateral donors and diplomatic missions or even NGOs would have required its own book.

Second, our twelve case studies vary according to the ambition of change sought by the proponents of learning. There is no general way of measuring such ambition, as it may take fundamentally different forms. One 'ambitious' lesson may seek sweeping changes to the formal structure of the organization or require substantial financial commitments while another may aim for a wholesale transformation of a politically sensitive doctrine on building security institutions or dealing with informal systems of justice. We selected cases reflecting each of these dimensions of ambition at different levels. At the same time, to keep our analysis firmly anchored on the political core business of peacebuilding, we did not choose any of the purely technical – although quite consequential – exercises of learning in which administrators strive for increased efficiency (e.g., in logistics).

Third, while all of our cases reached a minimum level of progress and entered at least the advocacy stage of the learning cycle, outcomes vary widely between rapid failure and abandonment, long periods of stalling and revival, to the successful adoption of a lesson whose destiny in terms of institutionalization often remains wide open. The missing extremes are rarely if ever observable in the peace operations apparatus. In the case of immediate failures, this is because lessons that never made it beyond the stage of knowledge acquisition at the level of a small, often informal group leave very little in terms of a paper trail which researchers might find. The opposite extreme, full-cycle success (including a completed feedback loop to evaluate and adjust the lesson implemented), has simply not been possible for most of the period under review in this book as the bureaucracy's learning infrastructure has only slowly built up its support systems for training, evaluation, and review.

Research Context

This book draws on three main strands of research: the study of international organizations, organizational learning, and peace operations. First, we build on the revival of scholarship combining the analytical approaches of organization studies and international relations (IR) in studying international organizations.[3] The rebirth of interest in international organizations as organizations rather than just negotiating tables for the great powers has gained momentum with the publication of Michael Barnett's and Martha Finnemore's 'Rules for the World: International Organizations in Global Politics' (2004), which builds on their seminal 1999 piece in 'International Organization' (Barnett and Finnemore 1999). Since then, a number of studies have been published that zoom into the work of international bureaucracies (see e.g., Weaver 2008; Biermann and Siebenhüner 2009a). While these studies differ in their assessment of their work,[4] they share a concern with better understanding a unique set of organizations mandated to execute some of the most ambitious tasks in global governance and whose work affects the lives (and often the survival) of millions around the world. Peace operations are a prime example. We need a better analysis of the work of international bureaucracies in this field because 'millions depend on UN peace operations as the main bulwark between state collapse and hopes for peace' (Roy 2009: 15). In turn, peace operations with their complex range of activities offer rich and challenging empirical material for refining concepts and methods for the study of international organizations.

Second, we draw on a rich literature on organizational learning in different academic disciplines. Within the discipline of IR, we build on the pioneering work conducted by Ernst B. Haas in the 1980s.[5] While there are a number recent studies dealing with learning in international organizations (see, e.g., Senghaas-Knobloch et al. 2003; Böhling 2007; Siebenhüner 2008), understanding knowledge-based change in international organizations is still a niche concern in IR. While there is a broad literature on organizational learning in other disciplines, most of it has so far ignored international bureaucracies as research objects. The two most prominent volumes which took stock of research on organizational learning do not make any reference to international bureaucracies (Dierkes et al. 2001; Easterby-Smith 2005). At the same time, research in organization studies, public administration, and business administration as well as a long tradition of scholarship on learning in military organizations have valuable insights to offer that we incorporate in our conceptual framework. In turn, we hope that our study helps to lay the groundwork for a comparative agenda on learning that includes public, non-profit, and business organizations.

---

[3] See Benner et al. (2009) for a detailed discussion of the broader research agenda on international bureaucracies.

[4] Barnett and Finnemore, for example, put a lot of emphasis on the power-seeking nature and the pathologies of international bureaucracies, whereas Biermann and Siebenhüner argue that 'international bureaucracies [are] more often interested in resolving political problems than increasing their power as such' (Biermann and Siebenhüner 2009b: 8).

[5] Haas (1990) focuses on issues of sustainable development and his work remains mainly typological without engaging in an in-depth tracing of learning processes.

Third, we contribute to the literature on UN peace operations and peace- and statebuilding more broadly (for surveys of the field, see Call and Cousens 2008; Fortna and Howard 2008). Research in this area has produced a number of excellent overview studies (Chesterman 2004; Paris 2004; Caplan 2005; Berdal 2009). With the exception of the book by Howard (2008), none of the contributions deals with the issue of organizational learning in greater depth. This book is the first one to focus at organization-wide processes of learning in the UN peace operations apparatus. We aim to provide an assessment of the development of the UN's learning capacity in this field, as well as to add to the understanding of the ambitious civilian-led institution-building components of today's multidimensional peace operations which have greatly increased the complexity and dilemmas of such undertakings (Paris and Sisk 2009). As such, our in-depth tracing of developments and lessons learned in four core areas of peace operations (police, judicial reform, reintegration of former combatants, and mission integration) also seeks to be of value to the broader political debate on the future of peace operations.

Method

Introducing their landmark study on international bureaucracies, Michael Barnett and Martha Finnemore (2004: IX) observe: 'There has been an important revival of interest in international organizations, but remarkably little empirical research gets inside these organizations to see how they work.' Opening up the 'black box' of international organizations requires in-depth empirical analysis before jumping to general conclusions. We benefited from access to internal documents as well as officials, diplomats, and key policymakers at the UN and among member states to reconstruct the paper trail as well as the bureaucratic and political reality of our twelve case studies of attempted learning. Over five years we conducted extensive personal interviews with over 250 UN officials, diplomats, activists, and experts at UN headquarters in New York and in peace operations in Asia (Timor-Leste), Africa (Liberia), and the Caribbean (Haiti). Since many UN officials frequently rotate between missions we had the opportunity to talk to veterans of a number of additional field operations during these trips, complementing our desk research and telephone interviews to illuminate key aspects of our case studies that took place in the Democratic Republic of the Congo, in Sierra Leone or Sudan.

To guide our research into the heavily politicized international bureaucracy that manages UN peace operations, we relied on a multidisciplinary framework bringing together insights from international relations, public administration, business management, and organization studies. Combining classical insights into bureaucratic decision-making with approaches that account for the role of knowledge and political power, we adapted the concept of organizational learning to the context of international bureaucracies. We understand organizational learning as a knowledge-based process of questioning and changing organizational rules to change organizational practice – in our case, UN peace operations.

We use the method of process tracing to track learning processes along a cyclical model of learning through the three stages of knowledge acquisition, advocacy, and institutionalization that we introduce in Chapter 3. The operationalization of learning falls into two parts: the change of rules – to the extent to which those rules are formally condensed in written form – is made visible in written documents (standard operating procedures, training, and guidance documents). The other part of learning – the questioning and advocacy – is made visible in a mixture of written notes (lessons learned reports, memoranda/proposals for change, as far as such documents are accessible), complemented by semi-standardized interviews with staff placed at the 'nodes' of the learning process.

Outline of the Book

Chapter 2 outlines the trends that define the learning challenge in peace operations, followed by an overview of the UN's institutional response: professionalizing its operations with the goal of becoming a learning organization. Three key trends define the reality of peacekeeping in the twenty-first century: growth, a new formula for the use of force and the increasing scope of mandates to include complex institution-building in post-conflict settings. As a response to these trends, a new generation of peace operations managers led a comprehensive reform effort with the goal of building an effective learning infrastructure and, ultimately, of transforming the peace operations bureaucracy into a learning organization. In closely following their efforts and the obstacles they encountered, the institutional context for learning in UN peace operations becomes clear as it shapes each of the twelve case studies of learning attempts at the core of the book.

Before we get to the case studies, Chapter 3 elaborates a framework for the study of organizational learning in the UN peace operations bureaucracy. We briefly survey the relevant academic literature from the fields of international relations, public administration, and organization theory to identify building blocks for a framework of organizational learning in an international bureaucracy. Based on these elements, we present our definition of organizational learning and the learning cycle as a heuristic model for analyzing the process dimension of learning. We then discuss the range of variables that help or hinder the learning process. We distinguish between broadly structural properties that make up the learning infrastructure of an organization on the one hand, and political factors covering the dimension of human and social agency on the other hand.

Chapters 4–7 present our twelve case studies of learning in four key fields of peace operations: police assistance, judicial reform, reintegration of former combatants, and the crosscutting challenge of mission integration. Each of the four chapters in the second part of the book follows the same basic outline. First we introduce the key challenges and particularities with regard to learning in the respective field of activity. Then we present three case studies of (attempted) learning before closing with an analysis of the crucial factors affecting the learning processes in each field.

Chapter 8 summarizes the findings and presents a research agenda and our conclusions for the future of learning and the evolution of UN peace operations.

2

Twenty-First-Century Peace Operations: Learning Challenges and the Evolution of Organizational Capacity

This chapter sets out the context of UN peace operations that shaped the requirement as well as the constraints for organizational learning over the past decade. This context is defined by three political trends which have profoundly changed the nature of peace operations since the 1990s, and the institutional response of the 'peace operations bureaucracy' – a fragmented organization that consists of the field missions themselves as well as various departments and agencies involved in strategic and support roles.

The core of the peace operations bureaucracy is the Department of Peacekeeping Operations (DPKO) in the UN Secretariat.[1] The department assists the Secretary-General and the intergovernmental bodies such as the Security Council, the General Assembly, and their various committees and working groups in their policymaking roles. DPKO is also the key bureaucratic actor (and some areas the only one) to plan, equip, deploy, supply, and control each of the fifteen to nineteen peace operations deployed globally at any one time during this decade. At the same time, many of the tasks of modern peace operations require the collaboration with many other departments and agencies within the UN system and beyond, and the need to coordinate with these actors has been an increasingly critical task for DPKO.

This chapter begins by analyzing the three defining trends for peace operations in the first decade of the twenty-first century and by explaining the learning challenges that result from each. The second part of the chapter turns to the peace operations bureaucracy, charting its institutional response to these challenges and the obstacles encountered along the way. Beginning in

---

[1] In 2008, the administrative part of DPKO was spun off as a new Department of Field Support (DFS). As our case studies are most concerned with political and operational questions that remain in DPKO's hands, we refer to DFS only where necessary.

2000, a comprehensive reform effort took shape with the goal of building an effective learning infrastructure and, ultimately, transforming the peace operations apparatus into a learning organization. By following these developments closely, the institutional context for learning in UN peace operations becomes clear as it shapes each of the twelve case studies of learning attempts analyzed in Chapters 4–7.

Trends and Challenges in UN Peace Operations

As the 1990s drew to a close, UN peace operations were in crisis. Post-Cold War euphoria about humanitarian intervention had waned and, in the eyes of many, the instrument of blue helmets had been discredited by the failure to prevent the 1994 genocide in Rwanda and the 1995 massacres in the Bosnian town of Srebrenica. As a result, the Western powers had largely turned away from the UN for peace operations. The fiftieth anniversary of peacekeeping in 1998 was such a somber occasion that the UN's top peacekeeper, Under-Secretary-General Bernard Miyet, felt it necessary to affirm that 'there is still a role for the United Nations peacekeeping operations' (UN DPI 1998). Less than a year later, there were fewer peacekeepers under the blue flag than ever before or after in the post-Cold War period. The UN deployed less than 15,000 soldiers, police officers, and international civilian experts globally, which is less than a fifth of the 75,000 deployed only four years previously. The state of peacekeeping in early 1999 looked nearly the same as it did in 1988, almost as if the 1990s had never happened at all. Most missions, many of which had existed for decades, followed the traditional model of ceasefire monitoring between the territories of erstwhile belligerents. The only two exceptions were the operations in Bosnia and Haiti, where UN Civilian Police officers attempted to retrain and reform local security agencies. And in New York, amid the increasingly confrontational North–South politics, the majority of developing countries in the General Assembly forced the Secretary-General to send home all military personnel that (mostly Western) governments had provided free of charge to the organization, depriving DPKO of a substantial part of its capacity.

Then, in quick succession, everything changed. In June 1999, the Security Council presented the Secretariat with the unprecedented mandate to establish a transitional administration for Kosovo alongside a NATO force in charge of security. A few months later, in October, the Council dispatched UN blue helmets to East Timor to replace an Australian-led peace enforcement mission and to establish another temporary government for the tiny island nation's transition to independence. In parallel, it tasked DPKO to deploy a further 6,000 troops to Sierra Leone. In November, it mandated another mission to the Democratic Republic of the Congo that would later become the largest and most expensive peace operation for years to come. In short, the turn of the century marked a world made anew for peacekeeping. Within just twelve months, UN peace operations tripled in size, marking the dawn of a period of renewed confidence and sometimes overconfidence in peace operations. The first decade of the twenty-first century would stretch the UN peace operations apparatus to its limits.

Three fundamental trends define this period, each of which poses a major learning challenge to the UN peace operations bureaucracy. First and foremost, peace operations have grown rapidly in terms of complexity, budgets, and personnel. Combined with a high turnover rate, the result has been that the vast majority of personnel have little or no experience in the tasks they are being asked to perform and critically depend on access to knowledge and guidance as well as capturing the lessons of departing staff. Second, complex civil wars became the dominant operational environment for peacekeepers. In many of these situations, the UN's traditional adherence to the principle of nonuse of force, except in self-defense, effectively left both blue helmets and local civilians at risk. In response, the UN experimented with more nuanced ways of using force within the paradigm of peacekeeping rather than peace enforcement, which required new instruments and doctrine for military and police forces as well as new ways of information sharing and analysis. Third, peace operations shifted from mere peacekeeping to peacebuilding. In order to create the foundations for a lasting peace, UN missions were tasked to build or rebuild the full range of state institutions in a series of countries emerging from conflict. Peacekeepers were utterly unprepared for these new tasks and had to make up their expertise on the fly – often literally, on the flight to their deployments.

Rapid Growth: Missions, Budgets, and Personnel

Rapid continuing growth has been the most obvious feature of peace operations over the past decade. While the number of active missions only fluctuated between fifteen and nineteen in the 1998–2010 period, each year saw about two missions closing down and another two new missions opening. For each new mission, political and technical assessments must be made, plans and budgets drawn up, troop and police contributors found, civilian professionals hired, legal agreements with the host country negotiated, equipment shipped, and a myriad items procured. Also, there are fifteen existing missions at any given time, each of which requires constant headquarters support. Broken equipment needs to be replaced, uniformed contingents and staff found for the next rotation of personnel, operational progress monitored, and, on occasion, whole missions reviewed and reconfigured so as to adapt to changing contexts on the ground.

For almost every closing mission, a more ambitious operation was established somewhere else. As a result, the size and complexity – and therefore, cost – of peace operations rose sharply, resulting in a tenfold budget increase for all missions combined from US$800 million in 1998 to US$7.9 billion in 2010. Effectively, peacekeeping became the signature activity of the UN Secretariat. The rest of the Secretariat pales in comparison: the combined spending for all other activities amounts to barely a third of the peace operations budget – and that does not even include the huge contributions made by many humanitarian and development agencies of the UN in peacekeeping contexts.

A far cry from the improvised transport and travel arrangements of its early days, the peace operations bureaucracy now operates a fleet of more than 250 aircraft, tens of thousands of vehicles, a logistics base in Italy, and a satellite communications network with hundreds of ground stations, among other things. The most critical dimension of growth, however, has been personnel. After the establishment of the United Nations Mission in Kosovo (UNMIK) in June 1999, it took less than twelve months for the number of troops, police, and civilian employees to triple from less than 17,000 to nearly 50,000. After a brief dip in 2002/2003, the number doubled again from 40,000 to more than 80,000 in a period of less than two years. In mid-2010, UN peace operations reached 125,000 personnel. Given the rate of rotation and rapid turnover, this means that almost 200,000 individuals passed through the system in 2010 alone.

Most military and police units serve for six to twelve months before returning home. Roughly the same is true for individual police officers who are rarely allowed by their home governments to extend their tours with the UN beyond a year. During a human resources review in 2008, officials found an average turnover rate of 28 percent for civilian professionals, 88 percent of whom are working on short-term contracts of one year or less – meaning that more than a quarter leave each year and need to be replaced. The high turnover also leads to a very inexperienced overall staff: 44 percent of staff had less than one year experience, while nearly 60 percent had fewer than two years of experience in peace operations. Key civilian functions such as judicial reform and policing have been particularly hard hit, with a vacancy rate of 30 percent in some missions (UN DFS 2008a, 2008b). In most cases, the UN is unable to provide any substantive training to its new employees, mainly for lack of funding. In addition, given the cumbersome recruiting process and the resulting high vacancy rate, there are very rarely full and formal handovers for even the most senior positions, leading to an instant loss of institutional memory and experience in the field (Figure 2.1).

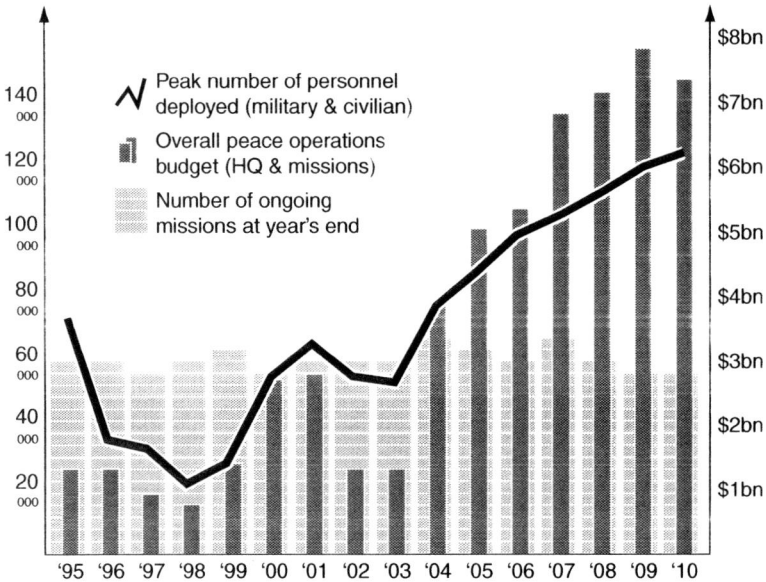

Figure 2.1 UN peace operations: missions, personnel, and budgets, 1995–2010

Throughout the decade, this enormous growth taxed beyond their capacity the established systems for generating military and police units, recruiting civilian experts, individual police officers, and candidates for senior leadership positions. The same is true for training, procurement, logistics, and communications. To find, for example, qualified judicial experts in the numbers required, to integrate military and police forces from a rapidly expanding pool of contributing countries into UN command and administrative structures on the ground, and to do all of these things more quickly posed enormous challenges. Arguably, the most difficult challenge relates to knowledge and learning. More specifically, getting all these newly recruited civilians with little or no peacekeeping experience up to speed, providing them with doctrine and guidance on how to go about their job, and enabling them to document and share their experience and lessons across the UN system. This is the overall issue addressed in this book.

Modern Civil Wars: Sovereignty and the Use of Force

It was barely a year into the period of renewed faith in peacekeeping when the Revolutionary United Front (RUF), a rebel group in Sierra Leone, reminded the UN and the world that the structural weaknesses at the heart of its failures in the 1990s had still not been addressed. In May 2000, after a series of calculated provocations, the RUF detained more than 400 blue helmets at various locations throughout the country and stripped them of their weapons and equipment including, in one case, a helicopter (UN Secretary-General 2000: 8–9; Reno 2001: 222). A rapid intervention of British paratroopers defused the immediate crisis, but at the same time it put the broader challenge for the UN into bold relief: in its newfound confidence in peacekeeping, the Security Council was increasingly sending peace operations into modern civil wars, raising difficult questions about the use of force in peace operations.

Traditionally, the blue helmets were bound by the principle of 'non-use of force except in self-defense,' which had been prominently reaffirmed as late as 1995 by Secretary-General Boutros-Ghali's 'Supplement to An Agenda for Peace' (Boutros-Ghali 1995: para. 33). This proved to be a dangerous trap in modern civil wars where there are often many more violent actors than parties to a peace agreement. War profiteers, breakaway groups, and even signatories of a peace deal who hoped for a quick strategic gain had all the incentives to exploit the UN's strict adherence to the principle of nonviolence. And even where blue helmets were allowed to use force in self-defense, some contingents were so badly trained and equipped that they were easily overpowered by a determined rebel force. From Sierra Leone in 2000 through a string of crises in Haiti and the Democratic Republic of the Congo to Darfur, the UN found itself time and again in a dilemma that echoed the lessons from Rwanda and Srebrenica: rather than protecting the blue helmets, which had been the original intent behind the principle of nonuse of force, or saving civilians under the immediate threat of violence, which is arguably one of the highest goals of the UN as a whole, the traditional constraints on the use of force endangered both.

This realization led to a vivid policy debate and a gradual shift in doctrine on the use of force in peace operations. Just a few months before the hostage crisis in Sierra Leone made international headlines in May 2000, Secretary-General Kofi Annan established a panel led by the former Algerian foreign minister, Lakhdar Brahimi, to make recommendations that would prevent another peacekeeping disaster like the ones in Rwanda and Srebrenica. The publication of the panel's report in August 2000 marked the beginning of a long debate on 'robust peacekeeping' and its limits that shows no sign of resolution, even a decade later. In the meantime, events on the ground from Sierra Leone to the Congo and Darfur forced policymakers in New York and national capitals to make decisions. As a result, while the disputes over policy dragged on, the practice of force structures, equipment, and rules of engagement on the ground became more complex and diverse, which posed new challenges to the peace operations apparatus, particularly in terms of command and control as well as the integration of military, police, and civilian components of its missions.

Both the doctrinal debate and the related evolution of practice on the use of force were defined by a fundamental rift that played out in different ways on the political-diplomatic stage and within the senior levels of bureaucracy. At both levels, the debate and the evolving practice on the ground sparked a number of concrete learning challenges for the peace operations bureaucracy itself, in addition to shaping the overall context within which UN peace operations function.

On the level of member states and their diplomatic representatives in New York, it was the broader North–South split that defined the debate. Northern governments and civil society organizations who advocated humanitarian intervention and the emerging concept of a 'Responsibility to Protect' generally pushed for a more proactive doctrine on the use of force. If peace operations were to become effective tools against state failure, civil wars, and mass atrocities, blue helmets would at the least need to be able to control the forces of violence, that is, to become 'robust peacekeepers' willing and able to employ force to deter aggression or save civilians under imminent threat of lethal violence. What the North regarded as a progressive, morally enlightened policy was seen in the South as a frontal assault on the fundamental norm of state sovereignty and national self-determination, values that had been hard won in the battles of decolonization. For many hardliners among the Group of 77, the main developing-country bloc at the UN, the concept of 'robust peacekeeping' was closely linked to the broader debate about conditional sovereignty – a debate to which UN Secretary-General Kofi Annan had made a number of controversial contributions (Annan 1997a).[2] Unlike the Western caricature of this position which saw the sovereignty argument as mostly a shield for abusive dictators, what many developing country leaders actually valued was the partly legal, partly symbolic function of nonintervention as 'the great equalizer' in their painfully unequal relations with the great powers.[3] Furthermore, the many developing countries who were also large troop contributors feared that peace operations would become more dangerous for their soldiers. The Security Council, they reasoned, might be willing to adopt stronger mandates but its permanent members and other nations with modern militaries would likely continue to deny the UN vital components of a robust force posture such as helicopters and small, highly trained forces to counter serious threats.

Inside the UN bureaucracy, a growing number of staff embraced a broader set of acceptable options for using military force on the part of the UN as inescapable if the organization was to avoid repeating the failures of the

---

[2] The US invasion of Iraq in 2003 only deepened the distrust on the part of the South, notwithstanding Kofi Annan's outspoken opposition to the war.

[3] The quote is from Jean-Marie Guéhenno, Interview, April 2009.

1990s. Many, championed by the Brahimi team, supported a doctrinal shift toward mandating and equipping peace operations to 'project credible force' for the purpose of 'defending themselves...and the mission's mandate,' a commonly used shorthand for protecting public order, the political process the UN is supporting with its presence and even civilians where that is part of the mandate (United Nations 2000: 1, 9). In extreme cases such as situations of impending mass atrocities, 'peacekeepers may not only be operationally justified in using force but morally compelled to do so' (ibid.). At the same time, even the proponents of such a policy strongly reaffirmed the call for the Secretary-General and the Security Council to abstain from actual peace enforcement mandates which would have severely overtaxed the UN's weak force generation and command and control systems as well as its identity and legitimacy as a neutral arbiter. Another faction within the peace operations bureaucracy echoed the fear on the part of many troop-contributing countries, in particular, that those Security Council members with first-rate military forces would cynically adopt robust mandates while failing to produce the resources and military assets necessary to implement them. In this view, peacekeeping could only be effective in a traditional context, with very limited mandates and based on the full consent of all the parties to the conflict.

The debate unfolded in twists and turns following the publication of the Brahimi report. It was shaped by the impact of a series of critical challenges to the various missions on the ground. With each new crisis situation, as the reality of civil war drove the UN a little further away from the traditional principle of nonuse of force except in self-defense, new learning challenges emerged. A defining crisis occurred in the Democratic Republic of Congo (DRC) in 2003. In response to warnings of impending genocide in the eastern part of the DRC, DPKO managed to secure unprecedentedly robust rules of engagement as well as a mandate to field brigade-sized reinforcements to the region. Forces on such a scale needed to be raised and a command staff established that would be able to run tactical enforcement operations within controlled limits of physical and political risk. But military peacekeepers were not the only international actors on the ground. The challenges and opportunities of having humanitarian agencies within and outside the UN on the ground reinforced the need for better integrated systems for information collection, analysis, and operational control.

At about the same time, the United Nations Mission in Liberia (UNMIL) was established, and for the first time with a much stronger force posture than what had been standard practice before. Due to US political and financial support as well as Nigeria's readiness to deploy in strength, UNMIL was able to provide a considerable degree of stability that, in all likelihood, prevented many of the challenges that Liberia's fragile peace process had seen earlier. To do so, however, required a capability to deal with civil unrest and low-level violence with instruments other than lethal force, which neither military peacekeepers nor traditional 'civilian police' (CIVPOL) were able to provide. After Liberia came Haiti, then Côte d'Ivoire, and then again the DRC. Realizing that there was often no way back to the good old days of low-risk peacekeeping, policymakers in permanent representations and the capitals of member states began to agree on pragmatic solutions on a mission-by-mission basis as DPKO's leadership managed to reestablish trust with a rapidly expanding pool of troop-contributing countries.[4]

While the practice of peace operations was changing mission-by-mission on the ground, the larger question of doctrine on the use of force remained unsolved until late 2006, when the senior leadership of DPKO decided to take up the issue once more. As part of its broader guidance development agenda, work began on a restatement of the high-level principles for the conduct of UN peace operations in a document that could serve as the 'capstone' of a growing body of guidance intended to cover every major aspect of multidimensional peacekeeping. This 'capstone doctrine' provided an opportunity to clarify fundamental matters of strategy and operations, particularly on the use of force, from the vantage point of the UN bureaucracy. The principal goal of the authors was to consolidate the practical experience of the previous years in a comprehensive statement of doctrine. In the process, a key priority was to engage internal opposition within the bureaucracy and create a consensus around the doctrinal changes that were already tacitly underpinning operational practice. To that end, the handbook was introduced as a working document by the Secretariat, so it would not formally require the endorsement of member states. Nonetheless, the writing team went to great lengths to consult with member states in a series of workshops around the world, with a view to have the product recognized by the membership through the General Assembly's Special Committee on Peacekeeping Operations.[5]

---

[4] At the same time, those who were always skeptical of the willingness of developed countries to share the risks of 'robust peacekeeping' have been vindicated: the disparity in risk between North and South has been rising even further with almost no unit-strength deployments from developed countries outside the Middle East. Military peacekeepers are generally deployed in battalions of about 350–400 personnel, while formed police units (FPUs) comprise about 120 personnel.

[5] The consultation approach did not entirely succeed in avoiding line-by-line negotiations with member states. Partly owing to the larger political rifts among the membership and the contemporaneous debate about intervention in Darfur, diplomats carried the discussion on the use of force into the Special Committee on Peacekeeping Operations, which required the Secretariat to abide by whatever language the member states would agree on. This explains the somewhat circumscribed way of reinterpreting the traditional principles rather than straightforwardly changing and complementing them with additional ones, which was the original intent of the writing team (UN DPKO 2006a, 2007).

A little bit over a year later, the product that emerged from this process recognized the new reality by reinterpreting the three basic principles of consent of the parties, impartiality, and nonuse of force except in self-defense. According to the new 'Principles and Guidelines,' UN peace operations are to 'manage' the consent of the parties, including, 'as a last resort, the use of force,' and the limits to the use of force are expanded to include 'self-defense and defense of the mandate.' This effectively opens the door to initiating combat at the tactical level within the framework of consent of the major parties on the strategic level (UN DPKO/DFS 2008: 31–5). While strongly affirming the doctrinal foundations for robust peace operations, the document insists even more poignantly on the minimum conditions for their successful deployment, including a credible peace process (commonly referred to as a 'peace to keep') and the appropriate forces and supplies to implement the mandate. Viewed from early 2008, when the 'Principles and Guidelines' were published, almost a decade of debate and practical experience had shifted many of the previous opponents of the Brahimi agenda on the use of force into the supporters' camp, particularly within the bureaucracy.[6] Among member states, however, it only served to highlight a deepening divide linked to many developing countries' persistent mistrust of the North and the growing sense of influence on the part of emerging powers.

These occasionally fierce arguments notwithstanding, the point of reference for the use of force in peace operations has de facto changed. A number of concrete learning challenges have emerged from this shift, the most important of which will be examined in Chapters 4 and 7. Peacekeepers developed a new capability to fill in the gap between unarmed 'civilian police' and all-out military force, and began to establish doctrine for the tactical collaboration between military and police forces. Also, to improve awareness of their more complex and more dangerous operational environment, peace operations created a number of integrated mechanisms for communication, information sharing, and intelligence analysis between military, police, humanitarian, and other mission components. The broader context of the debate about the use of force, and the related political rifts among member states, touches on many of our cases as well.

---

[6] As Marrack Goulding, a former UN Under-Secretary-General for peacekeeping between 1986 and 1993, wrote later in his memoirs: 'for a long time, the ... doctrine was that coercion cannot be combined with consent-based peacekeeping ... I adhered to it throughout my time in the Secretariat ... But now I realize that we in the Secretariat adjusted too slowly to the demands of the new types of conflict which proliferated after the end of the Cold War' (Goulding 2002: 17).

Peacebuilding: Laying the Foundations for Sustainable State Institutions

As a third major trend, the scope of tasks for peace operations expanded rapidly based on the recognition that a shaky political settlement and the quick holding of elections without a minimum level of effective statehood in place virtually guaranteed a renewed outbreak of violence. In the language of Secretary-General Boutros Boutros-Ghali's 1992 Agenda for Peace, the UN was asked to conduct a new set of tasks under the catchphrase of 'peacebuilding' to complement preventive diplomacy, peacemaking (by judicial, diplomatic, or military means), and traditional peacekeeping. While many international actors use the term peacebuilding in different ways (Barnett et al. 2007), the practice of UN peace operations has mostly followed the canonical definition of the Agenda for Peace: 'rebuilding the institutions and infrastructures of nations torn by civil war … which will tend to strengthen and solidify peace in order to avoid a relapse into conflict' (Boutros-Ghali 1992: para. 15, 21).

Throughout the 1990s, the major powers had been reluctant to commit to sustained peacebuilding efforts and pressed instead for the swift implementation of 'exit strategies,' usually based on the quick, and often premature, holding of elections. In 1999, however, when diplomats from the five permanent members of the Security Council and a few other pivotal states together with senior UN officials drafted the mandates for unprecedented transitional administrations in Kosovo and East Timor, they went to the extreme opposite side of the spectrum. Less than a year after the fiftieth anniversary of UN peacekeeping, which had been a somber occasion marred by soul-searching and self-doubt, the peace operations bureaucracy was suddenly asked to set up interim governments, civil administrations, police services, justice systems, and much more in two small provinces at opposite ends of the world.

The UN as a whole had only very limited experience, and only with some aspects of these tasks. In addition, all these bits and pieces were scattered between DPKO, running peace operations, and the development program (UNDP). Altogether, the UN could not produce more than a few experienced civil administrators, police, and national security managers, and hardly any judges, prosecutors, and judicial administrators. How to find these professionals and how to actually build these institutions with motley teams comprising largely Western 'experts' in complex war-torn societies with complex historical legacies were the most daunting of all the learning challenges that the peace operations bureaucracy would face during the following decade. To what extent was the general expertise gained in other countries applicable at all, and how could generic knowledge be applied in a way that remained sensitive to each specific societal and cultural context? How were UN peacebuilders to strike a balance between local ownership and agency – not only a normative expectation but also simply a practical reality – on the one hand

and the apparent need for foreign guidance by virtue of the breakdown of the previous political order on the other?

These and many other learning challenges resulted from the trend toward comprehensive peacebuilding as institution-building that came to expand far beyond the exceptional cases of the transitional administrations in Kosovo and East Timor. As the Security Council mandated more missions to assist the building or rebuilding of governance institutions in places like Liberia and Haiti, the UN senior leadership found itself in a fundamental dilemma. Given the powers accorded to these missions by a Security Council that was seen (at the time) to be dominated by Western powers, and the practical dilemmas of effectiveness and legitimacy that the UN encountered on the ground, overtones of neocolonialism and the loaded debate on humanitarian intervention were impossible to avoid (Chesterman 2004; Caplan 2005). As a result, the notion of intrusiveness that was rooted in disputes about the exceptional cases of Kosovo and East Timor came to define the debate about institution-building as a whole.

The debate began when the Brahimi panel took the organization to task for the 'fundamental deficiency in the way it . . . conceived of, funded and implemented peacebuilding strategies and activities' (United Nations 2000: ix).[7] The report spelled out a number of sweeping proposals, starting with a plea to promote elections only with a keen eye toward the local political context rather than as a substitute for a sound exit strategy. Systematically covering most areas of peace operations practice, it went on to call for a fundamental rethinking of police assistance and activities to support the rule of law. Finally, to deal with the challenge of coordinating the many different actors on the ground, the panel pushed for the 'structural integration of UN peace operations and the "UN Country Team" of humanitarian and development agencies at the field level' (Ahmed et al. 2007: 17).

Amid the increasingly hostile North–South politics at the UN, the Secretariat faced the same rift among the membership that also poisoned the debate on intervention and the use of force. On the one hand, the mainly Northern proponents of comprehensive institution-building saw themselves finally acting on the lessons of earlier failures to invest into the foundations of sustainable peace. On the other hand, the mainly Southern stalwarts of sovereignty saw themselves as potential targets of humanitarian interventionism followed by a liberal peacebuilding regime that would not be much different from the humiliating and often harmful dictates of the Washington Consensus. Some

---

[7] While this assessment had come as much from observations in Kosovo and East Timor as from more traditional peace operations, a discussion of the even greater shortcomings in transitional civil administration was kept very short and buried deeply in the report. Senior UN officials, explained the panel's Project Director later, 'were reluctant to address the needs of such missions in the Brahimi report, viewing "transitional administration" as . . . beyond the scope of peace operations' (Durch et al. 2003: 34).

might have hardened their opposition because they saw their opportunities for graft and corruption threatened. However, most of the governments who were actually in a situation to receive peacebuilding assistance saw things in a more nuanced way. Some welcomed it, hoping for sensible implementation, while others remained skeptical. Overall, the rift through the UN membership on the fundamental issues surrounding institution-building made it harder to achieve progress on allocating resources for these activities as a number of the case studies in this book will demonstrate.

Beneath this broader rift among the UN's member governments, the peace operations bureaucracy was also deeply ambivalent about the increasing scope of tasks it was asked to fulfill. On the one hand, experience had amply demonstrated that without long-term institution-building, all efforts at nego- tiating peace accords and stabilizing the security situation would be quickly reversed. The Brahimi report, using the window of opportunity created by the rapid surge in missions and Annan's honeymoon period as Secretary-General, could be an opportunity to take member states to task in funding these needs and developing the necessary capacity. On the other hand, not only did the organization lack any experience in establishing state institutions in a distant country but many thought that it should not be its place to effectively rule entire countries, however transitory its mandate to do so. Not least, there was also a concern that member states would fail again to provide the means to implement these mandates, spoiling the unique opportunity that the Brahimi report was intended to exploit.

In subsequent years, the deep ambivalence about institution-building among senior managers internally, and the even deeper political rift between member states externally, defined the debate about each successive new peace operation or change in mandate. The planning and implementation of the new missions in Afghanistan (2001) and Liberia (2003) illustrate the two extreme points of the debate: in Afghanistan, owing in part to its particular history and the preferences of the United States but also reflective of internal resistance within the UN to a larger role, the UN established a political opera- tion with a 'light footprint.' It had no military component and focused mainly on political affairs while more intrusive activities such as building a military force, police services, and a justice system were outsourced to individual 'lead nations.' In contrast, Liberia became a 'must-win' case for the UN for two reasons. First, the UN needed to prove its continued relevance after the international tensions over Iraq. Second, conditions in Liberia were much more favorable than in Afghanistan due to the size and geographic accessibil- ity of the country as well as the relatively benign regional environment that emerged once the war in Sierra Leone was over. If the UN's idea of multidi- mensional peace operations comprising peacekeeping and peacebuilding ele- ments could succeed anywhere, it would have to succeed in Liberia. Therefore, the UN mounted a comprehensive mission with a sweeping mandate that called for police restructuring and judicial reform on top of the more traditional security, disarmament, and reintegration tasks. Yet again, the experience on the ground in both countries brought out the same problems that the Brahimi panel had already highlighted: nobody knew how to build peace, establish an effective and accountable justice system, or set up a functioning police service respectful of human rights.

Nonetheless, by 2003, institution-building in a basic sense – laying the groundwork and assisting local political elites with rebuilding and improving the institutions of their state – was accepted as an essential task, even if the peace operations bureaucracy had little capacity or experience to do so. Institution-building has posed and continues to pose tremendous learning challenges for the UN peace operations bureaucracy, arguably even greater ones than those posed by the extraordinary growth of the organization as a whole and the shifting patterns of violence in modern civil wars. Most of the cases analyzed in this book are related to the institution-building challenge, including the reform, restructuring, and rebuilding of police services (Chapter 4), capacity-building in the judicial system (Chapter 5), the link between short-term disarmament and long-term social and economic reintegration of former combatants (Chapter 6), as well as the strategic planning and coordination challenges that are posed by longer deployment timeframes and merging short-term concerns of security and relief with long-term concerns of development (Chapter 7).

Creating an Effective Learning Infrastructure for Peace Operations

Taken together, the trends of rapid growth, changing notions on the use of force, and the new task of institution-building defined the learning challenge for peace operations in the twenty-first century. Any of these three sets of issues alone would have presented a tall order for a peace operations bureaucracy fragmented by the historical evolution of the UN system and the political interests of member states. Having to face all these challenges at the same time had a contradictory effect on the Secretariat. On the one hand, the threefold pressures provided ample evidence of the need for building a professional organization with a strong learning infrastructure to match these challenges. On the other hand, they also brought many urgent operational priorities with them that laid claims on resources, time, and attention to the detriment of longer term institutional investments.

It was against this backdrop that in early 2000, barely seven months into the new surge in demand for peacekeeping, Secretary-General Kofi Annan commissioned the Brahimi report. Its analysis and the political reform process that it sparked aimed to professionalize peace operations in order to meet the new challenges and avert another catastrophic failure on the scale of Rwanda and Srebrenica. The panelists minced no words when describing the dismal state of affairs where the Secretariat's learning infrastructure was concerned: 'lessons learned in Headquarters practice are not routinely captured, . . . comprehensive training programmes for new arrivals are non-existent and . . . user-friendly manuals and standard operating procedures remain half-complete' (United Nations 2000: 37). While the many operational challenges would have required 'to exploit cumulating field experience [and] to feed it back into the development of operational doctrine, plans, procedures or mandates, . . . not enough has been done to improve the system's ability to tap that experience or to feed it back into the development of operational doctrine, plans, procedures or mandates' (ibid.: 39).

By UN standards, this assessment, like many others throughout the report, was unusually candid. Because the document had the backing of an eminent panel and chairman and the strong support of the Secretary-General himself as well as that of key members of the Security Council, it provided a rare political opening for the Secretariat to push for far-reaching change. Reformers within the peace operations community, led by Jean-Marie Guéhenno, the incoming head of DPKO, gathered under the banner of the Brahimi report and made its analysis and the spirit of its recommendations their guiding paradigm.

The daunting challenges borne out of the rapid growth of peace operations, their increasingly frequent deployment into complex civil wars, and the growing need for peacebuilding had already cast their shadows in the various crises of 1999/2000, when the UN had struggled to man and equip four new missions on three continents, to reinforce the struggling operation in Sierra Leone against the repeated challenges from armed spoilers, and to provide political and practical guidance for the many new tasks that the Security Council had given to the new transitional administration missions in Kosovo and East Timor. The capacity of the system to withstand these pressures had again become overtaxed. As a result, the reformers were convinced that another disaster on the scale of Rwanda or Srebrenica was only a matter of time if the UN would keep doing business as usual. The only way to avoid this fate was to finally undertake substantive reforms in terms of doctrine, funding, management, and culture. The establishment of an effective learning infrastructure was at the heart of this reform agenda that grew out of the Brahimi report, was championed by Guéhenno, and driven by a cohort of younger managers whose formative experience of peacekeeping had been in the field during the existential crises of the 1990s. Their efforts faced significant obstacles in both the cultural and the structural DNA of the organization.

Implementing reforms to promote learning was not merely a technical challenge – it meant going against and changing some of the core tenets of the entrenched organizational culture of the UN peace operations apparatus. Indeed, for the Brahimi report and the decade-long effort that was launched under its name, overcoming these internal obstacles was a goal in its own right, in addition to rallying member states in support of a higher budget and more responsible Security Council mandates (Durch 2004; Ahmed et al. 2007).[8]

Constant Crisis and Constructive Ambiguity: Traditional Organizational Culture

The Brahimi reform agenda challenged the core of the entrenched organizational culture of peacekeeping that had developed over a half century of institutional history. It is based on a traditionalist interpretative frame that views UN peace operations as a feeble endeavor deprived of necessary resources and political support to implement its mandate with any degree of professionalism. As a result, peacekeepers saw themselves forced to operate in a climate of constant crisis in which they had 'always been very good at taking experience and knowledge and expanding it into another field, learning to do things on the fly.'[9] On the flip side of the same coin, critical introspection and any kind of standard operating procedures that might limit whatever precious political room for maneuver had been left by member states became a threat rather than an opportunity to improve the effectiveness of their work. Based on such a frame, the organization produced cultural norms that prized political flexibility or, in the words of one insider, 'constructive ambiguity' and disregarded efforts to openly discuss previous failures in order to draw lessons or develop standardized doctrine to mainstream such lessons into future practice.

The roots of the traditional culture of peacekeeping reach back to the early days of the UN. In May 1948, when the Security Council asked the Secretariat to set up the very first peacekeeping operation, the UN Truce Supervision Organization (UNTSO) for Palestine, there was neither precedent nor experience on how to put the idea of a neutral UN presence in a war-torn area into

[8] In the following discussion of organizational culture, we concentrate on the divide between a traditional and reformist organizational culture that uses different frames. We describe a longer term process of attempting to change the organizational culture of the peace operations apparatus. The degree to which this change was achieved has a bearing on the learning processes analyzed in the empirical part of this chapter. Here, organizational culture features as part of the institutional infrastructure (as introduced in Chapter 3). However, since we describe a longer term shift, organizational culture rarely has immediate effects discernible in specific moments of the learning processes analyzed in this book.

[9] Interview with a long-standing senior DPKO official, May 2009.

practice. The task of planning its deployment, defining a doctrine, recruiting staff, finding accommodation and office space, establishing a radio network, and a myriad of other vital issues fell on the American UN official Ralph Bunche, then the principal aide to the UN mediator for Palestine, Count Folke Bernadotte of Sweden. With a tiny staff of his own, Bunche put together the practical foundations of the mission while the actual observers, drawn from a carefully balanced mix of nations, were slowly arriving throughout the summer (Urquhart 1998 [1993]: 161).

Eight years later, when the UN fielded its first armed peacekeeping force in response to the Suez crisis, Bunche had become one of two Under-Secretaries-General for Special Political Affairs in the Secretary-General's office in New York. His special assistant at the time, Brian Urquhart, was the only staff member who had any military experience, and was therefore put in charge of the hastily assembled working group to set up the UN Emergency Force (UNEF). In his words, the ad hoc culture of UN peacekeeping in the 1950s comes vividly to life:

> The process of setting up UNEF took place in Bunche's conference room on the thirty-eighth floor and proceeded more or less around the clock as the situation demanded.... Innumerable problems, great and small, had to be resolved urgently, mostly by improvisation.... The problem of uniforms and identification was quite literally vital, since some of the UN troops wore British-style uniforms [with Britain a party to the conflict]. What was needed was distinctive headgear for a distant sniper to recognize. A UN-blue beret seemed to be the answer, but it was impossible to procure enough berets in time. American plastic helmet-liners, however, were available in quantity in Europe, and were ready, spray-painted UN blue, in time for the first UNEF detachments to wear on their entry into Egypt. Identity cards in four languages had to be formulated... Tent stoves were another problem.... The nights and days passed quickly in dealing with a hundred similar details. (Urquhart 1998 [1993]: 268–9)

As UNEF settled down into a more orderly routine within a year and a half, UN Secretary-General Dag Hammarskjöld ordered an eight-month project, immense in light of the few resources available, to put together a 'manual,' in Hammarskjöld's words, to 'provide fundamental guidance for any future plans or efforts relating to a United Nations force' (quoted in Urquhart 1998 [1993]: 289). In the years to come, however, setting up each new operation would be the same political, operational, logistical, and force generation scramble all over again. Urquhart's description of ONUC, the vast and tragic operation in the Congo established in 1960, captures best the dilemma that came to define the organizational culture of peacekeeping for over half a century:

There were seldom any simple answers even to the smallest problems. Later on, some critics derided our efforts as amateurish or disorganized, but neither rules, nor precedents nor organization existed for a situation like the Congo in 1960. Under Bunche's leadership ONUC had, for the most part, to improvise as it went along. Bunche's insistence on personally controlling and checking all the activities of ONUC was also criticized later. To those of us on the spot this seemed the only sensible way of managing a vast emergency enterprise put together in a hurry, where many of the staff were new and untried, and where a single mistake could, and often did, have massive repercussions. (Urquhart 1998 [1993]: 319–20)

The political and organizational pressures of the early years therefore created a culture of ad hoc decision-making in a climate of constant crisis. Staff and resources were scarce, and the political wiggle room between the crushing might of the great powers was in most instances very small. As a result, the operating style of the 'founding fathers' of peacekeeping exemplified and prized a reliance on personal relationships instead of formal, depersonalized reporting chains, case-by-case considerations instead of general templates, and preserving 'constructive ambiguity' whenever instructions, mandates, or budgetary regulations were put on paper, in order to maximize whatever political room for maneuver remained available to the UN.

Over time, the frame of a crisis-driven mode of operation solidified and formed the core of the organizational culture of peacekeeping. At headquarters, the tiny staff in the Office of Special Political Affairs had its plate full with the whole peace and security portfolio, including preventive diplomacy, peacemaking, and peacekeeping. Other departments provided the necessary administrative and logistical support for field operations. Upon Bunche's death in 1971, Urquhart succeeded him in the post of Under-Secretary-General for Special Political Affairs in charge of peace and security. When Urquhart retired in 1985, the British diplomat Marrack Goulding became the first peacekeeping chief who had not been among the founders of the UN Secretariat in 1945. Goulding inherited a political team of seven and an even smaller military staff – effectively, an office no different in size and structure than the one with which Ralph Bunche and Brian Urquhart had set up the first peacekeeping operation thirty-seven years before.

With the end of the Cold War, UN peacekeeping saw a sudden surge in demand. Between 1989 and 1991, the Security Council mandated eight new peace operations, among them two large and unprecedentedly ambitious missions to oversee Namibia's transition to independence and to implement a settlement to the civil war in Cambodia. In February 1992, the new Secretary-General Boutros Boutros-Ghali established DPKO, initially with Goulding in charge. Hundreds of new temporary posts were created in various Secretariat departments to help carry the rapidly increased burden of supporting peace operations. To fill the few dozen additional political and leadership posts in the new department, the UN drew on a mixture of civilians (mostly diplomats) seconded by their governments, retired military officers, and regular Secretariat staff. Some of these officials were just returning from field assignments in Namibia or Cambodia, while many others came straight from their capital or their most recent diplomatic assignment with little experience in peacekeeping. Many in this generation went on to play major roles in the UN throughout the 1990s and beyond, including Iqbal Riza, later to become Kofi Annan's Chief of Staff; Shashi Tharoor, a one-time contender for the Secretary-General's office; Hédi Annabi, the second-in-command at DPKO between 1997 and 2007 who was often called 'DPKO's living institutional memory' and who tragically died in the earthquake on January 12, 2010, in Haiti; and Dmitry Titov, who defused many crises as director of the Africa division in Annabi's Office of Operations and took over the new rule of law office in 2007.

Thrown into the furious pace of the peace operations machinery, struggling to raise troops and staff to feed another fivefold increase in uniformed peacekeepers and the twofold increase in missions in a twelve-month period between 1992 and 1993, the newcomers easily absorbed and reproduced the organizational culture of constant improvisation that the 'founding fathers' of peacekeeping had created so many years before. In fact, they had little choice in the matter: because of the persistent refusal of member states to fund a more robust headquarters capacity to direct and support the slowly growing list of peace operations, there were no resources to develop a more professional organization to undertake conflict analysis for the support of strategic planning and crisis decision-making (Kühne 1999; Malone and Thakur 2001). As a result, the culture of improvisation, muddling-through, and management of the moment was in many ways a logical consequence of the external constraints placed upon the peace operations bureaucracy. It was not perfect, however, even by the standards of its own proponents. Luiz Carlos da Costa, another long-time senior official who also died in the 2010 Haiti earthquake, argued in an interview in 2009, that in retrospect, DPKO's excessive cultural self-confidence made it also miss many opportunities to partner with other organizations before institutional rivalries could erupt. Nonetheless, the traditional culture of peacekeeping clearly worked in holding the place together through a series of crises throughout the Cold War, as long as the number and scope of missions were limited.

With the number and scope of operations rapidly increasing after the end of the Cold War, the drawbacks of this organizational culture that resisted building a professional and self-critical organization slowly became apparent. In March 1993, when Kofi Annan took over the peacekeeping department, DPKO 'still operated in an atmosphere of chaos,' as one of Annan's biographers observed (Meisler 2007: 67). About fifty staffers directed and supported operations comprising 80,000 blue helmets across the globe with the assistance of little more than a hundred logisticians and administrators dealing with finance and personnel. In the first eighteen months of Annan's tenure, DPKO grew to about 400 staff including the merger with the unit that covered finance, personnel, and logistics support as well as large numbers of temporary hires and loaned personnel from various governments. However, following the withdrawal of American troops from Somalia and the disillusionment with UN peacekeeping in the US Congress, the sensible buildup of organizational capacity suddenly stopped. Despite the continuously rising operational demands placed on the organization by the Security Council, particularly in the Balkans, the financial masters of the UN failed to invest in its organizational capacity to deliver.

This left Annan little budgetary room for maneuver to implement his ambitious agenda. As a first step toward professionalizing the peace operations apparatus, he established a 24/7 situation center to keep in touch with increasingly risky situations on the ground. Beginning in 1993, the senior leadership of DPKO also began to establish the organization's first Lessons Learned Unit. Despite strong support from internal oversight bodies, troop-contributing countries, and the General Assembly at large, it took Annan until April 1995 to create a unit of two: a head of unit and one research assistant.[10] Under the prevailing organizational culture at DPKO, the approach to learning and introspection remained fundamentally defensive. For senior officials, who prized political flexibility and ad hoc improvisation above all and who were reflexively opposed to standard operating procedures on substantive matters of policy implementation, the absolute need to maintain internal coherence and 'constructive ambiguity' for the future severely constrained the effectiveness of 'learning lessons.' Learning was confined to the level of individuals and small groups behind closed doors, where it became a luxury that often took second place after the demands of constant crisis management. Like in many tight-knit social systems put under persistent pressure, the constant perception of urgency and crisis fostered defensiveness against outside 'interference' and internal deviance or criticism, promoted groupthink, and stymied open discussion and learning (Janowitz 1959; Hermann 1963). In one telling example, Jarat Chopra, a young participant to a series of conferences held in 1995 to review the earlier UN operations in Somalia recalls:

> Hard lessons cannot be learned politely, yet the same diplomatic approach that failed to respond to the social and political environment in Somalia failed to yield lessons at the meetings.... [Even] limited proposals were marginalized. If knowledge is power, in the U.N. knowledge is dangerous and officials [are] secretive, which is organizationally suicidal. By far the majority of 'lessons' were banal

---

[10] We have explained the genesis and effective paralysis of DPKO's Lessons Learned Unit in the 1990s at greater length elsewhere (Benner and Rotmann 2008: 45–6).

conclusions that have been known for decades, such as the need for clearer mandates and more resources. Despite calls for frank discussions, a diplomatic environment prevented cool analysis; what is acceptable to say may not be useful to know. Self-criticism in sessions was transformed formally into self-justification as a whole. (Chopra 1995)

Chopra's observations are just one illustration of the general reaction of the traditionalists when the majority of world opinion turned against the UN following its failure to mobilize and lead an effective response to the genocides in Rwanda in 1994 and in Srebrenica in 1995. Most of the more senior officials defended themselves and the institution by pointing to the responsibility of member state governments: 'the responsibility lay with member states, but the blame fell on the Secretariat,' as one senior official argued in an interview in May 2009. The consequences were drastic: the 'lull' in peace operations between 1995 and 1998 resulted in huge financial pressure on DPKO, which lost 27 percent of its professional staff. But in the view of these senior officials, the UN as an organization had worked as well as could be expected under the circumstances. It was the member states that had created the circumstances, in particular those dominating the Security Council and holding the purse strings. They had deprived the organization of credibility and resources by withdrawing their blue helmets at the first sign of trouble in Rwanda and limiting their rules of engagement to fit an unrealistic fantasy of peacekeeping while organized, premeditated violence was unfolding. Ultimately, in this view, member states had failed the UN and their own lofty pronouncements of 'humanitarian intervention' when they had sent lightly armed and defensively mandated peacekeepers into a war zone in the first place. In comparison to such grave political and ethical failings on the part of politicians in world capitals, whatever might have gone wrong within the UN bureaucracy was hardly more than a glitch.

Critical Analysis and Learning: The Reformist Challenge to Organizational Culture

In the mid-1990s, a new generation of civilian managers joined the peace operations community. Spending their formative years with the UN on the ground, mainly in the large missions in the Balkans, many of these younger officials experienced the traditional organizational culture of peace operations as dysfunctional and dangerous. Watching the crises of Rwanda and Srebrenica unfold, they took issue with the instinctively defensive response of their superiors in the field and the peacekeeping establishment in New York. From their perspective, as accurate and necessary as it was to criticize key member state governments, the UN as an organization should not be allowed to hide behind diplomats and policymakers in Western capitals to avoid critical intro-spection. Aside from the failures of high politics and the personal responsibil-ity of senior decision-makers, they found the organizational culture of peace operations at fault as well. In their view, the culture that had emerged from forty years of directing and supporting traditional peacekeeping during the Cold War was inadequate for the scale and scope of modern peace operations. In the different context of robust peacekeeping or peace enforcement in complex civil wars, these shortcomings of analysis, information sharing, excessively cautious decision-making, and anticipatory obedience to member states that were rooted in the traditional culture had contributed to the UN's share of failures in Rwanda and Srebrenica.

As a result of widespread internal dissent along these lines, a split emerged in the hitherto monolithic organizational culture of peacekeeping. A new, competing interpretative frame held the traditional culture partly responsible for the political and managerial shortcomings in responding to the situations in Rwanda and Srebrenica. From this perspective, a more professional culture based on open self-assessments, common standards, and organizational learning would be required to avoid the repetition of these failures in the future.

This clash of interpretations first played out over the suggestion of an internal inquiry into the UN's actions during the crises. In 1996, Jordanian diplomat Prince Zeid Ra'ad Zeid al-Hussein became the Deputy Permanent Representative of his country to the UN in New York. He had spent the preceding years as a Political Officer with the UN Protection Force (UNPRO-FOR) in Bosnia, where he had been deeply affected by the events in Srebrenica. When he floated the idea to conduct a thorough investigation to be conducted by the Secretariat itself, senior officials in DPKO reacted defensively. 'The Secretariat had no wish to expose its dirty laundry,' as a close observer of the UN in the Annan years described it (Traub 2006: 125). Using his newly acquired leverage on the diplomatic stage, Zeid rallied the ambassadors of Bosnia and Croatia to create public pressure on the Secretariat until the General Assembly commissioned 'a comprehensive report, including an assessment' of the UN's reaction to the events in Bosnia (UN General Assem-bly 1998).

Annan agreed to conduct an unusually candid investigation that would not shy away from institutional self-criticism and asked his Chief of Staff, Iqbal Riza, to supervise the process. Riza delegated the work to two young political officers who had served in the Balkans, David Harland and Salman Ahmed. Riza, Harland, and Ahmed all supported the need to expose the failures as a means to create pressure for organizational change. Therefore, Harland and Ahmed conducted a detailed investigation over six months and wrote a report that, while 'unsparing on the member states who shaped the policy,' was 'no less harsh on the UN professionals who carried it out' (Traub 2006: 54). Cast in the voice of the Secretary-General himself, the report minced no words in its conclusion: 'Through error, misjudgment and an inability to recognize the scope of evil confronting us, we failed to do our part to help save the people of Srebrenica from the Serb campaign of mass murder' (UN Secretary-General 1998: 108). By not using military force to stop the impending violence against Bosnian Muslim civilians in Srebrenica, 'the management of UNPROFOR' had failed to 'adapt mandates to the reality on the ground' (UN Secretary-General 1998: 106), a lapse that was, in Traub's words, 'a matter less of shortsightedness than of institutional culture and entrenched principles' (Traub: loc.cit.). 'The report suggested that these failures had their origin in the culture and collective psychology of the Secretariat, which had come to see itself as a bulwark against the 'culture of death' – a phrase used by Boutros-Ghali – that it could not accept the imperative to use force' (Traub 2006: 126).

As a direct challenge to the prevailing organizational culture, Harland's and Ahmed's draft report got a frosty reception with DPKO senior management. Many officials 'objected, sometimes furiously, both to assertions of specific actions and to the report's broader moral claims about the failed doctrine of neutrality' (Traub 2006: 127). Amid 'fierce line-by-line arguments' with senior DPKO officials, Riza and Assistant-Secretary-General John Ruggie had to protect the two authors 'from the wrath of their seniors' to preserve the draft's candor (ibid.). In the words of another close UN observer, the report's 'sheer thoroughness and ... its readiness to present facts in an unvarnished form even though they might be disturbing and uncomfortable for the organization ... rather forced the hand of the UN senior management with respect to the question of just how far to go in terms of airing the linens of self-criticism in public' (Berdal 2001: 46).

The 1999 Srebrenica report marked a turning point in terms of self-criticism. A month later, it was followed by the report of an independent panel on the Rwandan genocide that Annan had commissioned as well (UN Security Council 1999). Together with a third report on the failure of the UN sanctions regime against Angola and the Brahimi report itself, otherwise critical observers now found the organization to be 'less interested in ducking blame and covering itself from attack than it is in improving performance' (Malone and Thakur 2001: 11).

It was by no means assured that this would lead to a lasting and self-sustaining process of cultural transformation of the peace operations apparatus. For the time being, however, the series of self-critical reports, chiefly that of the Brahimi panel, provided the new reformist generation with considerable momentum. Under the new leadership of Jean-Marie Guéhenno, they aimed for nothing less than a wholesale transformation of the organization's culture: only by acknowledging mistakes – at least internally – would the organization be able to learn, and only in a more professional bureaucratic culture based on doctrine derived from the best available knowledge and constantly evaluated in practice would it be able to meet the ambitious expectations for peace operations set in Security Council mandates.

However, this transformation toward a learning organization did not come easily and proved to be a constant struggle for most of the decade following the publication of the Brahimi report. The gradual shift toward a more professional organizational culture was only one part of that struggle. Equally important and even more persistent were the structural and political constraints, most of them at least partly beyond the control of the Secretariat, that hampered peace operations generally and the evolution of its learning capacity in particular.

Structural and Political Constraints to Learning

The longstanding institutional deprivation of peacekeeping combined with the growing complexity of post-Cold War missions mandated to combine traditional and 'robust' peace operations with humanitarian assistance and elements of development cooperation has given rise to a number of structural features that have often dysfunctional effects.

The peace operations bureaucracy is a fragile, extremely decentralized, and highly politicized organization. It is fragile because of extreme turnover – on average, civilian staff stay for less than four years while military and police personnel are generally on six- to twelve-month deployments – and weak bonds between the individual and the organization. Soldiers and police officers owe their primary allegiance to their home country and naturally view a stint with the UN as nothing more than a temporary assignment. Civilians, almost all of whom are kept on short-term contracts of a year or less, might be more willing to identify with peacekeeping but the insecurity of their jobs forces them to always keep looking for another position. As a result, outside a small group of career UN officials in New York, the lack of a career structure limits the positive incentives the organization can put into place while implicitly penalizing any contribution to the common stock of knowledge. After all, from the point of view of an individual, each piece of knowledge or experience, if kept private, could be the ticket to their next job. Even worse, and beyond the politicization of appointments, the extent of global economic inequality makes it impossible to balance material incentives sufficiently to ensure high competence across the board.

The peace operations bureaucracy is also highly decentralized, both geographically and among different agencies. Ninety-nine percent of its personnel are deployed in the field, and field missions enjoy a high degree of political autonomy while being stuck in a regulatory straightjacket in matters of administration and procurement. Beyond the sheer geographical distance and time difference between New York and most mission areas and the lack of resources at headquarters, the way Security Council mandates arise from often difficult diplomatic compromises often allows key elements of strategy only to be defined in vague terms. As an unintended consequence, senior officials are required by events to fill the gaps in strategic guidance by taking decisions with strategic implications in a piecemeal fashion without being authorized and resourced to articulate a strategic plan. As a result, the Special Representatives of the Secretary-General (SRSG) heading each mission enjoy wide leeway in the most consequential political decisions, as long as they do not violate the boundaries set by the great powers. Personal inclinations and personalities often make a huge difference in what priorities are pursued, at what pace, and in what kind of relationship to local politicians or other UN agencies. This level of space for individual leadership and experimentation creates both opportunities for learning and obstacles for the implementation of guidance and best practices.

Internally, however, the senior mission management team has direct authority only over the military contingents, police units, and civilians assigned to the peace operation as such – and in case of military units, only to the extent that the troop-contributing countries allow their forces to follow UN orders. In addition, member states have found ways to control what many diplomats view as an unaccountable bureaucracy by tightening the administrative screws through the budget. Responding to their pressure, the organization set up detailed standard operating procedures regulating equipment purchases, leases on building space, hiring, and promotions. Taking both effects together, senior officials end up in the perverse position of enjoying ample freedom to decide key political questions of strategic importance, but very little choice in many of the mundane issues of everyday management (Figure 2.2).

Beyond the peacekeeping mission itself, DPKO and the SRSG as the top UN representative on the ground have no effective authority at all over other UN agencies such as UNHCR, WFP, UNDP, or the World Bank and their field offices (see Figure 2.3), despite the fact that a modern peace operation cannot implement its mandate without their support. Despite many solemn declarations in favor of 'coordination' and 'integration,' each agency is primarily responsible to its own governing and funding body, where a particular political setup among member states drives its strategic priorities. To identify and make use of the significant overlap among those priorities requires constant interagency coordination both at headquarters level and in the field. This has particular relevance to day-to-day management as well as organizational learning with regard to the peacebuilding challenge, where almost every UN task or function has to be performed in concert with agencies other than

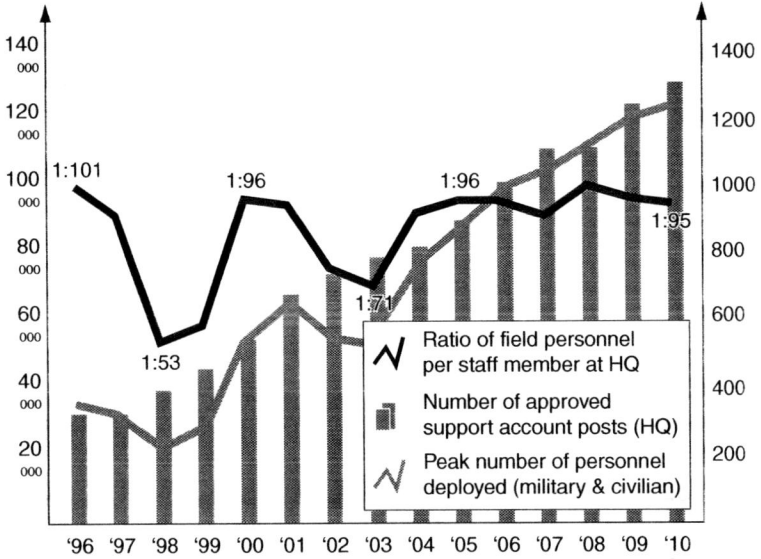

Figure 2.2 Overstretch: mission demands and headquarters capacity, 1996–2010

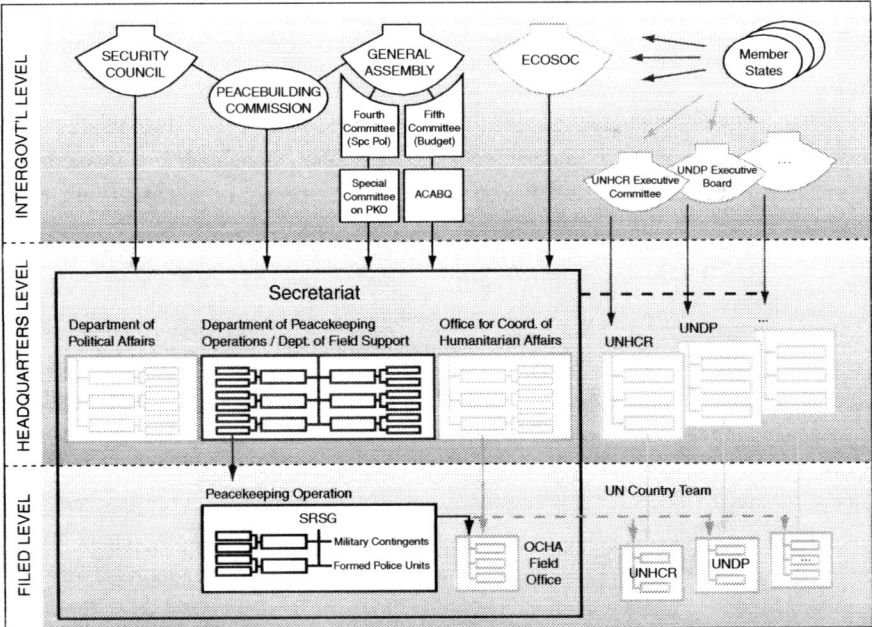

Figure 2.3 The peace operations bureaucracy in context: intergovernmental bodies and key organizations at headquarters and field level

DPKO or a peace operation itself. Rarely are peacekeepers the ones with the most experience within the UN system on these issues, and in many cases such as the reintegration of former combatants into society (Chapter 6), DPKO does not even have the status of a 'lead agency' and is just one of the players at the table – and certainly not the one with the deepest pockets – as soon as the immediate deployment phase is over and development agencies and the World Bank have adjusted their programs.

More recently, an upside has emerged to this fragmentation of responsibilities among the UN system as more and more departments and agencies began to develop their own learning infrastructures, as well. Among the first were UNDP's Bureau for Crisis Prevention and Recovery (even slightly before DPKO), the Secretariat's Peacebuilding Support Office, and the Office for the Coordination of Humanitarian Affairs (OCHA). After some initial competition in cases of overlap such as a big study on integrated missions that the humanitarian office had commissioned without DPKO involvement in 2005, the waves have calmed and collaborative learning and guidance development became possible in a number of cases, some of which we examine later in this book.[11]

Finally, the peace operations bureaucracy is heavily politicized. Member states, particularly the powerful permanent members of the Security Council, tend to navigate the bureaucratic maze of UN agencies, Secretariat departments, and field missions by politicizing senior appointments and using their budgetary levers to micromanage managerial decisions. In the 1990s, when the efficiency, effectiveness, and accountability of peace operations as a whole became a partisan political issue in the United States and a political wedge in North–South politics at the UN as a whole, political micromanagement began to extend far beyond the major political questions of each agency or mission and deeply into the operational details of implementation. As a result, member state diplomats in New York are now spending their time each year critically evaluating every single job paid for through the peacekeeping budget, every major equipment purchase, travel expense, or consultant fee. In effect, some of the permanent members of the Security Council are using these line-by-line budget negotiations to exert political control over a bureaucracy they regard as insufficiently accountable and unresponsive to their legitimate demands, while nonmembers are wielding the red pen to compensate for their lack of influence on the Security Council. The results are staggering costs in terms of time and attention on both sides and a tragic loss of flexibility on the

---

[11] While we cannot recount the evolution of learning infrastructures in another half dozen departments and agencies throughout the UN family without filling another volume and leaving the reader drowning in acronyms, we cover some of their roles as they relate to the issues and cases examined in subsequent chapters, particularly those on judicial reform (Chapter 5), reintegration of ex-combatants (Chapter 6), and mission integration (Chapter 7).

part of managers that constrains their ability to enact internal organizational reforms, build up an effective learning infrastructure, and implement any lessons that require institutional changes.

Learning to Learn: The Beginnings of Professionalization

Together with the emerging cultural rift of the late 1990s, these structural and political constraints provided the backdrop for the reform efforts that began in 2000, driven by the new generation of managers who gradually came into influential headquarters jobs from the field.[12] This cohort assembled around the new Under-Secretary-General for Peacekeeping Operations, Jean-Marie Guéhenno. In October 2000, the French scholar–diplomat whose career spanned analytical and managerial assignments across the foreign affairs and defense communities was given the daunting task of leading more than a dozen peace operations around the world while fundamentally rebuilding his headquarters at the same time. Guéhenno inherited a department all but overwhelmed with the operational requirements of five start-up operations in desperate need of staff, equipment, and guidance, one of which (UNAMSIL in Sierra Leone, in May 2000) had just suffered an almost fatal crisis.

Fresh from a series of field visits throughout the summer that had taken him to Sierra Leone, Bosnia, and Kosovo, Guéhenno arrived in New York determined not to leave the longer term challenge of institution-building by the wayside. He was convinced that the challenges borne out of the rapid growth of peace operations, their increasingly frequent deployment into complex civil wars, and the growing need for peacebuilding urgently required building a professional organization for peace operations, even if the incentive structure in the Secretariat – being much closer to the diplomatic circuit than to the field – would make it hard to remake DPKO into a 'good support system' for field operations. The stakes were simply too high to repeat the mistake of the mid-1990s, when the failure of Annan's internal reforms had contributed to the catastrophic failures in Rwanda and Srebrenica. At the post-Cold-War scale of tens of thousands of troops, police, and civilians in the field and hundreds of staff at headquarters in New York, it was not realistic to hang on to the ways of the past. Rather than relying on the genius of a few exceptionally talented pioneers to hold things together against the odds of a dysfunctional bureaucracy, the organization had to become sufficiently professional to allow the average qualified staff member to do a decent job within the system.

In Guéhenno's analysis, peacekeeping also provided better opportunities for reform than any other part of the UN system. The structure of the peace

---

[12] This section is based on extensive interviews with and some written accounts by most of the protagonists, conducted or collected between 2006 and 2009.

operations system as a whole provided for a potentially large supporting coalition of financial contributors (who want their money to be used efficiently and effectively), troop and police contributors (who want their people to be safe and making a positive difference that reflects well on themselves), and the recipient countries, mostly in Africa (the largest regional voting bloc, whose members want the increased stability peacekeeping can bring). Rather than 'implementing the lowest common denominator,' it should be the ambition of the international civil service to use these opportunities and strive 'to increase the scope of agreement among states in the service of the greater good.'[13]

Guéhenno joined peacekeeping at an opportune time, with the 'Brahimi Bonanza' in full swing as his deputy, Hédi Annabi, put it later. The Brahimi report, strongly supported by the Security Council and accepted by the General Assembly, provided positive momentum both on the internal, cultural front – were everybody understood the huge political and budgetary opportunity in front of them – and on the external front of member states. The report made a formidable set of demands to member states and the bureaucracy alike. Governments were asked to choose carefully when and where to employ a peacekeeping operation and to provide support commensurate with its mandate. At the same time, the Secretariat had to become more effective in managing the missions – among other things, by establishing an effective learning infrastructure. The key parts of this infrastructure, as sketched out in the Brahimi report, would be a 'revitalized' Lessons Learned Unit, new knowledge management systems, and the promotion of a learning culture within the organization.

Other than tossing out these crucial elements of a future learning infrastructure, however, the report did not provide a strategy for actually building it. The hard task of formulating and implementing such a strategy lay still ahead, and proceeded only slowly. There were three closely related reasons for this delay. First, the myriad demands of day-to-day mission management necessarily took precedence over Guéhenno's time and the resources of his overextended department. Second, the same logic of precedence applied to organizational capacity-building and reform. The units providing direct operational control and support were the first recipients of managerial attention, increased funding, and new talent, while the 'rear' parts of the organization had to wait their turn. Finally, the staffing needs of field operations, drawn-out budget negotiations, and the cumbersome recruitment system of the UN Secretariat greatly slowed down the speed at which Guéhenno could hire more of the young managers with field experience who supported his reform

---

[13] Interview with Jean-Marie Guéhenno, April 2009.

agenda. One of the first of these was Salman Ahmed, the coauthor of both the Srebrenica and Brahimi reports, who became Guéhenno's Special Assistant and a key figure in the implementation of reform.

As a result, it took more than two years until the reformers got around to a thorough analysis of the department's existing learning infrastructure. When they did turn their attention to this problem, they began with asking what was hindering the existing Policy Analysis and Lessons Learned Unit from acting as an effective driver gathering lessons from the field to feed into doctrine development, training, and implementation on the ground, with a swift feedback mechanism to enable the constant improvement of doctrine and training. They found that most of the modest growth in the unit's capacity since 1995 had been absorbed by servicing the intergovernmental committees, such as the General Assembly's Special Committee on Peacekeeping Operations. In as much as it had been able to work on its actual mandate, the unit had followed a reactive approach. Based on available capacity, members conducted or commissioned 'lessons-learned studies' of mostly closing missions in order to capture best practices. However, the intended recipients – senior managers and mission planners in the Office of Operations – rarely found the resulting reports sufficiently timely and relevant to be useful for their work. With a maximum output of two lessons learned studies or Secretary-General's reports per year between 1997 and 2000, the Lessons Learned Unit was largely unable to make itself relevant with regard to the key challenges faced by operational managers at the time. In the words of an official report issued much later, its output in terms of useful guidance materials had been 'limited, their quality uneven and their status often ambiguous, especially with regard to expectations of compliance' (UN Secretary-General 2007: 3; Benner and Rotmann 2008).

As a first step toward a more comprehensive strategy, Guéhenno secured significant extra funding for the learning unit and put a staunch proponent of organizational reform in charge: David Harland, Ahmed's coauthor in the Srebrenica investigation. Harland was able to hire almost his entire team from scratch, a rare event in the UN bureaucracy that brought another wave of young, reform-oriented analysts to headquarters. Most of the additional funds came from individual governments who wanted to support Secretariat capacity in this field, particularly the United Kingdom, Canada, and Norway, while a number of other European countries would pitch in on later occasions, including Germany.

With a new, expanded team, the number and analytical depth of the unit's reports increased significantly, and external consultants were hired to look into crosscutting challenges such as coordination and mission integration. The long-running endeavor to create a 'Handbook on Multidimensional Peacekeeping Operations' was completed in 2003, and a new Knowledge

Management Project was started to assemble an online Resource Center facilitating access to studies, reports, and documents on peace operations by the UN and external sources. Harland's willingness to open up to external expertise particularly in the scholarly community was part of a larger initiative driven from Secretary-General Annan's office who successively retained high-profile academics such as Andrew Mack (1998–2001) and Michael Doyle (2001–3) as Research Directors in his Executive Office. Over the following years, the Peacekeeping Best Practices Section (PBPS), once again renamed, issued studies and reports at a record quality and pace, in addition to its internal duties toward the intergovernmental bodies (Durch et al. 2003: 41; Benner and Rotmann 2008: 53).

Soon, however, Harland recognized that the unit remained stuck in an ineffectual paradigm. Much as the authors themselves or some external consultant might learn about previous failures or best practices, writing a study provided no institutional learning benefit as long as planners in the Office of Operations and decision-makers in senior management saw no point in reading it or acting on its recommendations. Focusing the bulk of available resources on studying closing missions was particularly ineffective because it almost never produced results that were seen as applicable to current challenges, for two reasons. First, almost every contextual aspect of a closing mission would be different from the current ones, both externally (in terms of different political situations in the Security Council and in the mission area) and internally (in terms of organizational changes within DPKO). Second, the single-case approach to writing those studies, without a guiding analytical framework and covering the whole range of possibly interesting questions about the mission, all but ensured that the product followed perceived political priorities rather than providing candid analysis and drawing useful generalizations for application in different situations. As a result, there was no institutional follow-up on 'lessons learned,' nor was there a standard operating procedure to collect the observations of serving officials in the field.

After a year spent on hiring staff, managing external consultants, and building up the Best Practices Section, Harland's team began to reinvent the unit as a hub to support a complete learning cycle. The problem was, however, that none of the other parts of that cycle – policy development, training, and evaluation – existed in DPKO. Apart from Security Council mandates for individual missions and general administrative regulations, there were no policies to help peacekeepers in implementing their mandates, and there was effectively no training provided by the UN. The existing training unit was part of the Military Adviser's office and already hard-pressed to deliver orientation sessions and introductory seminars on crosscutting topics such as human rights, gender equality, and civil–military coordination at military academies and training centers around the world, given that almost 200,000 troops rotated through UN peace operations every year. Only recently had the first four missions in the field created training centers to deliver a limited induction program to new staff, a high-level induction course for senior mission managers had been developed, and the UN Institute for Training and Research (UNITAR) had begun to build a program to systematically debrief SRSGs, funded by grants from member states and charitable foundations. Evaluations were conducted on a case-by-case basis, mostly by former senior military officers or senior mission leaders who would travel to a mission, conduct a few interviews, and deliver a report. While often useful to assess the specific situation of the mission in question, these evaluations were not designed to ensure compliance with any kind of general policies or procedures, or to investigate the effectiveness of such doctrine. Clearly, the reformers concluded, a strategy was needed that went beyond the narrow confines of tweaking the inner workings of the Best Practices Unit. The peace operations bureaucracy needed full-scale transformation.

Peace Operations 2010: Putting Learning at the Center of Institutional Reform

In the summer of 2005, an opportunity presented itself to get the ball rolling on the broader reform agenda. Guéhenno asked Harland to take over the job of Director of Change Management on an interim basis, while the previous incumbent went to serve in a senior management position in the field for a year. Harland quickly seized the opportunity to develop a broader reform agenda for DPKO based on what he called the 'unfinished business' of the Brahimi report, focusing on five core priorities: personnel (recruitment, training, rapid deployment), doctrine (need for standards and guidance on key tasks, as well as a process for the constant adaptation of such guidance), organization (clear division of roles and responsibilities), resources (improving efficiency and harnessing more funds), and partnerships (with other UN and non-UN agencies). In each of these fields, he identified 'weaknesses [that were] within the power of the Secretariat to change,' and drafted a five-year plan to do so. Guéhenno adopted this agenda for the department as a whole and presented it to the diplomatic community in October 2005. Given a catchy title ('Peace Operations 2010'), the program was further developed and distributed to peace operations personnel globally in November.[14]

Within the Peace Operations 2010 agenda, the work of establishing an effective infrastructure to support a full organizational learning cycle touched on almost every priority area, but was primarily associated with the priority of

---

[14] Quotes are from interviews with David Harland; the official presentation of the Peace Operations 2010 agenda can be found in Guéhenno (2005a, 2005b).

doctrine. This choice of language sparked instant opposition because many at the UN misunderstood the concept of doctrine as an exclusively military or militaristic term. It hardly helped that the term is often not consistently defined and employed outside military organizations, and until 2005, there was only an official UN definition for 'military doctrine' as the 'fundamental principles, practices and procedures that guide the *military component* of UN peacekeeping missions in support of mandated UN objectives' (UN DPKO 2001, emphasis added). However, doctrine in this sense as a set of principles and standard operating procedures to guide the actions of individuals on behalf of an organization is no stranger to civilian bureaucracies as well. As Guéhenno explained in his letter to DPKO personnel, the aim was 'to define and clearly articulate . . . what it is that UN peacekeeping can do and how, . . . followed by the development of effective guidance on how to achieve these standards. . . . We need uniform practices and procedures that . . . will be the basis for guiding you in carrying out your job. It will be a living doctrine that adapts to ongoing experiences and conditions' (Guéhenno 2005a: para. 11).

In defining its strategy, Harland's team conducted extensive research both internally and toward potential examples in other organizations. In 2004, the Best Practices Section had conducted a survey among field staff that revealed the extent to which people on the ground felt left alone by headquarters in New York. Fifty percent of the almost 600 respondents complained that the lack of guidance and documentation required them to reinvent the wheel 'very often' or 'all the time.' Forty-six percent said they had received no guidance materials or orderly handover from a predecessor at the start of their current job, and only 28 percent had received 'any kind of written instructions in the form of policies, manuals, best practices or otherwise' (UN Secretary-General 2007: 2). The reformers concluded that they had a 'knowledge-thirsty work-force,' but 'weak institutional support' in terms of an easily accessible repository of doctrine and guidance as well as effective knowledge management tools to support horizontal communication among different missions in the field (UN DPKO 2006b: 7). In trying to find the most effective ways to implement these ideas in an organization that was as fragile and decentralized as the peace operations bureaucracy, Harland's team drew on a wide range of outside experiences in some twenty other organizations, from international oil companies and the World Bank to the US and Indian armies (Figure 2.4).

Based on their findings, Harland's team set up three parallel efforts to build the groundwork of a full learning cycle 'that links the identification and sharing of best practices to the development of policies, guidelines and procedures that reflect those lessons [in] an institutional doctrine that can then be disseminated through training programmes' (UN Secretary-General 2007: 4): a Guidance Project to establish a doctrine development process and some of the most needed guidance materials, a 'knowledge toolbox' to enable better

A UN reformer's "ideal learning cycle"

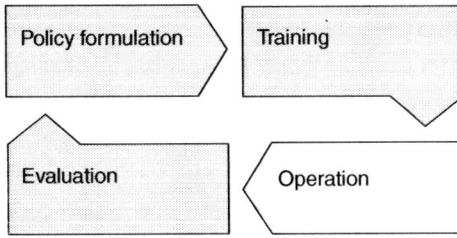

Figure 2.4 A UN reformers' 'ideal learning cycle'

informal communication and feedback from the field, and a revitalization of DPKO's training efforts. While the Guidance Project was bound to be a top-down exercise to establish officially codified policies and procedures, the knowledge management team was tasked to develop ways of informal bottom-up and horizontal knowledge sharing, the products of which could be used as a source of feedback to inform the formulation and improvement of guidance for as long as it would take to establish an effective evaluation capacity as well.

Harland's guidance team developed a hierarchical architecture to organize the various pieces of doctrine at different levels of abstraction, to be filled by policy directives, standard operating procedures (SOPs), manuals, and guide-lines for the various functional areas of peace operations. At the top of the pyramid, the so-called Capstone Doctrine would 'define the nature, scope and core business of contemporary UN peacekeeping operations.... It identifies the comparative advantages and limitations of United Nations peacekeeping operations as a conflict management tool, and explains the basic principles that should guide their planning and conduct' (UN DPKO/DFS 2008: 8). All the progressively more fine-grained and technical elements of doctrine in each of the functional areas of peace operations link these abstract principles to the mission-specific planning and implementation in the field. At the beginning, the guidance team would do all the legwork in terms of drafting policies and shepherding them through the approval process itself. As other units became willing to set aside their own resources or obtain additional ones to take responsibility for policy development in their subject area, the Best Practices Section would limit itself to the role of a 'learning hub' supporting the various doctrine development and knowledge management processes and helping management to prioritize among them. To put each individual unit in charge of their own policies was seen as the only way to ensure their full participation in the process, and the only way to achieve a substantial level of output without putting unrealistic demands on the Best Practices Section alone.

The knowledge-sharing toolbox followed a much less predetermined approach. The idea was to provide a set of tools that would be equally useful for horizontal communication among field staff and for knowledge collection efforts at headquarters.[15] The team urged senior officials to write End-of-Assignment Reports and conduct After Action Reviews to be shared on a new intranet platform, while officials at all levels were encouraged to write formal Handover Notes. Best Practices established online 'communities of practice' for practitioners to discuss their challenges and solutions among each other, and offered to conduct 'surveys of practice' on frequently asked questions among practitioners in the field, again sharing the results informally across the organization without prior review or approval by DPKO. All of these tools, no matter how well supported by the small team in New York, would impose additional work on often overworked and skeptical staffers in the field. Therefore, one 'Best Practice Officer' would be deployed to every mission to support the adoption of these tools in practice. As the flow of information from the field would grow, it would also become increasingly useful as a source for prioritizing and informing guidance development at headquarters.

DPKO's scattered military and civilian training units were merged into a new Integrated Training Service (ITS). Previously, its staff had been flying around the world to deliver lectures and seminars at the request of member states, too few to make much of an impact on the readiness and competence of blue helmets at large. As the complexity of peace operations and the number of contributing countries rose, demand for training quickly outstripped the unit's capacity, forcing its staff to play a constant game of catch-up and leaving insufficient time to even develop high-quality training materials. Based on this analysis, the new ITS first sought to limit its own training activities to a select number of courses for senior mission leaders and civilian newcomers to peace operations, and otherwise focus on producing training materials for national and regional peacekeeping training centers to use. In a second step, following a change of leadership in October 2007, ITS went even further and tried to have the functional experts in each field develop the actual curricula and training materials: contributing countries would remain responsible for military and police training, and civilian training would be assigned to the substantial sections in DPKO, for which ITS sought to raise funds to create a small training capacity for each. ITS itself would focus on strategy, standard-setting and quality assurance, as well as conducting a very

---

[15] Many of the ideas that evolved into the knowledge-sharing toolbox had their roots in the Brahimi report itself, which featured a somewhat technology-focused but well-crafted set of recommendations to improve knowledge management in peace operations (United Nations 2000: paras. 252–8).

limited range of crosscutting training programs such as the civilian induction course and the senior leadership seminars. While sound in theory, member states so far have neither provided the funds to create state-of-the-art training materials nor have troop contributors relented in their pressure on ITS to provide its traditional seminars which had always been popular with their military brass.

The Challenges of Implementation

Despite Guéhenno's personal endorsement and support, the reinvigorated reform program quickly encountered resistance within the department. The most skeptical officials were to be found in the higher echelons of DPKO and in its core element, the Office of Operations. Organized in regional divisions and desks for each field operation, the Office of Operations coordinates the political planning, deployment, and ongoing management of peace operations, drawing on the services and expertise of the rest of the department as required. As a result, the office enjoys enormous informal authority and regards itself as the best and most hardworking part of the organization. Justifiably proud of having held together many a mission in crisis with little more than their bare hands and starved for resources for a long time, Operations managers were the main carriers of the department's traditional culture of ad hoc improvisation.[16] At the same time, mutually destructive stereotypes poisoned the atmosphere among the different parts of DPKO, and the Operations crowd found themselves widely accused of arrogance and aloofness in dealing with the nuts-and-bolts parts of their own department.

When it came to organizational learning, many Operations officials had seen scores of 'lessons learned reports' that they ultimately found irrelevant for their day-to-day business. Given their rapidly rising workload throughout 2005 and 2006, it was hardly surprising that many found themselves not only unable to contribute to knowledge management systems or doctrine development but that some went as far as to question the wisdom of spending scarce resources on another exercise that was asking for their time and attention now while promising a payoff much later, if at all. More to the point, some officials feared that the drive toward professionalization and standard operating procedures would result in a technocratic, 'cookie-cutter' approach to peace operations that would level contextual differences and marginalize local knowledge even further. In making this argument, they echoed well-founded

---

[16] Since the establishment of DPKO in 1992, there are many cases in which budget increases benefited other units to a greater extent than the Office of Operations, sometimes because specific issues were more popular with member states, sometimes because other managers were more effective advocates for their needs.

warnings in part of the academic literature. As Michael Barnett argues, '[it] is [the] lack of knowledge [on the part of peace operations staff] about how to engineer a successful postconflict operation that poses the real problem. At present, many peacebuilders escape their uncertainty by relying on general models that frequently are developed from their most recent experiences in the field.' Like development economists in the 1970s, the danger is that peace operations professionals would be 'falling in love with their models and assuming that these countries were so simple that those models told them all they needed to know.' Instead of universal templates, Barnett argues that successful peace operations 'require judgment informed by a deep knowledge of local circumstances and views' (Barnett 2006: 109–10).

While undoubtedly well founded and in most cases brought forward without ulterior motives, it is somewhat ironic that allegations of bureaucratic universalism were raised in response to the efforts of 'a new generation of UN staff [who] . . . are self-critical and skeptical of cookie-cutter approaches' themselves (NYU-CIC 2004). Unavoidably, some of these questions were also fueled by the underlying cultural rift between this younger generation of reformers and the longer serving, generally older generation of traditionalists. In the evolution of organizational culture, the balance began to tip in about 2005. The new posts that the Brahimi reforms had yielded for DPKO had been filled mainly with reform-minded officials from the field for whom the Brahimi report embodied the guiding paradigm. In addition, Guéhenno's professionalization efforts bore fruit. A 2004 management review conducted by the UN's internal auditors recognized 'a number of worthy initiatives in that area [management culture] that were focused on change from crisis-driven decision-making to tackling longer-term systemic issues and from being reactive to becoming more responsive to the needs of the field' (UN Secretary-General 2004: 17).

Building on this sense of movement on the cultural level, Harland managed to convince a sufficiently strong coalition of supporters at all levels of the necessity and the merits of the proposed changes. Over a period of several months and with 'top cover' from Guéhenno, he set up a working group to drive the reform process and established a formal doctrine development procedure both of which were sufficiently inclusive to draw on the substantial expertise of supporters and skeptics alike, and to allow the latter a significant say, often effectively a veto, on policy decisions.[17]

When Jean-Marie Guéhenno left office in the summer of 2008, the internal political and cultural support for his reforms had become itself a part of the organization's identity. While each of the building blocks for an effective

---

[17] The doctrine development process is formally defined in an SOP dated July 2005 (UN DPKO 2005).

infrastructure of learning – and ultimately, to make the peace operations bureaucracy a 'learning organization' (UN Secretary-General 2007: 4) – remained unfinished business, there was no backlash from within the bureaucracy after his departure: despite the odds, he had achieved his initial goal to 'build an institution' and even long-time skeptics among DPKO's senior management praised him for 'transforming Best Practices into something really useful.'

In his final months in office, Guéhenno implemented the new Secretary-General Ban Ki-moon's plan to divide the core of the peace operations bureaucracy into a policy and management department (which retained the name DPKO) and a new Department of Field Support (DFS) to cover administration and logistics. On the coattails of that separation and a substantial if insufficient budget increase, the Secretariat convinced member states to fund a number of policy development positions in various parts of DPKO; create a stronger Policy, Evaluation and Training Division; and combine the Police Division, a small judicial section, the disarmament team, and a small new team on security sector reform into a new high-level Office of Rule of Law and Security Institutions (Figure 2.5).

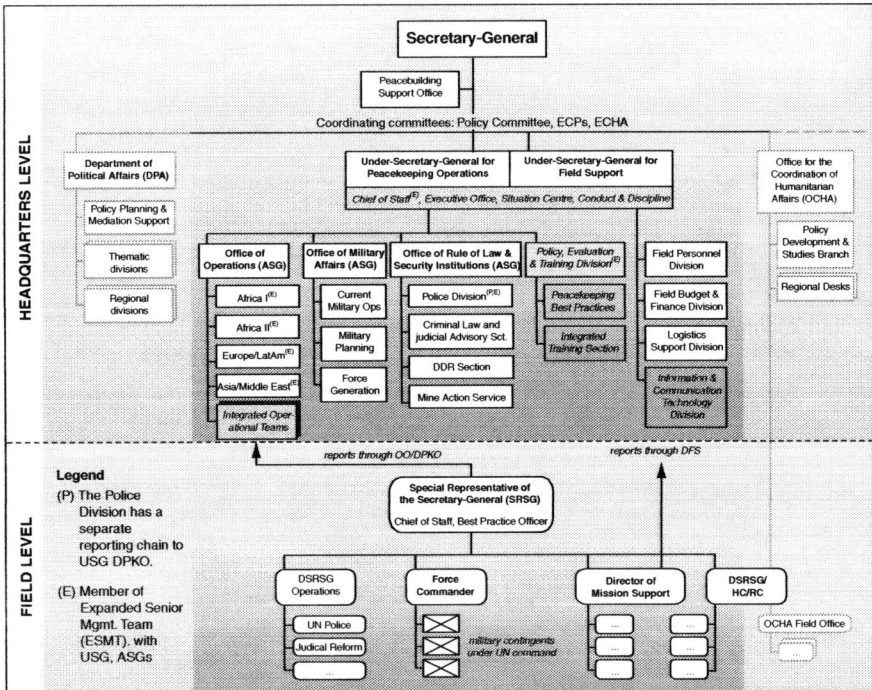

Figure 2.5 Inside the peace operations bureaucracy

Eight years after the Brahimi report and six decades after the first peacekeeping mission, it was the first time that the peace operations bureaucracy possessed a learning infrastructure sufficiently well resourced and integrated into decision-making processes to support a basic hum of modestly ambitious learning to take place. Until that time, as our case studies attest, most learning processes had been more of a fight against bureaucracy than a process supported by it.

A preliminary assessment by the Secretariat after the first two years (2005–7) lists the general outputs. Over that time period, the knowledge-sharing toolbox generated '78 After Action Reviews, 129 End of Assignment Reports and eight Surveys of Practice,' while the policy development system resulted in '24 policy directives, eight guidelines, 14 standard operating procedures and four manuals... on a wide range of operational tasks' (UN Secretary-General 2007: 9). Best Practice Officers were deployed to most multidimensional missions. Use of the new intranet platform and participation in horizontal exchanges through Communities of Practice has grown rapidly, with ten communities with a total of almost 1,500 contributors active and more requests for the establishment of new ones than the small knowledge sharing team could handle (ibid.). In addition, the new Principles and Guidelines document issued in February 2008 is the first high-level statement of peace operations doctrine in more than a decade.

However, beyond these statistics, the question remains how learning has played out in concrete cases – within concrete issues areas all of which have been wrestling with the overall trends and challenges in peace operations outlined in this chapter. What were the enablers and constraints on learning in concrete cases and what conclusions can we draw for the efforts to build a learning organization? In Chapters 4–7, twelve case studies across the policy areas of public security, judicial reform, reintegration of former combatants, and mission integration will present in-depth analyses of these questions. Introducing these case studies, Chapter 3 develops an analytical framework for investigating concrete processes of learning in the UN peace operations bureaucracy.

3

Analyzing Organizational Learning in the Peace Operations Bureaucracy

Chapter 2 detailed the efforts of the reformers in the UN apparatus to strengthen the learning capacity of the UN peace operations bureaucracy. But how exactly has it learned (or not learned) over the past decade? What are the key drivers and obstacles to learning? What patterns can we discern as to the relative importance of these influences? What are the conditions for learning to occur in international bureaucracies?

Answering these questions requires a clear conceptual framework to guide case selection and analysis. In thinking about organizational learning, conceptual clarity has never been easy to find. As Jack Levy wrote, 'the concept of learning is difficult to define, isolate, measure, and apply empirically' and any such effort requires 'sweeping a conceptual minefield' (Levy 1994: 280). This is particularly so because 'learning is a concept which cuts across virtually all of the major theoretical and meta-theoretical debates in the social sciences. A broad range of positions on questions such as the locus of social learning (who or what learns?), the nature of and "motors" driving such learning; developing corresponding criteria for distinguishing between learning and non-learning-based change phenomena; and the relationship between power and learning are visible in a diverse body of literature devoted to the concept' (Stern 1997: 69).

As a consequence, the danger of getting bogged down in meta-theoretical debates looms large in thinking conceptually about the analysis of organizational learning. We seek to avoid this risk by starting with a number of assumptions. First and fundamentally, we assume that *organizational* learning exists as a phenomenon distinct from *individual* learning, which is of course a necessary precondition. A number of scholars refute this possibility entirely.[1]

---

[1] Jack Levy (1994: 287), for one, argues that 'the reification of learning to the collective level – and the assumption that organizations or governments have goals, beliefs, and memories – is not analytically viable.'

We disagree; this position ignores the well-documented fact that organizations such as the UN peace operations bureaucracy work based on rules internal to the organization which exercise substantial and observable influence over its actions (Barnett and Finnemore 1999, 2004). Organizational learning can be one reason for these rules to change, which in turn influences the way officials work in these organizations.

Second, we choose not to engage in the value-laden exercise of judging whether what an organization learns – a 'lesson' – is accurate. Lise Morjé Howard (2008) and many others assume that organizational learning leads to greater accuracy in terms of what the organization 'knows' about the world, and also greater efficiency in terms of achieving the organization's goals through a better matching of ends and means.[2] Judging this would require a standard by which we can measure the accuracy and effectiveness of learning. In peacebuilding, like in many other fields of social science, outcomes are often uncertain, there is very little universally accepted knowledge about causal relationships, and fundamental assumptions are highly contested. Without an unquestioned scientific point of reference, scholars following the 'efficiency' school of organizational learning almost invariably fall back on 'their own causal assumptions and normative biases' (Levy 1994: 292). To avoid this pitfall, we choose not to make judgments about the validity of lessons and their contribution to efficiency or effectiveness. At the same time, our approach is not entirely value-free. We argue that organizations should become better at reflecting their failures and successes, especially if they work on complex and contested issues of peacebuilding that affect the lives of millions. In Michael Barnett's words, the burden on organizations such as the UN peacebuilding apparatus is to 'cultivate a spirit of epistemological uncertainty' (Barnett 2010: 211).

With these assumptions in mind, in the following pages we develop a framework for analyzing organizational learning in the UN peace operations bureaucracy. We begin by situating our approach in the different literatures on organizational learning, developing our definition of organizational learning and sketching the learning cycle as a heuristic tool to capture the process dimension of learning. After that, we discuss two clusters of influences that can both promote and obstruct learning processes: infrastructure and politics. We then identify four different patterns in which these factors interact. Finally, we explain the selection of the book's case studies that will examine the interplay of these patterns in greater detail.

---

[2] Howard, for example, contends that 'the results of cognitive change are only understood to be learning if they enable an organization to better engage with the environment' (Howard 2008: 15).

Perspectives on Organizational Learning

What is organizational learning? How can we define and analyze organizational learning for international bureaucracies such as the UN peace operations apparatus? One would expect that the discipline of international relations (IR) provides clear answers to these questions. Unfortunately, this is not the case. Precious few studies in IR have dealt with organizational learning; the pioneering work of Ernst Haas was a towering exception (Haas 1990; Haas and Haas 1995).[3] At the same time, turning to current research on organizational learning in other disciplines such as sociology, public administration, military studies, and business management does not provide readily available answers either. While each of these fields looks back on a longstanding and fruitful tradition of scholarship on organizational learning and has produced several valuable concepts, these should be taken with a grain of salt. This research shows a high degree of heterogeneity and 'has suffered from conceptions that were excessively broad, [...] and from various other maladies that arise from insufficient agreement among those working in the area on key concepts and problems' (Cohen and Sproull 1991: Editor's introduction). Furthermore, most of this research has focused on either business organizations or domestic administrations and all but ignored international bureaucracies as research objects. For example, the two most prominent volumes taking stock of research on organizational learning do not make any reference to international bureaucracies (Dierkes et al. 2001; Easterby-Smith and Lyles 2005). Thus, any concepts taken from this research first need to be adapted to fit the context of international political bureaucracies, which is as distinct from the market environment of companies as from the domestic political context of national armies or administrations. One way of doing so is to link back to some of the classics in the sociology of organizations, such as the work of Max Weber (1980 (1921)) or the debate on bureaucracies in the 1960s (Mayntz 1968). In recent years, these classics have also been rediscovered for the study of international organizations (Barnett and Finnemore 2004), providing some of the crucial building blocks of a framework for analyzing organizational learning in international bureaucracies.

In our definition of organizational learning, we therefore combine some key insights on the nature of bureaucracies from the classical sociology of organizations (stressing, among other things, the salience of rules) with the seminal work of Ernst Haas on learning in international organizations (which puts a premium on the importance of knowledge). Drawing on further research from related disciplines, we develop a learning cycle as well as an overview of the key influences that promote or obstruct learning in international bureaucracies.

---

[3] There is a rich tradition of scholarship on foreign policy learning that looks at states and state-level decision-makers but not at organizational learning (e.g., Breslauer and Tetlock 1991).

Defining Organizational Learning and the Learning Cycle

Max Weber was the first to systematically analyze organizational traits of bureaucracies, stressing the importance of rules for their basic logic of operation. In order to deal with the complex political circumstances that they are set up to address and stabilize, bureaucracies develop rules to reduce the complexity of their environment. Rules are at the core of what makes bureaucracies work. Michael Barnett and Martha Finnemore (2004: 3) have recently taken up Max Weber's lead for the analysis of international bureaucracies: 'Bureaucracies exercise power in the world through their ability to make impersonal rules. They then use rules not only to regulate but also to constitute and construct the social world.' Rules create organizational structures such as hierarchical reporting lines and the division of responsibility between units as well as standard operating procedures on how to deal with particular kinds of tasks. In the peace operations bureaucracy, rules establish a new mission or a rapidly deployable standing police unit as well as a standardized checklist to manage fuel consumption and complex, context-sensitive guidance on how to rebuild judicial systems in postwar societies. Rules also make up 'doctrine.' We use doctrine to describe a particular body of rules to guide the organization in implementing its mandated objectives (UN DPKO 2001; Ahmed et al. 2007). A temporary change in organizational action may also happen without an explicit change of the rules, but such change is only institutionalized – that is, made sustainable across staff rotations – when new rules reflect the change. Organizational learning in bureaucracies needs to address this core feature and lead to a change in the rules. At the same time, unlike some of the military learning literature (Nagl 2005), we do not assume that rules (e.g., doctrine) are always readily implemented. Therefore, learning can only be considered complete or successful when rule changes also lead to changes in practice.

From the work of Ernst Haas (and much of the literature on organizational learning in sociology and management), we adopt the focus on the importance of knowledge.[4] In our understanding of learning, we consider a process to be organizational learning only if it is significantly based on reflection and knowledge (Haas 1990). We also agree with Haas that there is no such thing as value-free, 'technical' knowledge, in particular in peacebuilding. Rather, knowledge is always informed by a normative claim to be valid or true – a claim that is necessarily subjective and often contested by the proponents of a different view.

---

[4] Here, Haas follows Max Weber who emphasized that knowledge is at the heart of bureaucratic power.

However, we do not share Haas' exclusive focus on 'consensual knowledge' developed by 'epistemic communities,' such as groups of like-minded scientists, as a basis for learning. In Haas' model, scientists reach a consensus on (re-) conceptualizing a problem and an adequate response (e.g., how chlorofluor-ocarbons damage the ozone layer and how we can mitigate this effect); an enlightened international bureaucracy adopts the (new) scientific wisdom through a political process and thereby 'learns.' While certainly viable for particular environmental issues, the model is of far less relevance when it comes to fields where there is no clear-cut scientific consensus within an 'epistemic community.' Peacebuilding is such a field. There is no 'science of peacebuilding' producing consensus on how to deal with the complex challenge of building a lasting peace after conflicts (Lipson 2010).[5] Therefore, we choose to cast a wider net in terms of the knowledge sources of learning. Knowledge informing organizational learning in peace operations does not have to be 'consensual knowledge' emerging from a circle of scientists. Knowledge can have a variety of sources (e.g., from within the organization itself, from local actors in the affected countries, from nongovernmental organizations), may draw on practical experience rather than scientific inquiry, and always reflects the particular views and perspectives of those from whom it emerges. For knowledge to be relevant to justify a change in organizational practice, it needs to be made explicit even if it may have been around in the form of tacit knowledge already (Nonaka 1994; Rid 2007).

Combining the emphasis on rules and knowledge, we define organizational learning as *a knowledge-based process of questioning and changing organizational rules to change organizational practice.* Conceptually speaking, learning may also confirm existing rules and practice. Since such cases pose much less of a political and institutional challenge to the organization, we focus on a more ambitious set of cases that attempt to change existing rules and practice.

In a political bureaucracy, particularly in a field as contested and heterogeneous as peacebuilding, the questioning of prior knowledge and the debate about lessons is never an apolitical exercise. In a review of political science contributions to organizational learning, LaPalombara (2001: 139) argues that economic rationality as the sole driver of learning 'is as rare in the public or political sector as it may actually be alien to it.' Instead, 'organizational "lessons" are formulated though a process of negotiation or bargaining. That is, "lessons" are ... the product of an organizational or political dynamic,

---

[5] In addition, even if there were such a scientific discipline, in the absence of a broadly accepted, monolithic body of intersubjectively shared knowledge, competing factions within an international bureaucracy would be expected to draw strategically on the opposing analyses offered by scientists. In recent years, an example of this problem could be observed in the debate about the causes of climate change.

rather than ... of the application of logic and pure reason to the past' (Lovell 1984: 134).

The process dimension of learning is best captured in a cyclical model similar to the policy cycle, a familiar heuristic tool for political scientists. In line with much of the organizational learning literature (March and Olsen 1976; Huber 1991; Crossan et al. 1999), we distinguish three stages of the learning process, each guided by distinct logics: (a) *knowledge acquisition*, (b) *advocacy*, and (c) *institutionalization*.

- *Knowledge acquisition*: Organizational learning begins when a small group of individuals within the organization acquires new knowledge through active research or passive reception from outside sources, or by converting its own experience into new knowledge. Outside sources of knowledge could be scholars, member states, or other organizations. The new 'lesson' – be it a small technical proposal or a fundamental critique of core assumptions – only becomes relevant for the organization at the small-group level, where the lesson evolves beyond an individual's secret idea. Those small groups do not need to correspond to formal units according to the organizational structure; they may include dedicated units like the Department of Peacekeeping Operations' (DPKO) Best Practices Section as well as informal groups of like-minded reformers from several layers of hierarchy or different duty stations, at headquarters or in the field.

- *Advocacy*: As the carriers of the new lesson spread the word within the organization, they translate new knowledge into policy proposals to change existing rules. At this stage, the learning process enters a stage of intergroup advocacy, arguing, and bargaining. Through a combination of arguing their case and building coalitions, the lesson's proponents try to build momentum and convince key decision-makers to accept their claim to new knowledge and the corresponding proposal to change rules, the details of which will often change during the advocacy stage in order to broaden political support. In doing so, they may draw on the higher echelons of the bureaucracy, member states, or a combination of the two, depending on the nature of the lesson at hand. The advocacy stage results in an authoritative decision on whether and how to change the rules.

- *Institutionalization*: Once a decision has been taken to formally change the rules, it must be codified and implemented. However, implementation does not follow automatically.[6] For the most part, institutionalization is a top-down process in which the new rules are merged into the existing

---

[6] The implementation challenge is exacerbated by the multisited character of many international bureaucracies (e.g., with a high number of quasi-autonomous field offices as is the case with the UN peace operations apparatus).

body of rules, disseminated among the relevant units, fed into training programs, and in which, ultimately, compliance is ensured. The learning process is only completed once the new rules are applied throughout the organization. In an ideal learning process, implementation is followed by formal evaluations as well as dedicated channels for bottom-up communication to activate a full feedback loop (Figure 3.1).

If these three stages are completed at least once, we speak of a 'successful' learning process. As we refrain from our own normative judgments about the validity of lessons, our standard of success refers only to the fulfillment of the process cycle. Ideally, the full cycle would repeat itself with the newly institutionalized rules or doctrine subject to continuous review and further learning. However, the cycle can be interrupted at any point. Stalled, incomplete, or abandoned learning processes are indeed common empirical phenomena. The use of the term 'learning process' in this book to refer to the objects of our case studies is therefore never meant to imply successful learning but denotes a process of attempted learning whose outcome could be anything from immediate failure through various stages of partial success or stalled progress to, ultimately, full completion of the learning cycle. Studies of learning 'should attempt to specify at what point in the cycle the learning process gets blocked' and why (Levy 1994: 289), which we will do in the case studies in this book. To do this, we need to be able to systematically assess the influences that promote or obstruct learning, which is another key element of our analytical framework.

Influences on Learning

Most scholars of organizational learning assume that traditional bureaucracies are by nature unlikely to learn. Building on Weber's emphasis on the formal rationality of bureaucracies and their propensity to standardize operating procedures, Barnett and Finnemore point out that the 'absence of a

A Cyclical Model of Organizational Learning

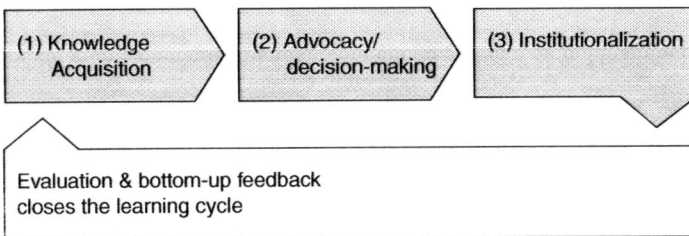

Figure 3.1 A cyclical model of organizational learning

competitive environment that selects out inefficient practices coupled with already existing tendencies toward institutionalization of rules and procedures insulates the organization from feedback and increases the likelihood of pathologies' (Barnett and Finnemore 1999: 723). Another analyst of the 'bureaucratic organization' contends: 'The bureaucratic system of organization is not only a system that does not correct its behaviour in view of its errors; it is also too rigid to adjust, without crises, to the transformations that the accelerated evolution of the industrial society makes more and more imperative' (Crozier 1964: 287). Therefore, most scholars hold that only major crises can overcome bureaucratic inertia and trigger learning processes in bureaucratic organizations. However, the default setting in everyday bureaucratic work is inertia and non-learning. This setting is far away from what the management literature describes as the ideal of the *learning organization* – one that purposefully constructs 'structures and strategies so as to enhance and maximize organizational learning' (Dodgson 1993: 377). Constant learning and feedback is the default for this kind of organization. As little scholarship as is there on the UN peace operations bureaucracy, most scholars implicitly or explicitly based their work on the traditional bureaucratic default setting of the 'non-learning organization.' Consequently, they found that only major crises such as the UN's catastrophic failures in Rwanda and Srebrenica appear to be able to trigger any sort of learning (Breul 2005; Seibel 2009).[7]

At least since 2005, the non-learning organization default is not an accurate description of the UN peace operations bureaucracy. The reforms detailed in Chapter 2 have sparked a nascent transformation toward a learning organization. As a result, the UN peace operations bureaucracy during the first decade of this century is not a pure non-learning organization where we could content ourselves with looking out for major crises and catastrophic failures as triggers for learning. Rather unsurprisingly, neither is it a perfect learning organization in which learning is the default. It is exactly this in-between state that makes the UN peace operations bureaucracy so interesting for detailed research on the influences promoting or obstructing learning.

Therefore, it is no longer enough to simply focus on catastrophic failures as the only triggers of organizational learning. We need a more nuanced understanding of the influences that can promote or obstruct processes of learning. We identified these influences both deductively from the literature on learning in various academic disciplines and inductively from exploratory

---

[7] Lise Morjé Howard's recent study on the peacekeeping operations of the 1990s is an exception in that it investigates learning from a broad range of sources well beyond the 'crisis factor.' At the same time, her inquiry remains mostly confined to individual missions and does not systematically analyze how learning actually works and how it is being affected by different influences (Howard 2008, 2009).

case studies (Benner et al. 2007). In conducting our earlier case studies, we found that it is important to go beyond existing frameworks of causes, factors, or influences on organizational learning, particularly in two dimensions.

First, many approaches try to explain a particular learning process with reference to one fixed constellation of causal factors. For the most part, however, organizational learning unfolds as a dynamic process over a substantial period of time, often years – time in which the organization and many other contextual aspects of a learning process are likely to change. Rather, we found that mapping the temporal dynamic of how the various influences interact throughout the stages of the learning cycle is more useful to explain the progress and ultimately the success or failure of each case.

Second, various frameworks for the analysis of learning focus on traditional organizational characteristics such as formal hierarchy and incentive structures at the expense of crucial political dynamics that play a particularly important role in international bureaucracies with their many political stakeholders. Even apart from those scholars who find no substantial difference between private and public organizations at all (Cook et al. 1997), a classic assumption is to expect a purely negative effect of political factors on learning (Argyris 1986; Senge 1990). According to more recent empirical studies, this hypothesis is 'incomplete, to say the least. Learning within public organizations can be either facilitated or inhibited by a process of politicization' (Dekker and Hansén 2004: 227). At the same time, few attempts to combine political and organizational factors to explain learning manage to avoid excessive heterogeneity and achieve full consistency among their explanatory factors.

Mindful of these conceptual challenges, we systematically group the relevant influences on learning into two clusters: *infrastructure* and *politics*. The infrastructure cluster covers broadly structural properties of the organization that are static at any point in time. While these factors can and do change over time (a crucial feature in many of our case studies in this book), they often at times evolve slowly and in a path-dependent way. The politics cluster covers the part of human and social agency, that is, the dynamic and often more volatile factors of leadership, political pressure, and bureaucratic politics within and beyond the organization.[8]

Infrastructure

An organization's 'learning infrastructure' describes those parts of its overall infrastructure or architecture that affect learning by providing a more or less

---

[8] We regard (infra)structure and politics as mutually constitutive in line with the results of the structure-agency debate in sociology (Giddens 1984).

fertile soil for learning attempts to grow and prosper. Building on the results from our exploratory case studies, we distinguish five influences on learning within the infrastructure cluster: formal structure, resource base, standard procedures, incentive systems, and organizational culture. While each of these factors is analytically distinct, all of them are closely interrelated. An example from the empirical overview of the evolution of the learning infrastructure in the UN peace operations bureaucracy (in Chapter 2) may illustrate this point, which ultimately runs through this entire book: the buildup of a resource base and standard procedures to support knowledge management and learning could only be effective together with a fundamental shift in organizational culture which, in turn, was to a large extent the effect of that investment into dedicated resources and processes. When an organization is comprised of distinct parts whose features partly diverge from that of the core or parent organization as a whole, the factors comprising the learning infrastructure for these suborganizations may also diverge from that of the whole. In the peace operations apparatus, this is most clearly the case for individual missions, and also for parts of the headquarters bureaucracy that are operating with significant autonomy with regard to knowledge management, doctrine development, and learning, such as DPKO's Police Division.

Key elements of *formal structure* such as the distribution of authority and autonomy within a formal hierarchy, the openness or rigidity of information flow and horizontal communication can support or impede the flow of proposals for a knowledge-based revision of rules. It can also provide or deny their proponents' opportunities to question existing assumptions and discuss with senior managers or colleagues from other parts of the organization. In the case of the UN peacebuilding apparatus, the way headquarter–field relations are structured is of particular importance. Similarly, 'boundary-spanning' structures serving to source knowledge from outside organizations (such as those working on similar issues or faced with similar challenges, local actors in the field, universities, and think tanks, and also the organization's own principals, i.e., member states) can play a potentially supportive role, particularly in the knowledge acquisition phase (Thompson 1967; Ansell and Weber 1999; Böhling 2005).

Resources comprise dedicated units, posts, funds, and knowledge repositories to support knowledge management and learning. Most critical is probably one seemingly mundane element: time. Protected staff time for knowledge management tasks (such as documenting and reviewing experience) and adequate numbers of posts to cover the core functions of learning support (such as doctrine development, training, and evaluation) are likely to be a key factor. In an organization operating under constant stress such as the UN peace operations bureaucracy, the allocation of dedicated human resources to strategic objectives such as learning needs to be protected from day-to-day operational demands. Easily accessible, if modest funds are helpful to draw on outside expertise, particularly to refine proposals and develop doctrine or training materials in support of institutionalization. A growing and easily accessible 'knowledge base' of reports and studies may support doctrine development as well as the informal cross-fertilization of knowledge and the generation of lessons.

Standard procedures are at the heart of bureaucratic organization. The substance of standard operating procedures on reporting or decision-making as well as the existence and acceptance of dedicated procedures to support knowledge management and learning determine largely if learning will always be a 'fight against bureaucracy' or if it may be in part embedded in bureaucracy itself. In the peace operations apparatus, such procedures include a defined doctrine development and decision-making process as well as technical and social tools such as online communities of practice, document repositories, regular-lessons-learned studies, end-of-assignment reports, after-action reviews, and evaluation mechanisms. Ideally, these tools and procedures should cover all three stages of the learning cycle from knowledge acquisition to institutionalization.[9]

Incentive systems are hugely consequential for the way humans within organizations work, particularly in terms of initiating proposals, advocating for change, and implementing changes after the formal decision is made. Many knowledge-based organizations such as business consulting firms have created strong incentives linking each individual's contribution to the collective knowledge and learning base to medium- and long-term career prospects (Crucini 2002; Engwall and Kipping 2002). Not only have such incentives been traditionally lacking in the UN system, the whole human resource system for peace operations is built in a way that sets adverse incentives for the majority of field staff operating on short-term contracts. The lack of career prospects for these staff members might actually discourage many to contribute to a common knowledge base.

Finally, *organizational culture* refers to the interpretative frames and cultural norms that are prevalent within subunits or the organization as a whole (Barnett and Finnemore 2004: 39). The effect of culture can promote or obstruct a learning process. For example, advocates of ideal–typical learning organizations have pointed out that a culture that promotes learning needs to be one 'that fosters inquiry, openness, and trust' (Lipshitz, et al. 2002: 84; see also Argyris and Schön 1978). However, culture must not necessarily be

---

[9] As detailed in Chapter 2, it has only been quite recently that the UN began to invest in developing routines and tools for knowledge management and doctrine development for peace operations (Benner and Rotmann 2008). To what extent these innovations have already made a difference on learning will be one subject of our case studies.

homogenous within the entire organization; an organization can have competing subcultures, each with their own interpretative frames. For the case of the UN peace operations bureaucracy, we discussed the competing interpretative frames ('traditionalists' vs. 'reformists') in Chapter 2.

Politics

The 'politics' cluster comprises different kinds of political dynamics which may influence a learning process, originating both within an organization and from interaction with outside actors and events. Within the politics cluster, we distinguish the effects of three crucial dynamics which are closely interrelated: leadership, external political pressure, and bureaucratic politics. Not all of these dynamics are present in every learning process and some of them may combine in a way that makes them impossible to distinguish.

Leadership refers to the role of individuals, often in concert with others, to promote a learning process beyond their formal positions of authority (or lack thereof). In large and complex organizations such as the UN's peace operations bureaucracy, effective leadership coalitions between people in complementary positions on different levels of hierarchy, in different parts of the organization, or even in different organizations, including external partners, are often necessary to effectively support a learning process. The active support of senior officials within the organization may mobilize often scarce resources, help build momentum for advocacy, and provide political cover for the proponents of a lesson (Seibel 2009). Similarly, important roles are taken by mid-level managers, who are often well connected and therefore well positioned as influential advocates, and committed individuals on the working level who are willing to go beyond the call of duty in developing the details of a proposal or repackage it in a persuasive memo (Rid 2007: 19–21). A supportive influence of leadership may also result from an effective leadership coalition across organizational boundaries. Such coalitions may draw on officials in partner agencies within the UN system for best practices or a healthy dose of peer pressure, on experts in think tanks for knowledge or advocacy support, and even on particularly committed diplomats in embassies or member state capitals for external (often financial) resources. As this latter example illustrates, the boundaries between individual leadership and official, if often informal, political support or pressure from member states are often hard to establish. Leadership is also required to create and/or exploit the rare but nonetheless potent opportunities for learning created by a widespread perception of crisis for the organization at large, an example of which is Kofi Annan's skillful use of the Brahimi panel to turn the powerful memory of Rwanda and Srebrenica into an opportunity for a new wave of peace operations (Durch et al. 2003).

Political pressure emerges primarily from member states as the principals of the United Nations and may either promote or obstruct a learning process (Dekker and Hansén 2004).[10] In contrast to the rare case of a leadership role of diplomats (often in the face of friendly indifference on the part of their home ministries), political pressure refers to a deliberate policy toward the UN, if not necessarily toward a particular learning process or lesson (Seibel 2009). Member states define the political and fiscal space in which the UN Secretariat operates. Member state interests and attitudes are therefore a key element in internal debates about whether a lesson is politically desirable or feasible. Often, the mere fact that an influential member state shows a particular interest in a specific subject, regularly inquires about progress, and occasionally provides targeted funding may be enough to support a learning process. Conversely, political power applied by member states may also severely obstruct learning when influential countries oppose a particular lesson or if a learning process falls victim to an unrelated political conflict among states. Specific member state obstruction can also directly affect the behavior of bureaucrats, self-censoring specific proposals known to be opposed by key member states.

Bureaucratic politics within the organization and the wider UN system may result in similar forms of obstruction against a particular learning process. The study of bureaucratic politics consistently discovered that bureaucracies often fail to pursue the 'right' and most appropriate policies because individual units and partially autonomous suborganizations follow 'competitive, not homogeneous interests; [their] priorities and perceptions are shaped by positions; problems are much more varied than straightforward, strategic issues; the management of piecemeal streams of decisions is more important than steady state choices; making sure that the government [or the UN] does what is decided – and does not do what has not been directed – is more difficult than selecting the preferred solution' (Allison and Halperin 1972: 44). In the face of even the most well-intentioned proposal for change, many bureaucratic–political conflicts may arise from the fact that individual actors have incentives to safeguard and maximize their influence and power (Halperin and Clapp 2006: 25–6). Similar to the effects of political pressure, however, bureaucratic politics need not all be detrimental for learning. For example, savvy leaders could tap into the currents of bureaucratic politics to rally support from those who might not be convinced of the lesson alone but may stand to profit from it in terms of influence and power.

---

[10] The media may be another important source of pressure on the bureaucracy. None of our case studies showed a significant effect of media pressure beyond that being channeled through member states. While the agenda-setting role of the global media should not be underestimated, it is probably most significant for the rare, if crucial, moments of fundamental crisis such as those of Rwanda and Srebrenica.

The effects of bureaucratic politics and political pressure are greatly compounded when a lesson's underlying claim is contested among different actors. After all, a lesson and proposal for change might be seen as representing the specific perspective of a particular organizational unit and threatening the interests of others. It is often impossible to empirically distinguish if such a claim about a piece of knowledge or a specific lesson is based on interest in its validity or tactical calculation. In almost any substantive aspect of peacebuilding, it is rare that claims about cause and effect are not contested. As a result, learning is prone to be politicized and caught up both in bureaucratic politics and in broader ideological conflicts between the member states.

Patterns of Influences on the Learning Process

For any point in time in our case studies, we qualitatively assess to what extent we find the interplay of influences in these two clusters to promote, to constrain, or to remain neutral toward the learning process at hand. In doing so, we consider the substance of the lesson – the issue it seeks to address, the ambition of the proposed change, and the way it is perceived or politicized – to be a crucial determinant to the conditions of its success or failure. As a result, no single influence or cluster is always necessary or sufficient on its own for a learning process to be completed. A positive effect from any one cluster may or may not be sufficient in the absence of obstruction from the other, depending on how 'hard' (i.e., ambitious or contested) the lesson turns out to be. As an example, the same moderately developed learning infrastructure may well be able to successfully support a small-scale technical proposal (taking a positive value for that process) while being utterly inadequate to steer a fundamental turnaround on a sensitive political issue through the bureaucratic decision-making process (in relation to which it would take a neutral value, at best).

When the effects of infrastructure and politics are in conflict, we generally expect political influences of adequate strength to be sufficient to determine the outcome in the short term, either promoting learning over a weak infrastructure or obstructing learning in spite of a supportive one. This is a consequence of the way we initially defined these two clusters, locating individual authority and agency as well as the short-term effects of political power in the politics cluster. Over the medium- and long-term, for example, after a formal decision has been pushed through, even sustained political attention may not always be sufficient to ensure institutionalization in the face of a deficient infrastructure. While politics might therefore not always prevail in promoting learning, it is likely a very effective force of obstruction, no matter how well developed a learning infrastructure may be.

Table 3.1 Patterns of interaction between the politics and infrastructure clusters

		Politics		
		Promoting	Neutral	Obstructive
Infrastructure	Promoting		*Infrastructure-driven (progress)*	*Politically inhibited (stalling or failure)*
	Neutral	*Politically driven (progress)*	*Infrastructure-inhibited (stalling or failure)*	
	Obstructive			

Based on these considerations, we expect the interaction of effects from the infrastructure and politics clusters to exhibit one of four distinct patterns at any point in time (Table 3.1). The process may be *politically driven*, that is, promoted by political influences such as leadership or political pressure largely independent of the effect of the infrastructure cluster. It may be *infrastructure-driven*, that is, promoted by the infrastructure to advance along the learning cycle while the politics cluster remains neutral. In other words, in the absence of political obstruction, an enabling infrastructure can promote learning. Conversely, in the absence of supportive influences of either politics or the infrastructure, we consider the process *infrastructure-inhibited* and learning will stall or ultimately fail. Finally, a *politically inhibited* process is determined by obstructive politics, regardless of the infrastructure effect.

Each of the learning processes examined in our case studies can be described as a sequence of these patterns throughout the stages of the learning cycle and empirically explained with reference to the dynamics of interaction among the various influences. Following this framework and identifying these four distinct patterns of interaction between the individual influences on each learning process helps us in three particular ways in dealing with our research question. First, it organizes our findings in a way that directly addresses our initial hypothesis on the dominance of political factors, as stated earlier. How do we find one cluster substitute for the weakness of the other, or undermine the others' strength? Second, it allows us to juxtapose clearly identifiable dynamics with key properties of the lessons themselves: for example, do heavily politicized lessons require a politically driven learning process to succeed, at least among our twelve cases? Third, it guides our research toward answering a key policy question: to what extent did the investment into an effective learning infrastructure for peace operations pay off for the UN over the past several years? Based on the analyses of our twelve cases, we will use the concluding chapter of this book to identify further regularities among different kinds of lessons, relevant patterns of influences, and the stages of the learning cycle.

4

Replacing and Rebuilding Police: Toward Effective and Legitimate Public Order

In the morning of May 24, 2006, a group of UN-trained and certified riot policemen, along with renegade soldiers and demobilized ex-guerrilla fighters, launched a four-hour assault with automatic weapons on the armed forces headquarters of Timor-Leste in Tibar, just west of Dili, the country's capital. One soldier was killed. On the following day, 25 May, 'loyal' army units attacked the police headquarters and, ignoring a UN-brokered ceasefire, killed ten unarmed police officers and injured more than thirty, including two UN police advisers. The confrontation was the culmination of weeks of open violence that pitted rival elements of the nascent Timorese security apparatus against each other. Later on the same day, an advance company of Australian paratroopers landed in Dili paving the way for an international rapid reaction force to restore order at the request of the Timorese government. By mid-August, the UN was back in its erstwhile protectorate, mandated with executive powers to maintain public security and rebuild – or better: build for the first time – a police force that is credible in the eyes of the population. It had barely been fifteen months since the last peacekeepers had left on May 19, 2005, touting Timor-Leste as a 'safe and peaceful country, which was able to assume responsibility for its own security' (UN DPI 2005).[1]

Timor-Leste represents probably the most obvious example of an apparent UN success story in rebuilding law and order after conflict that had in fact failed miserably to achieve anything but the most superficial and short-term indicators of stability (Hood 2006: 61). That was hardly a surprise for insiders, as a former national security official with the UN transitional administration (UNTAET 1999–2002) reported: 'When asked what posed the greatest threat to Timor Leste's security in 2004, a senior officer in the high command of the country's defense force ... stated simply, "The police"' (Rees 2006: 6). 'The

---

[1] See UN DPI (2006), ICG (2006: 12–13), and Perlez (2006).

police' was entirely the creation of the UN transitional administration in East Timor. In addition to performing executive policing duties ranging from crowd control to criminal investigations, the UN mission had been tasked to 'rapidly' establish a 'credible, professional and impartial East Timor police service' (UN Secretary-General 1999: para. 57). Refashioning a former pro-independence guerrilla army and former members of the oppressive Indonesian security institutions into a professional and democratic army and police turned out to be too challenging a task for a UN mission in a hurry. UN police were overwhelmed by its hugely ambitious mandate and lacked both capacity as well as doctrine and guidance to live up to the expectations set by the Security Council. Writing in 2000, Sergio Vieira de Mello, the head of UNTAET himself argued: 'UN police are slow to arrive and seldom effective. They are made up of police officers from up to sixty different countries, all with their own attitudes towards policing, uneven training standards and varying levels of individual competence.' By early 2006, ample warning signs of trouble existed but were lost in communication between mission staff in Dili and the UN headquarters in New York.[2]

Timor-Leste is just one example of the challenges associated with the enormous expansion of UN police that began in the 1990s and accelerated after 1999. The role of police in peace operations has shifted from a mere afterthought to a core element of the stabilizing mission. This rapid evolution presented the UN peace operations apparatus with enormous challenges both operational and doctrinal. Operationally, each of the broader trends in the development of peacekeeping – rapid growth, changing patterns of conflict, and the institution-building mission – had a massive impact on the police. The surge in demand alone was striking. In 1988, there were just thirty-five unarmed UN 'blue berets' deployed in a single mission to Cyprus. A decade later, in 1998, the UN had over 2,000 police deployed globally. In the sixteen months between July 1999 and November 2000, this number more than tripled from 2,411 to 7,800 with new missions being established in Sierra Leone, Kosovo, and East Timor. In January 2011, there were more than 14,300 police officers from eighty-five countries deployed in UN peace operations. Nearly 99 percent of UN police are concentrated in eight large multidimensional peace operations, six of which are in Africa.[3]

As late as 1998, almost all UN police officers were recruited as patrolmen with no regard for special skills or experience. Today, the UN seeks a diverse set of occupational specializations from forensics to management, and more than

---

[2] Interview with senior DPKO police official, May 2007.
[3] DPKO figures include only police deployed to DPKO-led operations, including some political missions such as UNAMA in Afghanistan. In addition, there are a small number of UN police officers serving with political missions led by DPA. The figures have been collected from a variety of official sources (Boutros-Ghali 1995: para. 11; UN DPKO not dated, 2010a, 2010b).

half of UN police are now constabulary forces or 'formed police units' (FPUs) in UN terminology.[4] Not only would it have been entirely impossible to meet the rapid growth in demand with a recruitment model in which every single police officer would be screened, interviewed, selected, and deployed individually. Their missions and the conflicts into which they were deployed also became by several orders of magnitude more demanding. Since 2000, executive roles in interim law enforcement spread from the two formal transitional administrations to a variety of 'robustly mandated' peace operations such as those in Liberia, Côte d'Ivoire, and Haiti. The Security Council's move toward sending peace operations into complex and only partly resolved civil, social, or regional conflicts called for different skill sets, tactics, and equipment – including riot control, and also forensics, criminal investigation, expertise on organized crime, and many other specialized skills. As part of this trend, constabulary forces became standard issue for UN police components in order to fill the gap between military and civilian police capabilities. Similarly, the general trend toward peacebuilding as institution-building found its reflection in the field of police as UN officials increasingly recognized that police reform is much more of a political and managerial challenge than one of technical training and advice. The proliferation of such mandates required rare management experience, combined with a willingness and ability to engage with the local environment that are hard to find in any police service.

These operational challenges, combined with short deployment times, the almost universal lack of pre-deployment training, and the fact that only few police officers deploy for a second tour, made the need for effective guidance and common standards more pressing than ever before – and in turn, the lack of doctrine compounded the operational problems. However, the development of doctrine to guide these increasingly complex operations has been lagging behind. 'Structural shortcomings of doctrine and strategy have limited the operational effectiveness of UN police activities,' warned the Henry L. Stimson Center (Smith et al. 2007: 29). Indeed, to deploy police officers from up to seventy different countries with different legal systems and widely diverging human rights records, the great majority of whom had never served in a UN mission before, to post-conflict settings without clear doctrine and guidance seemed like an irresponsible and dangerous gamble to the reformers in the UN peace operations apparatus.

---

[4] Finding a generic term that captures the functional essence of such police forces amid different national police traditions and diverse sets of requirements practiced by different international organizations proved a challenge we have not been able to fully address. Similar to other terms such as 'gendarmerie' or 'paramilitary police,' the term 'constabulary' has its share of misleading meanings in some national contexts such as Britain, where it refers to any kind of police organization. Nonetheless, we use 'constabulary police' to describe any organized police force operating in formed units under civilian authority and bound by domestic law regardless of the particularities of UN, EU, or NATO regulations and practice.

In 2000, the Brahimi report marked the first time that these issues received high-level political attention. Three critical reports written by Richard Monk, then the UN's police commissioner in Bosnia, and internally championed by Wolfgang Weisbrod-Weber, then the Balkans director at the Department of Peacekeeping Operations (DPKO), had sparked concern among senior officials and landed their author an invitation to be part of the Brahimi panel as the only police expert among diplomats, generals, and UN bureaucrats.[5] In its report, the panel called for a 'doctrinal shift in how the Organization conceives of and utilizes civilian police in peace operations' and for the role of UN police to be 'better understood and developed' (United Nations 2000: para. 40). This formulation was the closest the drafting team came to calling for better operational doctrine in the face of clear warnings from member states that it had already been 'pushing the edge of the envelope with the few doctrinal points it had made' (Ahmed et al. 2007: 18). Five years later, in a study for DPKO's Best Practices Section, legal expert and experienced peacekeeper Bruce Oswald stressed that 'peacekeepers cannot, and should not, expect that their actions involving the use of force, limiting freedom of movement, and detaining individuals are justifiable solely on the basis of necessity or the "fog of peacekeeping." Rather, their actions must be guided by sufficiently detailed principles and standards so that they and the local population are clear about the parameters within which peacekeepers will undertake law and order functions' (Oswald 2005: 10).

Turning the demands for better guidance and doctrine into action turned out to be fraught with difficulties. Some of these difficulties are inherent to the project of having foreigners build or rebuild a police service after war: just by their presence, whether in actual law enforcement or as advisers to local police officers, UN police constantly call into question the credibility and capacity of their local counterparts. While there is a lot of knowledge on the technical basics of forensic analysis, criminal investigations, and the human rights requirements for treating detainees, many of the more complex questions about how to create effective and accountable police services surpass what can easily be expressed in doctrine and guidance documents (Carothers 2003). What is more, even if there was a better overall analytical knowledge base, balancing the universal technical aspects and the normative context-specific aspects of policing and police assistance presents a huge challenge to guidance development. As part of the criminal justice system, the role of police in society, its powers, and procedures are not only a technical matter to be optimized under the tutelage of objective subject-matter experts. To be legitimate, many of these issues must be the subject of political debate and

---

[5] Richard Monk and William Durch, personal communication, August 2010.

contestation. Doctrine developers are therefore required to constantly balance the need for general guidelines to help officers on their first or second deployment avoid mistakes and to constantly reinvent the wheel with the danger of universal technocratic prescriptions to complex idiosyncratic problems where solutions need to be tailored to the local context.

* * *

In terms of professional culture, police officers, like the military, are used to being trained according to doctrine and adapting their general rules for each specific situation. On a very basic level and despite huge differences in cultural and professional backgrounds of individual UN police officers, this should give police a certain advantage in implementation, provided the UN manages to produce useful doctrine in the first place. Perhaps partly because of that professional affinity with the concept, doctrine development efforts began a bit earlier in the field of police than elsewhere. Similar to the military and unlike the civilian branches, UN police has long had its own institutional home within the peace operations bureaucracy, beginning with the tiny Civilian Police Unit that was created in 1993 and evolved into what is now called the Police Division. While other parts of the UN system became increasingly involved with police reform (UNDP), human rights monitoring (OHCHR), or drug enforcement training (UNODC), DPKO always remained by far the largest and officially the lead UN actor on police issues.

In the latter half of the 1990s, the unit produced a couple of handbooks and guidance documents that were helpful for its own work – not an insignificant factor, given the growth and turnover at headquarters a few years later. The most comprehensive one was called 'United Nations Civilian Police Principles and Guidelines,' a concise and accessible booklet published in December 2000 to help member states, police commissioners, and senior mission leaders prepare for deployment (UN DPKO 2000). Like most of these publications, the 'Blue Book' was partly overtaken by events as key missions began to operate under entirely different legal and political rules, and was largely ignored in the field. Rapid turnover, dire need for staff, and the reality of UN human resource management did not provide any means to hold field staff accountable on anything but administrative rules. For a long time, DPKO's institutional infrastructure also provided insufficient resources for an effective learning infrastructure for the police.

Throughout the 1990s, the Civilian Police Unit was short-staffed and had little bureaucratic standing. In the words of the Brahimi report, it was formally tasked 'to support all aspects of United Nations international police operations, from doctrinal development through selection and deployment of officers into field operations.' Like the Military Division, the police had its own autonomous learning infrastructure centered on its small policy and planning unit. The department's overall Lessons Learned Unit focuses on the civilian branches of DPKO and keeps out of uniformed territory. This division of labor remains the same today, and, with the exception of occasional crosscutting reports, it is being observed. Until 2000, however, the police unit was able to 'do little more than identify personnel, attempt to pre-screen them . . . and then see that they get to the field' (United Nations 2000: para. 179).

Partly as a result of the Brahimi report, member states agreed to strengthen the unit and elevate it to an equal standing with the Military Division, which gave the professional considerations of police officers a voice among senior decision-makers. This was also the result of the strong support provided by the new head of DPKO. Jean-Marie Guéhenno saw strengthening the rule of law as a key task of sustainable peace operations from the outset of his tenure. Of the three 'pillars' of police, courts and prisons that made up the common image of rule of law institutions, the police appeared the most fundamental and the least controversial. The idea of UN meddling in their justice systems met strong resistance from many developing countries who were, at the same time, eager to find practical solutions to the security problems posed by fragile states. Countries like China, otherwise very defensive about the principle of national sovereignty, regarded the police as more a technical than a political challenge in a post-conflict context. As a result, a strong focus on the technical capacity-building challenges of the police was Guéhenno's strategy to avoid destructive political fights while moving forward on at least one leg of the rule of law tripod – a strategy that also leveraged the support of the police-contributing countries.[6]

A new Policy and Planning Unit for the police was established on paper. In reality, the 'unit' was left without a dedicated manager, with each person reporting directly to the Police Adviser – a post that was vacant for almost two years (mid-2001 to early 2003) because the UN had problems finding qualified and politically acceptable applicants. Without effective leadership with sufficient bureaucratic clout to expedite the cumbersome UN recruitment procedures to fill its new posts, the policy unit drifted. Hardly any time and resources were invested into guidance development and support for organizational learning.

By mid-2003, with the newly funded posts out of the Brahimi process finally occupied and enjoying a temporary slump in field deployments, police officials managed to catch up with most of the mission planning and administrative guidance tasks that had fallen by the wayside during the preceding years. Still, there was little capacity to focus on organizational learning or practically useful guidance for police commissioners in the field.[7] This began to change

---

[6] Interview with Jean-Marie Guéhenno, April 2009.
[7] Personal communication with a former UN police commissioner, September 2010.

only in 2005, following the appointment of Mark Kroeker as the new Police Adviser. Kroeker, an American police officer, combined substantial field experience with the UN in Bosnia and Liberia with a penchant for the broader institutional reforms that Guéhenno's team had been advocating. Kroeker's tenure left a huge impact within the UN policing community. Some of his short, pointed quotes were still pinned on office walls at the Police Division long after his departure, and his leadership style is universally credited with revitalizing a team that had been demoralized for years. Member states finally strengthened the division's management capacity by funding two Section Chiefs for mission management and policy development. As a result of the UN's dysfunctional recruitment process, it took about sixteen months from the time the budgetary post was established in July 2005 to actually hire a manager for the latter unit, now called the Strategic Policy and Development Section.

Despite these difficulties, this period in 2005/6, just before the next wave of demand for UN police in Darfur, Chad, and again Timor-Leste hit the division, marks some of the earliest and most significant advances in guidance development of the whole peace operations bureaucracy. All the cases studied in this chapter made most of their progress in this period. For a time and a limited number of cases, the combination of an emerging policy development capacity with the leadership provided by a dedicated, politically astute Police Adviser and a strongly supportive Under-Secretary-General Guéhenno at the top made effective drafting, internal and external advocacy, and decision-making possible.

To compensate for the lack of internal capacity at least in part, Kroeker established formal forms of outreach to external experts in Doctrine Development Groups, created an International Policing Advisory Council (IPAC) to tap into the support of the 'wise men and women' of international policing, and promoted the use of doctrine and guidance from other international organizations such as the Organisation for Security and Co-operation in Europe (OSCE) and the European Union, wherever possible. This approach recognized the long-standing contributions of other UN agencies, think tanks (mostly in the Anglo-Saxon world), and member state governments (such as Canada, the United Kingdom, and the Nordic countries), many of which partially substituted for the weak internal learning infrastructure over the years. Nonetheless, and despite a modest growth of Police Division resources that began in Kroeker's tenure, an internal review noted that by December 2008, 'the policy guidance available to police officers in the field was [still] based on traditional paradigms with little direction on how to implement their interim law enforcement or police reform mandates' (UN Secretary-General 2010a: 59).

By mid-2010, eleven planners and doctrine developers were responsible for more than a dozen different operations with fundamentally different mandates and deployed in vastly different local contexts, comprising over

13,500 officers. Unlike five years earlier, a capacity for police doctrine development existed at a level that enabled the Police Division to come up with a 'Strategic Doctrinal Framework' with the goal of developing a 'common international police peacekeeping doctrine by mid-2012. This doctrine could serve as the basis for training curricula for police to be deployed into any international operation, as well as detailed job descriptions for operational specialties, and the fundamentals of a more broadly standardized pre-deployment training policy. Officers trained to these standards could in principle serve in a UN, NATO, EU, AU, or coalition operation with common expectations and understandings of police roles and competencies' (Durch 2010: 18).

* * *

In the following sections, we examine three of the most pertinent learning challenges that UN officials identified and pursued in this field since 2000: developing standards for constabulary police units to maintain a civilian, democratic role in line with UN principles rather than a paramilitary police force; creating a rapidly deployable team of experienced and highly competent police experts to support struggling missions and start new ones; and building effective and accountable police institutions beyond the short-term fix of vetting and training individual officers. As a reflection of the Brahimi report's priorities and the general trends in UN peace operations, most of these learning processes were attempts to catch up with the expansion of mandates and responsibilities on the ground.

Our *first case* is the attempt to develop basic standards for the roles and functions of constabulary police forces, a newly discovered resource that promised more reliable and rapid deployments, in theory at least, to fill the 'security gap' that emerged in the early weeks and months of every peace operation after civil wars. As financial and recruitment advantages led demand for FPUs to grow quickly, it also exacerbated the challenges of bringing organized forces from very diverse national backgrounds in line with the UN's ideals of how to conduct police work in the sensitive gray area between 'civilian' policing and military operations. UN officials chose this case to employ DPKO's new guidance development procedures in one of the first substantive attempts at creating doctrine for peace operations.

Our *second case* is the establishment of the Standing Police Capacity, the latest in a series of attempts to overcome the UN's structural inability to deploy even small advance parties rapidly and effectively. After many previous failures, DPKO officials developed a proposal together with member states' representatives that now allows the UN to rapidly deploy a core police team to new missions or strengthen existing missions at critical times.

The *third case* is a conceptual shift in how to build police institutions, from a focus on individual training and technical support toward a holistic, political view of the institution and the need to turn around its leadership, culture, and regulations to make it effective and accountable. This endeavor had a slow start; only gained speed with a crucial leadership transition at the Police Division; and despite a quick 'success in principle,' it continues to be hampered by the weakness of the organizational infrastructure for doctrine development, training, and evaluation. The following pages go more deeply into each of these cases.

Toward a Civilian Constabulary: Standards for Formed Police Units

During the crucial 'golden hour' of the first few weeks after a peace agreement, UN peacekeepers always faced a dangerous security vacuum. As Sergio Vieira de Mello (2000) discovered in Kosovo and East Timor: 'Unlike other nation-building tasks, the maintenance of law and order can not wait. If there is no law from day one, criminal activity thrives.' This security vacuum posed two interconnected challenges. In terms of quantity, traditional UN police officers were much slower to recruit and deploy than military units. In terms of quality, there were particular challenges that neither military forces nor traditional UN police were well prepared to deal with. In the context of immediate postwar instability, violent civil unrest, labor strikes and political demonstrations, organized crime, and similar problems in the gray area between military stabilization and civilian law enforcement overtaxed both sides. On the one hand, soldiers lacked the equipment and training for a very careful, gradual and proportional escalation of force in line with strict human rights standards and the expectations of local populations. On the other hand, lightly armed patrolmen were equally overwhelmed because they lacked any effective means of responding to large-scale violence and had little other option than to withdraw (Oakley and Dziedzic 1998: 518–20).

By 2003, the UN had drawn a principal lesson from this experience and introduced a new component into the peace operations toolkit: from now on, constabulary police or 'formed police units' (FPUs), in UN parlance, would be included in any large-scale mission.[8] Like the military, constabulary police operate jointly as units and use a wider range of weapons than civilian police

---

[8] Pioneered by NATO in Bosnia, the UN introduced constabulary police first in its missions in Kosovo and East Timor in 1999. It took until the UN Mission to Liberia (UNMIL) in 2003, however, that what had been grudgingly accepted by the senior leadership of the UN Secretariat for the 'special case' of transitional administrations with executive mandates was extended to mainstream peace operations, as well. The impulse for that change came from within the Police Division itself – another case of organizational learning that we examined elsewhere (Benner et al. 2008; Rotmann 2009).

officers. Like the police, they are trained in nonlethal combat techniques and hold a fundamentally civilian or rule-of-law-based approach to the use of force (Hansen 2002: 70). Finally, in terms of quantity and rapid deployment, the UN found whole units of 120 officers each to be much easier to find and deploy than a comparable number of individual police officers. In the eighteen months between September 2003 and April 2005, the number of FPUs deployed more than doubled, and the number of missions which deployed constabulary police tripled – at which point it became much harder to find capable units available for UN deployments even in developing countries, and the growth rate slowed.

In practice, however, it had already become apparent in the earlier experiences by NATO in Bosnia and Kosovo and by the UN in Kosovo and East Timor that the mere deployment of constabulary police did not guarantee their effective use on the ground. The record was sobering for both organizations. It took longer than expected to obtain the necessary forces, particularly for deployments outside the European continent. In addition, while European countries with standing constabulary forces such as France, Italy, and Spain did contribute to the Kosovo mission, they largely preferred to do so under NATO rather than UN command. For East Timor and later missions in Africa, the UN had to find formed police elsewhere, and turned to developing countries that were all too eager to send their riot police abroad as they were financially compensated in the same way as for military units. Training standards and human rights records varied, however. After the units arrived, their capabilities were sometimes misunderstood and underutilized by both military and civilian police leaders who did not always have previous experience in working with formed police. In a number of instances, formed police commanders complained that their units were kept in their barracks, not allowed to go on patrols or gather intelligence, and in various cases not allowed even to make their own situation assessments before implementing the missions assigned to them by higher authorities. The lack of clear command and control arrangements for mutual support with the military led to a number of operational failures. Over time, each individual mission appears to have learned from these failures, but none of these local innovations spread beyond its point of origin, at least not within the UN (Hansen 2002: 72–3; Perito 2004: 326–7).

The division of authority between constabulary police and military forces is a crucial case in point. In response to an incident of civil unrest on October 1, 1998 on a major overland road near Capljina in Bosnia, the senior NATO officer on site ordered an Italian carabinieri unit against the objections of its commander to forcibly remove a group of protesters. While the military officer acted in accordance with the chain of command, the resulting escalation of violence caused a number of casualties among civilians and police officers alike and damaged both the effectiveness and legitimacy of NATO's Stabilization Force (SFOR) (Perito 2004: 162–4). Subsequently, SFOR command developed the so-called Blue Box doctrine that specified command and control arrangements in joint military and police operations. In case of civil unrest, an Area of Responsibility (AoR) for police action would be established in a particular territory and for a defined period of time. Within this 'blue box,' the senior constabulary police officer would have authority not only over his own units but also over all military forces present, allowing the police to employ their nonviolent tactics to greater effectiveness. On the outside, the military would retain command and control. For NATO forces in Bosnia, the new doctrine worked well in a series of further incidents.

In Kosovo, the parallel setup of constabulary units within the UN Mission in Kosovo (UNMIK) Police and NATO's Kosovo Force (KFOR) with different and overlapping mandates led to a series of clashes over respective authority and roles, as well. The lack of a doctrine on joint operations was felt at various points, including the mishandling of the 2000 Mitrovica riots and the subsequent reluctance of military commanders to use the largely non-Western UN constabulary units for mistrust of their attention to human rights when required to use force against civilians. As a reaction to these experiences with civil unrest in 2000, UNMIK and KFOR quickly developed a local command and control doctrine that included setting up a Joint Operations Center and Regional Operations Centers to coordinate the respective day-to-day activities as well as flexible command arrangements based on the level of tension in each area (Blume 2004: 97; Perito 2004: 187–234). Still, it took the persistent leadership of two successive police commissioners over three years until the agreed principles of pragmatic cooperation were put into practice in a regular manner.[9]

None of these local learning processes in the field were even so much as formally recognized at headquarters during that time. What little guidance existed for the use of FPUs was mostly written by entrepreneurial officers in one particular field mission for its own use. The Liberia operation (UNMIL) was the first in which headquarters even defined the role of constabulary police in terms of actual tasks in its official mission plan, dated September 11, 2003: 'law and order' support to the local, UN-installed interim police force, dealing with civil disturbance in major population centers, capacity building for a future Liberian constabulary police force, and generally supporting the protection of civilians and property (UN Secretary-General 2003b: para. 68). UNMIL's subsequent concept of operations, dated January 2004, for the first time included a comprehensive plan for the police component. Drafted between the newly reinforced Civilian Police Division in New York

---

[9] Personal communication, former senior UN police official, September 2010.

and the very active input from UNMIL Police Commissioner Mark Kroeker in Monrovia, it was the first such concept that devotes several pages to the roles and capabilities of FPUs and their function within the overall mission. While hardly very specific, those few pages already pointed to a number of doctrinal challenges: when and what kind of force to use against violent protesters; internal discipline and respect for human rights in order to make a positive contribution to the population's sense of safety and security; and how to work together with the military, to name just a few.

Seven months later, in August 2004, the concept of operations for the new United Nations Stabilization Mission in Haiti (MINUSTAH) came out with an all but identical section on constabulary police forces (UN Secretary-General 2004c: para. 93). While these planning documents marked significant conceptual improvements over earlier ones, the substance of guidance for FPU contributors and mission leaders on the ground remained very limited. Beyond the envisaged roles and basic requirements for constabulary police units, almost no details were provided on the internal organization of FPUs, their rules of engagement, and their relationships to UN military forces. Senior leaders on the ground were once again left to their own devices to figure out how to use constabulary police effectively, and headquarters had no formal standard to hold police-contributing countries accountable to specific levels of quality. In the field, the results varied widely and changed often abruptly with changes in senior police positions.

At this stage, knowledge in the form of a lesson that worked locally and that was reported to headquarters had become available to the UN, but there was no recognizable organization-wide advocacy effort for substantive guidance after the initial introduction of constabulary forces into the Kosovo and East Timor operations. At a time of extraordinary operational pressures on headquarters in New York, while the new resources obtained after the Brahimi report were only slowly converted into actual manpower, there was neither an effective learning infrastructure nor a pressing political need for high-level leadership attention that could have driven such an effort. As individual crises arose, they were managed in keeping with the traditional organizational culture of the peace operations bureaucracy.

For several years, despite ample accumulation of knowledge from experience and experimentation in the field, the doctrinal gap of defining the precise roles, requirements, organization, and tactics of UN constabulary police remained unfilled. Like many other instances of learning at a particular place and time, and despite repeated efforts by UNMIK Police Commissioner Stefan Feller to raise the issue with UN and NATO headquarters, the solution found in Kosovo for military–constabulary cooperation remained a local innovation, with no institutional follow-up, while outside experts repeatedly blamed this lack of guidance for inadequate crisis prevention and response (e.g., Hansen 2002: 15; Dahrendorf 2003: 58). In fact, because of the sheer diversity of national models and backgrounds from the UN drew its FPUs, the core character of UN constabulary police had yet to be defined: when to negotiate, when and how to use force, whether to use rubber bullets or tear gas, how to work with the military, and, ultimately, how to maintain a distinct police identity according to the UN's civilian and democratic ideals (Hills 1998, 2001; Mobekk 2005). The parallel rise in demand for peace operations exacerbated this learning challenge as it required DPKO to raise dozens of FPUs annually. From 2005, what had started in part as an attempt to relieve pressure on military force generation rapidly turned into another 'seller's market' where the UN had to accept almost any FPU it could get its hands on.

* * *

On February 7, 2005, Mark Kroeker took office as the new Police Adviser at UN headquarters in New York. As Kroeker arrived from UNMIL in Liberia, Under-Secretary-General Guéhenno's broader reform agenda began to take shape and doctrine development became a priority for the department. DPKO's senior management team introduced its formal guidance development process in May and approved it officially in July (cf. Chapter 2). Following this department-wide initiative, the Police Division quickly came on board and took on stan-dard-setting for constabulary police as one of its first substantive priorities.

They began by setting a number of more basic policies in motion, beginning with a set of administrative and disciplinary *Guidelines for Formed Police Units*.[10] On a mission-by-mission basis, Kroeker began to curtail the wide latitude of FPU commanders in terms of what weapons and tactics to use. Units from a number of countries had presented themselves in a way almost indistinguishable from a military light infantry company, setting an example in the eyes of local politicians and populations that was very counterproduc-tive to the efforts of senior mission leaders to promote a civilian, democratic police bound by the rule of law.[11]

Outside the UN, the need for training and common standards for constabu-lary police in peace operations had recently been taken up by the G8 at their June 2004 summit. Italy and the United States established a Center of

---

[10] Now wrapped in the formal guidance development procedures championed by the Best Practices Section, the drafting of administrative and disciplinary guidelines for other aspects of UN policing had already begun under the previous Police Adviser, Kiran Bedi. Starting in May 2005, the FPU guidelines were formally approved in November 2005 and revised again in May 2006 (UN DPKO 2005a, 2006c).

[11] While earlier 'rules of engagement' for FPUs had codified the widest possible latitude for commanders to the point where weaponry up to and including light vehicle-mounted machine guns were sanctioned as police equipment for UNMIL, over the summer of 2005 a series of revisions were issued in which approved search and detention procedures as well as the lists of authorized weapons for constabulary officers reflected a significantly more restrictive posture (documents on file with authors).

Excellence for Stability Police Units (COESPU) at the Carabinieri barracks in Vicenza, Italy. In April 2005, as an explicit reaction to the previous years' riots in Kosovo, the center convened a joint UN–NATO–EU conference on constabulary police doctrine in peace operations. The meeting took stock of progress in doctrine development and identified a series of gaping holes that were essentially the same for each organization. In line with the center's G8 mandate, its staff were to act as a 'focal point for doctrine development' on FPU affairs (COESPU 2005: 17–19).

Against this background, the Police Division began in early 2005 to draft a 'policy directive' on the *Functions and Organization of Formed Police Units*, with the main motivation of improving force generation and selection standards. The process stretched out over nearly two years until it was finally approved in November 2006. Despite this long delay, the substance of the end result is largely identical to the earlier pieces of informal doctrine in the strategy documents for Liberia and Haiti. The doctrine describes a wide-ranging set of preventive and reactive roles of FPUs, from the protection of mission personnel and assets through confidence building by regular joint patrols with local police, support for crowd control, intelligence gathering, and situation assessments to training and advisory tasks for the benefit of local constabulary police (UN DPKO 2006*b*: paras. 4.9–4.11).

This long delay in the advocacy stage for a basic policy document that only formalized existing practice had both external and internal causes. Externally, the assignment of an interorganizational drafting role to the G8 Center of Excellence in Vicenza consciously prioritized the prospect of shared standards over expected delays in the guidance development process. Expecting some progress within a few months, the Police Division put its own drafting process on hold for a while. It was only after some time without progress on the part of the G8 center that DPKO restarted its own efforts.[12] A second external influence was a short-lived attempt by member states to gain more control over the bureaucracy's internal guidelines in general, not aimed specifically at police doctrine. In early 2006, the UN Special Committee on Peacekeeping Operations (2006: para. 102) used its annual report to stress 'the urgent need' for FPU doctrine to be 'propose[d] for its consideration.' In the partly collaborative, partly combative relationship between civil servants in the Secretariat and (often junior) diplomats in member state embassies, such language usually indicates a 'warning shot' expressing the need for greater consultation. From the diplomats' point of view, the threat to drag an issue into the long-winded and time-consuming arena of intergovernmental committees is often their only lever if they feel left in the dark by the bureaucracy. In this case, because

---

[12] Interview, senior police official, May 2007.

the warning shot was not directed at the FPU doctrine itself but rather reflected a general concern that the Secretariat might be trying to regulate political issues through the back door of issuing doctrine, a few informal contacts and briefings sufficed to assuage those fears. On the substance, member states had no problems with constabulary police: some were support-ive for either policy or financial reasons, while most were simply indifferent.[13]

Internally, the Military Division used the inclusive nature of the formal guidance development procedure to mount a string of delays. Because the policy addressed cooperation between FPUs and the military at least in pass-ing, the Military Division had a legitimate case to be part of the drafting process. It used its clout to caution against the overreliance on constabulary police which the Police Division saw as an attempt to defend their turf against encroachment from the new trend toward FPUs. Indeed, FPUs began to replace infantry battalions in a number of missions, reducing the military's default preeminence among the uniformed branches of peacekeeping and reducing its share of the growing budgetary pie.[14] At least one respondent who worked in the Military Division at the time agrees and adds that there was also a concern that too much reliance on the crowd control capabilities of FPUs might endan-ger the mission if military reserves were drawn down excessively.[15]

* * *

As one of the first pieces of formal guidance adopted under DPKO's new doctrine development system, the first generation of FPU standards and guid-ance was a significant step forward in terms of providing a reference for UN managers and staff to invoke in debates about the role and purpose of such units in missions around the globe. At the same time, it suffered from the most fundamental weakness that undercut the nascent body of guidance and the management of UN peace operations as a whole: no effective means of holding either Police Commissioners and mission management or police-contributing countries accountable to DPKO standards. As a result, the new guidance was never effectively institutionalized before the next cycle of learning and revision of FPU doctrine began in 2007.

The reasons were structural. Police Commissioners report primarily to the head of mission, the Special Representative of the Secretary-General (SRSG) on the ground, and not to the Police Division whose advice they often found to be of little use to their daily challenges. Police contributors were in an even stronger position vis-à-vis DPKO, particularly in the years following 2005 when the demand for constabulary police units shot through the roof. Similar to the

---

[13] Interview, senior DPKO official, May 2008.
[14] Interview, senior DPKO official, April 2009.
[15] Interview, DPKO military official, April 2010.

UN's experience with military contributors a decade earlier, police officials found themselves with almost no leverage to enforce standards of training or behavior for FPUs. As a result, some cash-strapped contributing countries cut corners when they saw an opportunity to get UN reimbursements and the prestige that came with being a significant contributor to peace operations. In one egregious case that became public, one unnamed developing country simply put a company of infantry soldiers into shiny new police uniforms, issued them batons, and sent them off to a UN mission as an FPU in exchange for its reimbursement. The Police Division, already scrambling just to find the quantities mandated by the Security Council, had no capacity to spare for effective quality control.[16]

These structural weaknesses cost two Kosovo-Albanian protesters their life in an incident that finally forced the UN's hand to act. On February 10, 2007, a rally of about 3,000 protesters organized by the Movement for Self-Determination (Vetevendosje) in Pristina turned into a riot during which two civilians were killed and two others wounded by rubber bullets fired by a Romanian FPU. According to subsequent investigations, the tragic outcome resulted from the confluence of many factors: a muddled chain of command, lack of command experience with serious public disorder, the omission of key steps to minimize escalation, and inappropriate tactics as violence did escalate. The consequent political crisis led to the resignation of the Minister of Internal Affairs and the sacking of the police commissioner by the SRSG. Investigators found the rubber bullets used to be 13 years old and hardened to the effect that they had penetrated the skulls of the two victims. In response, Richard Monk, the new police commissioner, banned the use of rubber bullets in Kosovo – a prohibition that Stefan Feller had already instituted in 2002 but that had been revoked in the mean time. DPKO followed by handing down a temporary ban on the use of rubber bullets in all its operations that was only partially followed by police commanders in other missions.[17]

Ultimately, it was the Kosovo incident combined with the mounting evidence of severe problems with training and equipment standards that forced the UN bureaucracy to reevaluate and tighten its policies on FPUs.[18] Starting in mid-2007, two years after Kroeker's doctrine development effort had begun, this became the signature effort for his successor in the office of UN Police Adviser, Australian Federal Police commissioner Andrew Hughes. Hughes launched a wholesale review process initially led by Richard Monk and subsequently championed by Andrew Carpenter, Chief of the Police Division's new

---

[16] Various interviews, DPKO police officials, and outside experts, 2006–9.

[17] Interviews, senior UN police officials, Timor-Leste, Liberia, and Haiti, 2007–9; internal documents and media reports (Associated Press 2007a, 2007b; Kraja 2007; UN DPI 2007; UNMIK 2008).

[18] Personal communication, senior UN police official, August 2010.

Strategic Policy and Development Section, that is supposed to culminate in a new 'UN formed police doctrine' to be issued. Together, Monk and Carpenter called together experienced FPU commanders for a first meeting of an FPU Review and Standards Team in New York in October 2007. Based on their often sobering experiences in the field, Monk compiled an interim report in January 2008 that identified a number of urgent requirements for a robust and coherent operational doctrine to be developed to which FPUs could be held to account. When ad-hoc teams were dispatched to test all thirty-eight deployed units for firearms proficiency, equipment operability, public order management, and command and control standards, twenty-four were assessed to have 'significant' deficiencies or worse. Supported by voluntary funding from member states, 'mobile assistance teams' were dispatched to provide remedial training. At the same time, largely driven by Andrew Carpenter, the division partnered with about a dozen police-contributing countries to spell out more detailed doctrine on the basis of the Monk requirements. As of August 2010, that effort remains unfinished business (Durch 2010).[19]

* * *

The attempt to set standards for the role and tactics of constabulary police in peace operations was one of the first big processes of organizational learning at the UN that spanned field missions and headquarters. The establishment of a foundational doctrine, if largely limited to defining the roles and capabilities of FPUs for force generation purposes, was one of the first pieces of substantive guidance that DPKO created through its new guidance development procedures. At a time when the department's learning infrastructure was still in a nascent stage, it was an unprecedented achievement for the peace operations bureaucracy to run a largely (but not entirely) infrastructure-driven learning process that succeeded to the point where an authoritative decision was made and partly institutionalized.

This success, if limited, depended first and foremost on a largely neutral political environment. As numerous police officials testified, the attitude of member state diplomats was one of benign indifference toward the whole idea of constabulary police. For key financial contributors such as the United States, it was good largely because it saved money. The one political influence came from intra-bureaucratic competition from DPKO's military arm. That conflict affected the advocacy stage quite negatively and delayed the result significantly, probably by more than a year. Ultimately, the deadlock was only resolved by Police Adviser Kroeker's internal advocacy.

The final flaw of the FPU standard-setting process up to 2007 and into the subsequent process of revision was the lack of comprehensive

---

[19] Richard Monk, personal communication, August 2010.

institutionalization in training standards, selection benchmarks, and field assessments or evaluations. In this, it reflected the weakest link in DPKO's organizational infrastructure for learning: the whole training system was being overhauled between 2007 and 2009, and an evaluation capacity was only slowly being developed since 2008. In their stead, the Police Adviser sent an expert team on an ad-hoc series of assessment visits in 2007/8 to induce at least some compliance and to gather information for the revisions that have been under way ever since.

Finally, this case is also a key example of the opportunities lost from the lack of effective institutional links between headquarters and field. Most apparent in the case of joint police–military operations, the pressure of daily challenges has often led to the emergence of pragmatic, creative solutions in the field that the learning infrastructure – at least up to 2005/6 – was in no position to effectively pick up, evaluate, and turn into a useful lesson for the institution as a whole.

Mission Start-up and Crisis Response: Creating a Standing Police Capacity

When the Security Council mandates a new peace operation, DPKO has to produce the required forces and personnel. While FPUs are 'generated' in a wholesale fashion from member states, individual police officers are much harder to recruit. Person by person, applicants need to be screened and interviewed for language abilities and basic competency. The more specialized the UN's needs – for example, when looking for mid-ranking supervisors with organizational reform experience, or forensics specialists, or narcotics investigators – the harder it is to find qualified and motivated individuals whose home countries are willing to release them from their regular jobs for a UN deployment. This is compounded by the fact that contributing countries have no financial incentive for deploying individual police officers, unlike military or constabulary units.

These adverse incentives result in extremely slow deployment times and high vacancy rates in the field, particularly in the crucial start-up phase of a mission. 'The first six to 12 weeks following a ceasefire or peace accord is often the most critical period for establishing both a stable peace and the credibility of the peacekeepers' (Smith et al. 2007: 39). Yet in 2007, it took on average nine months until the authorized number of individual police was deployed. The UN Mission in Sudan (UNMIS), six months into its deployment, had only 101 of its mandated 715 police officers and did not reach 90 percent of authorized strength until fourteen months later. Without qualified staff, it is unlikely that the mission could have much of an impact on the political and security situation in the country in this period. Even more critical than the numbers are important leadership positions, some of which often remain vacant for many months into the mission while many of the crucial strategy development and planning tasks, high-level engagement with the host government and the donor community, as well as the internal management of UN police remain neglected.

The early days, weeks, and months of the police deployment to Kosovo provide a typical case in point. While many observers at the time claimed that the Kosovo mission was a particularly hard case for the UN because of the unprecedented mandate and short lead time, neither of these factors turned out to be very uncommon in later cases. In turn, however, the Kosovo mission benefited from an extraordinary degree of political attention and support particularly from the United States and Europe, which has rarely been available for other operations.

After the Security Council had authorized a UN interim administration and NATO stabilization forces on June 10, 1999, advance elements of both organizations entered Kosovo very quickly on 12 and 13 June, respectively. While thousands of KFOR troops quickly deployed throughout the territory on the heels of the departing Serb forces over the following days and weeks, it took the UN almost three weeks to get at least a temporary team of thirty-five police officers into place (Blume 2004). Over the following two months, additional police trickled in, bringing the numbers up to 735, or 15 percent of mandated strength. In contrast to the KFOR troops, who brought all of their equipment and supplies with them, UNMIK Police had nothing. As Till Blume (2004: 94) reports, 'no infrastructure, no office furniture, no radios, few vehicles, no stationery, and 'no law' were available to start working [with]. In the first two months of the mission . . . , police officers were literally sitting around in Pristina and drinking coffee, because they could not do much without the necessary basic equipment . . . and experienced personnel for organized crime enforcement.'

When the inflow of officers picked up, UNMIK Police became largely bogged down with processing the new arrivals. With no prior organizational planning and very few police with peace operations experience, the bare-bones leadership in Pristina had their hands full inventing a functional structure and procedures while selecting further layers of management and integrating planeloads of new colleagues into the nascent institution. As a result, it took months until UN police were able to actually work on their assigned mission. In the mean time, the great majority of Serbs still living in Pristina had fled in the face of systematic ethnic persecution by Albanian extremists, a wave of organized crime had become entrenched, and the confidence of the general population into the UN had taken its first serious blow (Hochschild 2004).

* * *

The rapid deployment challenge was not a new problem in 1999, and it had always been particularly serious for police. A few years earlier, the member states had established the UN Stand-by Arrangements System (UNSAS) as a mechanism to pledge personnel and equipment to the Secretariat for deployment at fifteen, thirty, sixty, or ninety days notice. The system had failed immediately because almost no government was willing to give up the right to make case-by-case decisions whether and under what conditions to deploy. While the pledges made member states look good on paper, the strings attached in practice rendered UNSAS mostly useless as an instrument to speed up deployments.

The Brahimi panel recognized this problem and proposed a start-up capacity of 100 senior police planners to be 'on call' and available at seven days notice for planning support and mission start-up in the field (United Nations 2000). The idea was to bridge the gap until individual negotiations with UNSAS participants or other police contributors would be completed and countries would be found to deliver the required personnel. While quickly implemented by the Secretariat, the proposed standby police roster failed to catch on with member states. By late 2001, a model UN police headquarters for field operations and generic job descriptions for 100 posts in initial field deployment teams had been developed but member states failed to nominate a sufficient number of qualified candidates and many retained time-consuming veto provisions for each effective deployment decision (Durch et al. 2003: 80–1). For most governments, the setup of the on-call roster akin to a military force generation mechanism just did not fit the incentive structure and the domestic challenges of recruiting and contributing police (Weinlich 2011). When after two years, the Police Division still lacked a fully staffed roster, even the most stalwart supporters such as Britain, Canada, and the Scandinavian countries became disillusioned. By mid-2004, there were only six contributing countries left (UN Secretary-General 2003a: 23, 2004a: 34).

Back in 2000, when the Brahimi report was written, there had been a third option under discussion besides standby arrangements and on-call rosters: a standing UN police. Like the suggestion of a standing army of blue helmets, proposals for a standing UN police service under the control of the Secretary-General date back nearly five decades. Supporters argued that a UN police service, designed as an unarmed group of experts in post-conflict and transnational policing issues with no enforcement powers, should be easier to realize than the utopian vision of a UN army that had always provoked an intense backlash in many countries, chief among them the United States. Up until and including the time of the Brahimi report, however, member states had always made it clear that they would not allow the UN to have any kind of standing forces under its own control, including police (United Nations 2000: para. 90).

This political opposition notwithstanding, the 'friends of UN police' from Canada, Australia, and New Zealand to Britain and the Scandinavian countries kept the idea alive and continued to work out the details together with like-minded experts in academia. In 2001, Finland hosted a workshop with a number of police contributing countries to discuss a smaller 'headquarters unit' of 100 police officers. Optimized for rapid deployment, the unit would be meant to conduct technical assessments and strategic planning as well as manage the start-up phase of a new mission (Lewis et al. 2002: 9). Five years later, a new unit with the unwieldy name of Standing Police Capacity (SPC) would look remarkably similar to the ideas discussed there.

* * *

Following the high-profile falling out between the UN and its most powerful member state over the latter's invasion of Iraq in 2003, UN Secretary-General Kofi Annan convened a panel of eminent personalities from all over the world to make the case of the UN's continued relevance while providing another push for political and organizational reforms, in a process similar to the Brahimi report but much broader in scope. The High Level Panel on Threats, Challenges and Change would combine the high-profile grappling with the composition of the Security Council and the full range of peace and security issues that many countries in the world wanted to see raised to the highest level of attention with practical recommendations to improve the Secretariat's ability to fulfill its mandates (NUPI 2006). The panelists themselves were mostly interested in the issues of high politics rather than in the technical reforms. When the basic contours of the panel's report had emerged, the panel staff began looking for relatively uncontroversial internal reform ideas that would fit the thrust of the report, needed some more support from the membership, and would therefore benefit from the panel's official endorsement without derailing the report politically.

Several DPKO officials vividly remember what followed. In a regular meeting of the management of the Police Division with Under-Secretary-General Guéhenno during the late summer of 2004, the discussion turned to the persistent failure of standby arrangements and on-call rosters to deliver real improvements in mission start-up capacity. Three new missions had been established that year, and 'rapid deployment' had been as far from reality as ever. In the words of one participant of the meeting, 'Under-Secretary-General Guéhenno turned to his Special Assistant, Salman Ahmed, and said something like, "we need to come up with something new here," to which Salman responded, "why not create a small standing police cadre?"' In the wake of a new spike in demand for UN police for missions around the world that had been established with widespread support among the key Security Council members and financial contributors, creating a standing police unit small enough not to be threatening to the members seemed just feasible. Guéhenno liked the idea and asked the Police Division to pursue it.[20]

While the Police Division came up with a plan, Guéhenno's office began to generate top-level political momentum for the proposal. In his regular consultations with the Fourth Committee of the General Assembly and its Special Committee on Peacekeeping Operations, Guéhenno floated the idea several times that fall.[21] The main source of political momentum, however, would be the run-up to the World Summit in September 2005, where the presidents and prime ministers would meet to mark the sixtieth anniversary of the UN. In little more than a year, there would be three major documents of high political significance, each of which would loosely feed into the next one: the High Level Panel report, the Secretary-General's response, and the pre-negotiated World Summit outcome document.

As a first step, senior DPKO officials injected the idea into the High Level Panel report. The panel's drafting team had been drawn from a largely New York-based expert community that had long supported peace operations and the reforms following the Brahimi report. Many of its members were former UN officials or otherwise close to the DPKO leadership. For the High Level Panel staff, the standing police proposal was one of those low-key, practical suggestions that could use the political capital from being mentioned in a high-profile report and later, hopefully, in the World Summit outcome document.[22] When it was unveiled with much fanfare on December 2, 2004, the report argued for 'a small corps of senior police officers and managers (50–100 personnel) who could undertake mission assessments and organize the start-up of police components of peace operations, and the General Assembly should authorize this capacity' (United Nations 2004: para. 223).

As the panel report and Guéhenno's informal consultations began to pay off in terms of political momentum, Mark Kroeker came on board as the new head of the Police Division in February and immediately embraced the SPC as a strategic priority.[23] He and his team decided to pursue the most inclusive conceptual development process possible in order to secure the broadest buy-in and avoid the opposition of countries who could have felt insufficiently consulted. According to one official who was closely involved, the emphasis on consultation had partly come from the lessons learned from a similar policy initiative that was already seen to be failing. Also with the

---

[20] Interviews with several participants (DPKO and Police Division officials, numerous occasions, 2008–9).
[21] Guéhenno presented the idea in an oral presentation to the Fourth Committee for Special Political Affairs on October 25 (Guéhenno 2004) and on December 15 formally as part of the Secretary-General's annual report to the Special Committee (UN Secretary-General 2004*b*).
[22] Interviews, senior DPKO officials, and close observers of the High Level Panel process, May 2007 and May 2008.
[23] Interviews with senior DPKO and Police Division officials (see also Weinlich 2011).

backing of the High Level Panel, DPKO's Military Division tried to rally the member states behind a Strategic Reserve of on-call troops that would be available to rapidly respond to crisis situations in any mission. It ran into opposition early and died slowly in 2005 (Weinlich 2011). In the police team's analysis, a lack of consultation with member states had been the major reason why the proposal had not found traction. They were determined not to repeat their colleague's mistakes.

The Police Division began in the early spring of 2005 to engage what they called a 'motor' of about a dozen strategically selected countries who had either traditionally been supportive of UN policing or were considered indispensable for success.[24] A working group was set up and co-chaired by a DPKO official and a British police officer seconded to the UK embassy for the purpose. While it had been intended as the first step toward broader discussion with the membership, the group's selectiveness quickly aroused suspicion. Pushing back on what many diplomats saw as another secret reform initiative by unaccountable Secretariat bureaucrats, the UN Special Committee on Peacekeeping Operations (2005: para. 83) issued a report that while endorsing the SPC idea in principle essentially rebuked the Secretariat and demanded all interested member states to be included in a working group. In hindsight, one participant described this moment as the project's 'first crisis' that threatened to kill the proposal early on, similar to what had happened to the Military Division's Strategic Reserve concept.[25]

Kroeker's team realized its mistake quickly and invited the whole membership of the Special Committee to the working-group meetings. Eventually, representatives of about twenty-four member states participated on a regular basis. In March of 2005, when the Secretary-General issued his official reaction to the High Level Panel report, the language was much more muted. His report 'In Larger Freedom' endorsed the proposal for a standing police cadre only in vague terms, omitting any specifics on its size or mandate (UN Secretary-General 2005b). On this basis, discussions in the working group continued. As one participating DPKO official describes it, Kroeker tried to frame the discussions as openly as possible. For example, he began by laying out the problem of slow police deployment as a challenge to be discussed, without homing in on a particular fixed solution, and took time to discuss alternative strategies that had previously failed, in the hope that participants would gravitate toward the intended answer on their own. Eventually, they succeeded as diplomats developed a shared understanding of the challenge and a common response (Weinlich 2011).

---

[24] Participants in this initial group included representatives of Argentina, Australia, France, Germany, Nigeria, Sweden, the United Kingdom, and the United States (Weinlich 2011).
[25] Interview, UN police official, May 2008.

Now, a new problem came up. With member states taking actual ownership of the proposal as DPKO had always hoped they would, the Police Division partly lost control of the process to diplomats who began to eagerly work on the draft concept paper themselves and, although most of them had no substantive police experience, kept making suggestions at a rate the DPKO officials could barely keep up with. Finally, on August 22, less than a month before the World Summit, the working group produced an eleven-page 'informal paper' that elaborated the size, roles, command and control arrangements, recruitment procedures, and operational guidelines of the new SPC, as it would be called (UN DPKO 2005c).[26]

From the '50–100 senior police officers and managers' proposed by the High Level Panel, its size went down to an 'initial operating capability' of twenty-five posts, with the possibility of later expansion.[27] The paper foresaw two distinct roles for the unit: first, to deploy rapidly (i.e., within a few days) to establish the nucleus of a new mission's police headquarters; and, second, to advise and assist existing operations in their institution-building tasks, which would include the possibility of conducting 'operational audits' of their performance. An executive role or possibility of building an armed constabulary police unit that would have resembled a standing UN army too closely was avoided. The paper further defines precisely the unit's operational guidelines, recruitment procedures, and command and control arrangements. Finally, in what should become a bone of contention in the following months, it mentions four 'locations considered' for the eventual establishment of the SPC: Bonn, Brindisi, Nairobi, and New York.

Based on this working-level agreement, the SPC proposal was folded into the draft World Summit outcome document and endorsed in September by the Heads of State and Government, complete with the limiting language of 'initial operating capability' but without mentioning a specific number of posts (UN General Assembly 2005: para. 92). In the intergovernmental negotiations on the resolution, it was one of the few items that were not deeply controversial among the membership and one of the easiest things to agree on when almost the whole document was being derailed in the final weeks of negotiations. In this sense, as one official argued later, the SPC probably benefited from the unsuccessful run-up to the summit.[28]

---

[26] Interviews with UN police officials, May 2008. For more details on the process, the role of member states, and DPKO's outreach to think tanks, see Weinlich (2011).

[27] As working group members recognized that it was politically not feasible to ask for more than twenty-five posts initially, the suggestion to use the label 'initial operating capability' in order to retain the option for quick expansion came from the UK delegate, according to another member of the group.

[28] Interview, UN police official, May 2008.

After the success with the summit outcome document, the SPC came into trouble a second time when the time came to get funding for it. As a result of continuing conflicts between member states over the location of the unit's headquarters, the whole supplementary budget for the various summit outcome projects was held up until the SPC was moved to the regular budget proposal, effectively delaying it by about six months.[29] In his annual report to the UN Special Committee, the UN Secretary-General (2005a: paras. 51–2) proposed as a temporary solution to the duty station controversy to keep the unit in New York 'at least' for its first year and pleaded with the committee for 'positive consideration.' But it was only after an informal bidding war between Italy and Germany had been resolved and a strategic decision by DPKO's senior leadership had found in favor of Brindisi, the location of a major peacekeeping logistics hub, over Bonn that the proposal was officially endorsed by the UN Special Committee (2006: paras. 99–101) and its budget approved without further delay (UN Secretary-General 2006a: para. 237).[30]

While the budgetary back-and-forth went on, the Police Division developed a Policy Directive in line with DPKO's new guidance development procedures as the doctrinal basis of the SPC. Compared to the August 2005 'informal paper' that had been drafted between the Police Division and interested member states, the May 2006 directive showed very few differences: in evaluating field operations, the SPC would not be directed by the Police Commissioner on the ground but by the head of DPKO in New York; planning and decision-making arrangements on field assignments were changed, giving DPKO's Operations division a say in SPC deployments; and the SPC was given an additional role in supporting the development and implementation of lessons learned and best practices (UN DPKO 2006a).

In recruiting the 'initial operating capability' of twenty-five police specialists plus two support staff, DPKO emphasized quality over speed – as a result, it took until early 2008 to get the small unit to full strength. The duty station controversy continued to simmer, as many developing countries found an interest in keeping the unit in New York in order to maximize their political control over it. Only in August 2009, the unit actually moved to Brindisi (UN Secretary-General 2010b: 34). In the first two years of its existence, members of

---

[29] After weeks of unsuccessful haggling, the General Assembly's Advisory Committee on Administrative and Budgetary Questions (UN ACABQ 2005: para. 64) excluded the SPC from the supplementary budget and advised the Secretary-General to resubmit the proposal with the general budget for 2006/7 a couple of months later.

[30] The pivotal role of the tug-of-war between Italy and Germany over the eventual duty station of the SPC was hinted at in vague language in the 2006/7 budget submission and confirmed in an interview with a senior DPKO official as well as a number of close observers (as well as Weinlich 2010). Another official argued that a further reason for the delay was an attempt by the Secretariat to get a fifty-strong SPC approved right away which failed in a 'misunderstanding' between the Special Committee and ACABQ.

the SPC were tasked with a staggering diversity of missions: helping out the Police Division with mission planning for Somalia, special investigations in Kosovo, as well as assessment and advisory assignments such as those undertaken by a two-person and later a four-person team in Timor-Leste kept the unit busy before it was fully constituted. Finally, beginning in late 2007, it got its first 'regular' assignment of one full 'team' (twelve SPC officers) as the start-up police component for the mission in Chad (UN Secretary-General 2008*b*).

For the unit's first commander, German federal police officer Walter Wolf, it was a challenge to balance the formal role and the intent of having a cohesive unit of experienced specialists for two specific tasks – mission start-up and crisis support – with the many well-founded political reasons to detach a few investigators here and a few police reform experts there to do the kind of work that the overstretched Police Division otherwise would have had to underwrite from its own personnel resources. When the Chad assignment came, the first on-call, rapidly deployable start-up capacity of substantive personnel (i.e., not logisticians and administrators) in UN history turned out to be so far ahead of its support base that SPC members were lacking almost all the necessary resources – from offices to cars to radios – to turn their rapid deployment into an operational advantage for the mission. As a result, the Department of Field Support put together prepackaged mission start-up kits including various small-scale items as well as entire jeeps that could be airlifted into a mission area from the UN logistics base in Brindisi on equally short notice. On a more substantive level, as well, the early arrival of UN police experts made the lack of judicial and prisons specialists even more glaring. Ultimately, the success of the SPC helped rally the membership behind an extension of the concept to a Justice and Corrections Standing Capacity to fill this gap (see Chapter 5).

* * *

The creation of the SPC, on the back of a string of failures to improve police availability for deployments, is an interesting example in many ways. It is a seemingly technical issue both in size and scope – a 0.5 percent personnel increase to fill critical gaps in implementing preexisting tasks – that was deeply affected by high politics both in a negative and in a positive way. After all, it is likely the political significance of national sovereignty and the funding deadlock created by the North–South divide that keep the UN from expanding such instruments as the SPC to a scale closer to that of the challenge in the field. Unlike many earlier attempts and most recently the case of the Strategic Military Reserve, this case turned out to be a politically driven learning success.

It was clear to Guéhenno and Kroeker from the outset that just for its funding, even the smallest new unit and clearly one that would be the first of its kind would be won or lost in the court of membership politics. Building a coalition of champions within the Secretariat, reaching out to the High Level Panel, and following a patient, consultative approach to the design of the SPC paid off when it placed the issue firmly in the 'technical,' uncontroversial column of the World Summit agenda. As Kroeker spent countless hours in meetings with member states' police and military advisers, he gave the supporters of UN policing a stake in the process. He was rewarded by their supportive political pressure in the endgame of intergovernmental negotiations. While this approach cost him a lot of decision-making autonomy and limited DPKO's influence on the outcome, it preserved the substance and made the eventual establishment of the SPC possible in the first place.

In the midst of a debate as politically charged as the one about standing UN police forces, the key to organizational learning lay not with the technical infrastructure of policy planners and doctrine development procedures, which were only weakly developed at the time. Instead, in this case it was only a wide-ranging and well-managed leadership coalition centered on Kroeker's and Guéhenno's teams at DPKO and reaching out to the Secretary-General's office, the High Level Panel staff, and most importantly, key allies among the diplomatic community from twenty-four countries that was able to overcome the budgetary inertia and the residual bias against a standing UN police force. As soon as political momentum was strong enough, the lack of infrastructure was easily overcome – at least for the modest initial strength of twenty-five professionals. Nor was there much damage from bureaucratic politics within DPKO, as the concept fell squarely in the Police Division's responsibility, served the needs of peace operations as a whole, and enjoyed senior management support.

Ultimately, it was only the deeply charged UN politics of North and South, spending and sovereignty that elevated a minor structural addition to the peace operations bureaucracy from a working-level issue into the political sphere. Only due to this context did it require a political solution, which Guéhenno and Kroeker drove to initial success. With the usual delays in setup, recruitment, and proving its worth to the satisfaction of the membership, the SPC was scheduled for expansion to thirty-nine professionals in late 2010.

Beyond Uniforms and Orgcharts: Building Sustainable Police Institutions

In line with the broader trend from peacekeeping to peacebuilding, the Security Council began in the 1990s to charge peace operations with building or rebuilding effective and legitimate police services. UN police dutifully began to screen local police officers in Bosnia or Haiti for human rights violations, to develop curricula, and to implement training programs to rapidly transform – often within three to six months – frequently undisciplined, incompetent, or even corrupt agents of an oppressive or embattled state into modern, professional, law-abiding and rights-regarding police officers. Such training and capacity-building, often with crammed timelines, remains an indispensable ingredient to effective police reform. At the same time, it took years and a number of harsh encounters with reality for the UN to even begin to realize that training, monitoring, and advising individuals were bound to fail as long as it left the surrounding institution at the mercy of the powerful political and economic pressures of the 'post-conflict' order.

In late October 1999, barely four months after its deployment to Kosovo, the UN began to set up another transitional government in the former Portuguese colony of East Timor.[31] The tiny new nation on an island off Australia's northern shore had just emerged from twenty-four years of Indonesian occupation and had never had an indigenous set of institutions to provide law and order. The Indonesian military and almost all the members of the Indonesian National Police had departed when UNTAET, the UN Transitional Administration in East Timor, arrived. Among the mission's many tasks in building a state for the newly independent nation was an unambiguous mandate from the UN Security Council to develop 'a credible, professional and impartial police service' (Res. 1272, 1999). For the interim period until the new institution could be established, UN police would need to provide public order themselves.

The first UN police officers arrived in January 2000 and began to focus on the most urgent task of public security provision. In the initial mission plan, no UN police officers were assigned to plan and establish the new Timorese police, nor were any efforts made to recruit specific individuals with training, management, or institution-building expertise for UNTAET's police component. Until a police development unit was set up nine months into the mission, senior UNTAET police managers put together a haphazard strategy with the 'overriding objective ... to recruit and train a large number of [Timorese police] officers (approximately 2,800) in a very short time (little more than two and a half years)' (Hood 2006: 63). As a result of time pressure and lack of expertise on the part of UN police officials, every element of their strategy experienced critical shortcomings: planning was undertaken without any effective and broad-based consultation with Timorese political leaders except a tiny clique around independence hero Xanana Gusmao, the selection of

---

[31] The following is based on a comprehensive review of official and scholarly literature on the police and security sector in Timor-Leste (Dahrendorf et al. 2003; UNMISET 2003; Rees 2004; Hood 2006; UN 2006; Goldsmith and Dinnen 2007; Wilson 2008).

cadets was biased toward Western cultural codes and English language abilities rather than competence and integrity, the acceptance and apparently superficial vetting of about 370 former Indonesian police officers into the new force undermined its legitimacy, and training was woefully inadequate. In particular, in training and subsequent on-the-job mentoring, the constant need for translation services from English into Portuguese, Indonesian, or local languages 'served to halve the amount of actual instruction provided' (Hood 2006: 64). With only three months of basic training provided and the quality and motivation of trainers and mentors varying widely, the actual impact could hardly be anything but insufficient.

For a long time, the work that was being done on recruitment and training of individual police, no matter how imperfectly, obscured the fact that the UN all but ignored the other part of its ambitious mandate: to make the new Polícia Nacional de Timor-Leste (PNTL) 'a credible, professional and impartial police service,' as the UN Security Council (1999) had modestly phrased the mandate. Without any institution-building experience in its own ranks, the UNTAET police component failed to establish any mark of an effective institution, from a shared vision of the PNTL's role in Timor-Leste's security sector through professional integrity to functioning management systems.

After the end of UNTAET's executive powers following the formal independence of Timor-Leste in May 2002, the subsequent mission did no better.[32] Ultimately, the 'original sins' of its creation combined with undue impatience at the diplomatic level played a major part in the breakdown of the Timorese police in May 2006 and the armed confrontation with the military that were mentioned at the beginning of this chapter. The collapse of security institutions in Timor required the deployment of another peace operation whose reform efforts had to start from scratch – an analysis that has been bluntly recognized by the UN itself on various occasions (UN 2006; UN Secretary-General 2008a).

* * *

UN peacekeepers had been charged to rebuild broken and distrusted police services in a number of places before. Prior experiences good and bad had accumulated through the 1990s, from Namibia and Cambodia to El Salvador, Haiti, and Bosnia. Compared to these other missions, East Timor, like Kosovo, was a special case in the sense that after the departure of the Indonesians and Serbs there were no formal, legitimate security institutions to rebuild. At the same time, many of the managerial challenges for UN police-builders were not so different, after all: like in many security agencies elsewhere, a vocal and

---

[32] For informed and largely balanced critiques, see Rees (2006), Hood (2006), and Wilson (2008).

powerful minority of Timorese or Kosovar police officers came from some sort of militia or military-style organization that was thoroughly politicized and run through personal networks rather than as a professional bureaucracy.[33]

Probably the least ambiguous success story in police reform was that of the UN Observer Mission in El Salvador (ONUSAL, 1991–5) working together with a few bilateral donors, particularly the United States. Despite many delays and obstacles along the way, international police experts and local leaders managed to reestablish the Salvadorian police as an institution that became much more professional and incomparably more legitimate than its predecessor during the country's civil war. At the same time, the assistance effort all but ignored the justice system as a whole, which created severe problems that came to haunt the police as well (Stanley and Loosle 1998).

From the experience of El Salvador as well as, similarly, from Namibia and Cambodia, a lesson emerged that was broadly validated in the contrasting results of police-building in East Timor and Kosovo. For postwar police development to be effective, the focus on individual officers in classic capacity-building programs would need to be complemented with holistic institution-building. Classroom instruction, on-the-job training and mentoring, as well as the physical rehabilitation of police stations and the provision of equipment had important roles to play, but only the systematic transformation of laws, regulations, and their practice from the boring administration of duty rosters to effective internal and external oversight could succeed to remake the police as an organization bound by the law, imbued with a culture of service to the population and professional management, and loyal to civilian political control.

In the view of some the most seasoned professionals who spent years in the trenches trying to reform corrupt, abusive police forces into effective and accountable police services, the key lesson is to learn about the institution as it is, and use this knowledge to nudge it toward what it should be.[34] There are two fatal mistakes that most short-term police developers and the UN as an organization continue to make, in this view. The first is to be fooled after a couple of years by the formal appearance of a semi-orderly police with uniforms and parades, and declare victory – like in Timor-Leste, in 2005. The second is to limit their own role to the technocratic delivery of capacity-building services to whomever happens to be formally in charge, thereby helping to entrench whatever powers managed to capture the police and

---

[33] Personal communication, former senior UNMIK official, September 2010.

[34] With regard to human resources, another common conclusion drawn by experienced practitioners is that such deep engagement with the institution and its political context in a foreign country requires a multi-year commitment by a core element of senior UN police officials in the same mission. Personal communication with Richard Warren, Stefan Feller, and Richard Monk, 2009–10.

perpetuating systemic corruption of the state. As many found out, aid is as much if not more of a lever for the recipient as soon as the donor is politically committed and accountable for providing it.[35]

Following this line of reasoning, the only way out of this trap is to deeply engage with the institution and learn how it really works, and how decisions are really made beyond the formal appearance codified in organizational charts drawn by international consultants or advisers. As Richard Warren, from 2002 to 2006 the Deputy Police Commissioner responsible for creating the Kosovo Police Service (KPS) and from 2006 to 2010 in the same position in Haiti, argues: 'The key is to embrace the institution in all its dysfunction and crookery, to understand its people, the rules and the relationships.' As the UN discovered time and again in previous missions, such knowledge is the only power available to outsiders to support police reform toward professionalization, transparency, and accountability. Only when the backbone of the institution – its management structure, career incentives, and accountability systems – is changed can the organization retain the recipients of externally provided training and equipment, promote the 'right people,' and create a climate in which those officers with dedication and integrity can afford to follow the rules and 'do the right thing.'[36]

As in many other fields of peace operations, no learning took place before 2003 beyond the level of individuals such as Kroeker in Bosnia and Liberia or Warren in Kosovo and Haiti, for there was no effective learning infrastructure at all. Even after the lesson was officially recognized and initial guidance issued in 2005, the learning process remained a bumpy ride. Even in 2009, in the words of a senior UN official, 'it remains an open debate within the Police Division' to what extent to focus on implementing the formally adopted lesson.[37]

* * *

With the establishment of two unprecedented transitional administrations for Kosovo and East Timor in the space of only four months in 1999, a tiny Civilian Police Unit in New York was asked to develop strategies for providing public order, enforcing the law, and building 'credible, professional and impartial police services,' in the language of the Security Council mandate for Timor – and all that within a few weeks, at most a few months' time while spending most of their long hours on the more mundane requirements of convincing member states to actually deliver the thousands of police officers who would implement their plans. Both in New York and on the ground,

---

[35] This restatement of the lesson is summarized from various interviews and e-mail exchanges with current and former UN police officials at headquarters and in various field operations.
[36] Interview with Richard Warren, May 2009.
[37] Interview with senior UN official, April 2009.

including in the ongoing operations in Bosnia, Sierra Leone, and elsewhere, the utterly inadequate rate of deployment and supply of resources directed the attention of mission managers and planners to the most critical and time-sensitive tasks, effectively ignoring everything else. Getting the new missions deployed and building up their personnel, setting up patrols, and working out the legal implications of their executive powers kept mission leaders and headquarters busy for years. At the same time, the institution-building parts of the mandate received scant attention beyond the establishment of training academies and mentoring schemes.

Inside the UN bureaucracy, there is no paper trail of debate or critical evaluations of such practice in the years until 2002. In the absence of formal evaluation mechanisms and an effective learning infrastructure, and in an organizational culture that was still dominated by a crisis management paradigm, this does not come as a surprise. Not only was there no bottom-up communication of problems or lessons from the field and headquarters understood its role more as logistical backstopping than to provide operational guidance and oversight, there was also a situation where senior managers concentrated on what they saw as acceptable among member states – which was to start the UN's endeavor into the field of rule of law reform at its most technical beginnings.

Most diplomats and UN officials saw the police as mostly a technical issue. Those who recognized the fundamental political dimension of policing often cast the challenge of police assistance as a continuum that began with basic, technical training and the provision of equipment before reaching its pinnacle in dealing with the organizational, legal, and political intricacies – a view in which it could not hurt to start slow, particularly given the meager resources of the UN. Finally, there was a strategic danger in going 'political': if police building came to be identified too closely with judicial reform which had already emerged as a very contentious topic in New York (see Chapter 5), the whole policing agenda would suffer. As a result, even Under-Secretary-General Guéhenno emphasized training and technical capacity-building over the politics of institution-building so as to avoid more of the destructive conflicts between the Secretariat and the developing country bloc that paralyzed so many other UN activities.[38]

In the wider community of experts, as well, the preoccupation with improving technical capacity-building and coming to grips with the political and legal implications of the UN's new executive law enforcement powers dominated the discussion. From the development of training curricula through the selection of international police officers to effective vetting and monitoring schemes to guard against human rights violations, most policy experts were

---

[38] Interview with Jean-Marie Guéhenno, April 2009.

busy with the operational priorities set by practitioners, while the more critically inclined academics wrestled with hard questions of legitimacy and neocolonialism that the Security Council's creation of modern protectorates had
raised.

The silence of the policy community on institution-building is striking,
however, in light of how prominently the issue had been framed in the
1996–8 series of conferences and publications on post-conflict police assistance run by a group around Michael Dziedzic at the U.S. National Defense
University. Their project coined the memorable and much-repeated labels of
deployment, enforcement, and institutional 'gaps' to capture the key challenges for post-conflict police assistance. Dziedzic's 'institutional gap' (1998:
14) pointed precisely at the lack of 'political development' of police institutions. Between March 1998 and August 2000, following up on the original
series, DPKO convened a series of three seminars on improving UN civilian
police operations. These meetings, however, produced a series of recommendations that hardly touched upon the substance of institution-building from a
political angle at all – but were picked up by the Brahimi report nonetheless
(Serafino 2004: 11). None of the influential policy literature at the time questioned the sole focus on training individuals as sufficient for institutional
reform. After all, the policy community remained preoccupied with analyzing
the challenges posed by executive mandates, the new feature of the Kosovo
and East Timor operations (Dwan 2002; Hansen 2002; Dahrendorf 2003: 58).

Perhaps ironically, the most in-depth treatment of the topic can be found in
DPKO's own 2000 handbook. Based on input from practitioners as well as recent
'lessons learned' reports about the operations in Bosnia, Haiti, and Eastern
Slavonia, the handbook lays out guidelines for 'reform and restructuring' of
police services as distinct from training and mentoring individual police officers.
It makes most of the points that previous and later critics would make about
the deficiencies of UN reform strategies in Timor-Leste, Kosovo, and elsewhere.
While likely a usable statement of high-level doctrine in theory, however,
the 'Blue Book' remained 'divorced from reality' as hardly anybody outside the
Police Division in New York was aware of its existence, let alone implemented
its principles (Hansen 2002: 43–4). In terms of police-building, much of these
addressed a political level of interaction with the host government that was of
little interest or importance to the booklet's audience of rank-and-file UN police
officers. At the same time, a few pages of bullet points, almost aphorisms, were
insufficient to impress those police commissioners whose previous experience
had not prepared them adequately for the task of supporting organizational
change from the outside in a volatile political environment.[39]

---

[39] Interview, senior UN police official, February 2010.

In effect, at a time of huge operational strains and without either political attention or a functional learning infrastructure, DPKO paid little heed to tackling the 'institutional gap.' Like in the 1990s, if organizational learning did take place locally in an individual mission such as UNMIK in Kosovo, it was the result of local innovation and experimentation. Its fruits were often forgotten when key staff changed and never effectively shared with headquarters and other missions, because there was no infrastructure to support an organizational learning process. There is little indication to believe that greater emphasis on the part of the research community could have remedied these problems at the time. Having begun to evolve on the heels of the rising interest in post-conflict policing since the mid-1990s, the English-language research community was still in its infancy. Very small, low in academic stature, and to a large extent based on consultant contracts which made many 'independent' researchers quite dependent on the practical trends on the ground, its capacity was probably exhausted by following the implementation of the Brahimi reforms, critically covering the persistent shortcomings in recruitment standards and deployment times and dealing with the profound normative and operational dilemmas of executive powers in transitional administrations.

* * *

Toward the end of 2002 and into early 2003, while DPKO's police unit had no boss and was still struggling to fill its new posts under the recent budget improvements, a number of internal and external reviews of key peace operations took place almost simultaneously. At the time, with the International Police Task Force (IPTF) in Bosnia just handed over to the European Union and police assistance in Sierra Leone a largely bilateral affair orchestrated by the United Kingdom, the two transitional administrations in Kosovo and Timor-Leste were clearly the most important, if the not the only missions that received any political attention.

The official independence of Timor-Leste on May 20, 2002, required a fundamental reconfiguration of the UN's involvement from a transitional administration to an assistance mission working with the sovereign institutions of the Timorese state. On the day of independence, the UN Mission of Support in Timor-Leste (UNMISET) took over from UNTAET. Together with the newly constituted government and a number of bilateral and multilateral donors, the new mission requested an assessment of international assistance needs in the security sector. In January 2003, the review team issued as its report eighty-two pages of clear and detailed assessments that did not shy away from harsh judgments about the international community's, and particularly UNTAET's, past performance. For a UN document, even more for a report that was jointly issued by a number of institutions, its clarity and criticism were striking. The report bluntly declared: 'there has been little attention paid to strengthening the key management and administrative support areas such as human resources management and finance. Equally, there is little or no planning and policy development capacity within the [PNTL, the Timorese police].... The focus of support from UNPOL has been on policing and the development and delivery of training. While this has been a necessary starting point in establishing the [PNTL] it is now necessary to provide assistance to strengthen its management and administration' (UNMISET 2003: 8). Beyond its harsh critique, the paper also made detailed proposals for such reforms to be undertaken in the future.

At least for the Timorese context, the report debunked the notion that any state institution, much less a police service intended to exercise the monopoly of legitimate violence within its territorial boundaries, can be anything but a thoroughly political institution. Experts such as Edward Rees, who wrote similar assessments for a study by King's College London, argued that to expect police officers and their superiors to use their UN-improved technical skills solely in accordance with impartial legal and bureaucratic rules to deliver their stated mission of law enforcement and public safety was to confuse wish and reality. While technical and human rights training, the refurbishment of police stations, and the weeding out of the worst of past offenders were very much necessary, all of these measures had little peace-building effect as long as senior leaders kept politicizing appointments and promotions with the force, undercut the formal commitment to human rights and the rule of law, as long as a weak legal framework and justice system failed to set clear boundaries, and as long as the highest officials of the country neglected to enforce the constitutional barriers between different security institutions. Specifically, the King's College study on East Timor reported that the mission had been 'slow to elaborate a comprehensive development plan for the [Timorese police], partly because no UNPOL had been assigned to the police development function in the original mission design. In the absence of a comprehensive strategy, UNPOL focused on training rather than the institutional development of the [PNTL]' (Dahrendorf et al. 2003: para. vi; Rees 2004).

While more than clearly spelled out in the project's case study on East Timor, the point was apparently not recognized as a significant crosscutting 'lesson' to be included into the final 'synthesis report' that the King's College team put out for policymakers. While the latter publication does make a passing mention of civilian oversight and cultural change in police reform, its only explicit recommendation on the matter keeps clearly with the prevailing orthodoxy: 'institution-building should be conducted in a training academy and be separated from executive policing functions' (Dahrendorf 2003: 58). To the busy reader, training, if only done right, was still sufficient to reform a police institution.

In April 2003, in light of the first downsizing plans for UNMIK, that mission's Inspector-General issued his own review. Similarly to the Joint Assessment Mission in Timor, albeit in much more bureaucratic and polite language, this report indicates that it found the mission's police reform efforts to be far more focused on training than on holistic institution-building. A later study by a former UNMIK national security official sheds some light on what critical observers were pointing at. 'The [Kosovo Police Service] was the UN's first experiment with the creation of a police service from scratch. In this case, as with the PNTL, there has been some success in the creation of a shell police service but there was little success in the creation of a "police institution" between 1999 and 2004.' UNMIK 'has generally failed to address the issue of institution building. Consequently, the institution building which is a fundamental part of the [security-sector reform] effort in Kosovo has been left to the attentions of technicians without the necessary expertise or political guidance' (Rees 2006: 19).

Locally at the level of the individual missions in Kosovo and Timor-Leste, these criticisms fared quite differently. In Timor, the assessment report was simply ignored, despite the appearance of worrying signs of deep cleavages within the security institutions. According to the International Crisis Group (ICG), echoing many similar complaints within and outside the UN, the mission leadership at the time '[failed] to question or even understand the implications of [the Timorese Interior minister's] politicization of the police' according to pre-independence political fault lines within the resistance movement (ICG 2006: 4–5, 17–18). UNMISET continued to work on training and mentoring programs that were challenging enough to implement, while being oblivious to the political forces that undermined the modest progress the mission was making. The result would be the utter lack of institutional resilience and integrity within the Timorese police service that all but enabled the crisis of 2006.

In Kosovo, the mission leadership reacted more constructively, despite the fact that the territory's unresolved status paralyzed its political development for several more years. By the time the Inspector-General's report was released, they had already brought in a former military engineer turned mission manager, Richard Warren, as the new Deputy Police Commissioner for KPS development. One of the erstwhile critics reported later: 'in recognition of KPS's lack of management or administrative capacity, UNMIK brought in a development partner (UNDP) to provide technical assistance to UNMIK and KPS in the development of an administrative division within the police service.... It has proved a success and is active in establishing and implementing the procedures, processes and systems which are the backbone of KPS's institutional administrative capacity' (Rees 2006: 20). A year later, the March 2004 riots in Kosovo opened a further window of opportunity to attract donor funding and push the political leadership of UNMIK toward more serious engagement with the police and the wider national security infrastructure of Kosovo (Rees 2005: 211).

While the missions in Kosovo and Timor-Leste were reconfigured, the summer and fall of 2003 also saw the establishment of a new peace operation in Liberia in which police reform was supposed to play a major role. The UN Secretary-General's mission plan (2003*b*: para. 66) for UNMIL mentions 're-structuring and reorganizing the Liberian National Police' as one of the mission's top police priorities but remains as vague as ever on how this was going to be implemented. In contrast, the mission's January 2004 concept of operations elaborates a 'long-term' focus 'on the redrafting and development of police legislation, policies and guidelines which will create the foundation of an accountable and responsive police institution answerable to the law of the country' (UN DPKO 2004: 18). This is the first time that this kind of document featured such a strong focus on the institutional dimension of police reform. Concepts of operations are drafted by DPKO in New York based on a prior 'technical assessment' of the needs on the ground and with some input from the mission leadership in the field.

Very similar language to that of the UNMIL concept of operations can be found in a technical assessment report on Haiti, dated April 2004. The proposed concept of operations for MINUSTAH, as the new mission to Haiti would be called, foresaw a large police advisory group to tackle management and internal oversight in addition to the classic training and mentoring tasks (UN Secretary-General 2004*c*). On the level of operational planning language, these concepts of operations for Liberia and Haiti signified a huge break with the earlier ambiguity and neglect surrounding the crucial substance of institutional reform. It appears as if this turn in the 'soft doctrine' issued by DPKO to the missions in Liberia and Haiti was primarily the product of the newly strengthened planning team at the Police Division – essentially a few experienced professionals who were much better able to tap into their own expertise and that of their own professional networks in the field to write down some of their own lessons.[40] Obviously, it was a whole different question to what extent those declarations were going to be implemented in practice.

The unambiguous priority for institutional reform expressed in planning documents, however, now allowed its proponents to point out practical deficiencies with much greater force. In March 2004, DPKO's Best Practices Unit informed the head of the Police Division that during a review of UNMIL's start-up phase in Liberia it had discovered that there was almost no police reform

---

[40] As it is often the case with official papers written 'by committee,' it remains unclear who the original author of the significant passages was. Our interpretation is supported by several interviews with individuals who participated in these discussions and some of the drafting on the New York side and in the field in Liberia at the time. We have not come across any contradicting evidence.

going on for several months, due to the slow deployment of the mission and budgetary barriers against hiring civilian experts with institution-building experience.[41] Despite the clear priority for police reform in the planning phase and the strong support of UNMIL's Police Commissioner Mark Kroeker himself, mission practice was largely limited to a vetting–training approach. In its regular report to the Security Council, the mission leadership blames the local authorities: 'The National Transitional Government of Liberia, however, has been slow to implement police reforms in compliance with its September 29, 2004 memorandum of understanding with UNMIL' (UN Secretary-General 2005c). In addition, the slow recruitment for the mission and its lack of police management and reform specialists allowed little opportunities for effective engagement on the management level while the lack of funds for equipping the Liberian National Police with basic equipment – it began with two cars for the entire organization, then five – further hampered reform. For more than two years, until some of these barriers were overcome, UN assistance to the police was limited to the establishment of a police academy, exercising some influence of the recruitment and vetting of new recruits, as well as providing advice (UN Secretary-General 2006b: para. 52; Blume 2007: 5–7).

At headquarters, those officials who had adopted aspects of the institution-building lesson individually over the years managed to sustain and reproduce their case in technical planning documents. Anything more than that was not seen as politically feasible at the time, both internally at the Police Division and externally toward member states – and there were plenty of other issues that needed work in UN policing. Internally, the focus on institution-building and the political dimension of police reform remained controversial. There were desk officers arguing that 'full-scale police reform is beyond the power of UN police' anyway, and that the UN should concentrate its very limited resources on the more technical tasks where it could make a difference in practice. Others believed that 'there is just no way around the fact that it is necessary from day one' to avoid a relapse into war. Kiran Bedi, the Police Adviser, embraced the traditional approach to training as capacity-building and emphasized other priorities during her tenure, including the development of community policing doctrine as a basis for classroom instruction and mentoring.[42] Externally, there was also some push-back from the Non-Aligned Movement (NAM).[43] While, in stark contrast to the headwinds against judicial institution-building (see Chapter 5), there is no evidence of actual negative interference against this low-level learning process by member

---

[41] Internal DPKO memo on file with authors.
[42] Interviews, DPKO police officials, 2008 and 2009.
[43] Personal communication, external expert, April 2010.

states, there were clearly many more low-hanging fruit available to make progress on the many challenges that UN police were facing.

As a result, there was no substantive support beyond the declaratory level on the part of the Police Division. No general guidance was developed and no steps were taken to target police recruiting more toward specialists in management and administration or create civilian posts for experts in organizational change to complement police officers. The Kosovo and Liberia examples show that without such guidance and support from headquarters, each mission still had to figure out for itself how to translate the strategic priority of institutional reform into operational practice. While locally successful, the creation and evolution of police reform strategy in Kosovo was not effectively tapped by headquarters to promote a learning process for the system as a whole.

* * *

To achieve official recognition for the political institution-building agenda, its proponents had to wait until 2005, when Mark Kroeker arrived from Liberia to take over the Police Division. When Kroeker came to New York in March, the number of peace operations with large police components had just about doubled within a year, and most of these missions were still inadequately deployed. Within a few months, planning for a huge police component for what would become the UN/AU mission in Darfur as well as a substantial police deployment to Chad began as well. Kroeker initially built up his own organizational infrastructure before he focused on doctrine development. When he did, what he called the 'three R's' of reform, restructuring, and rebuilding became a centerpiece of Kroeker's agenda, to the relief of some and to the chagrin of others in the Police Division. The internal debate about the feasibility and wisdom of holistic institution-building continued, but the onset of senior management attention set the pending learning process in motion again.

Kroeker initiated a redrafting of the UN Civilian Police Handbook, the first in five years in which UN police had seen plenty of new challenges and should have learned many new lessons. Published in December 2005, the new edition established an additional 'strategic priority' for UN police: 'reform and restructuring efforts aimed at supporting the institutional development and capacity-building of the local police' (UN DPKO 2005b: 32). To make it more attractive for its rank-and-file audience, however, Kroeker had the handbook designed to be smaller and dropped the detailed guidelines for police building that the previous edition had featured. They would find their place in a series of doctrinal publications under the new guidance development system, with a different target audience of Police Commissioners and their senior staff.[44]

---

[44] Interview, UN police official, February 2010.

As the first such document, an official DPKO policy on reform, restructuring, and rebuilding police services was drafted quickly in the second half of 2006 (UN Secretary-General 2006a: 85) and officially approved by Under-Secretary-General Guéhenno on December 13, 2006. In marked contrast to the earlier documents, it emphasized that 'an important element for sustainable success is to achieve a cultural change of police and law enforcement official's attitudes and behavior: this cannot be changed merely through recruitment and training' (UN DPKO 2006d: para. 5.13.17). 'Management tools, sound administration practices and fiscal controls should be given a very high priority' (ibid.: para. 5.13.11) and all necessary changes in laws and regulations are to be shaped in such a way that they promote transparency and accountability.

For several years, this policy directive remained the only piece of doctrine that spelt out at least the principles of holistic institution-building for the police. A number of more detailed doctrines on the 'institutional assessment' and 'institutional development' of police were announced with it but languished in the system while an effort to develop measurable indicators for rule of law institutions has been completed by early 2010. In practice, however, the very complexity of the subject combined with the dearth of substantive opportunities for training and exchange among senior police officials in the field led to a fundamentally unchanged situation as of 2008, at least.[45]

* * *

When policy analysts explained the reasons for the implosion of Timor-Leste's security forces in 2006 unanimously as a result of 'inadequate planning and deficient mission design arising from the dearth of institution-building expertise at UN headquarters' (Hood 2006: 68), it was clear that the first centrally driven push toward a political appreciation of institution-building by UN police had failed. A meager piece of doctrine setting out the principles, while a 'quantum leap' in the view of one critic of many years, was not enough to produce change on the ground. Looking to Timor in 2006 and 2007, there were few signs that anything had changed even after the UN's return with all their self-critical reports and the goodwill of the new Police Adviser, Andrew Hughes. Hughes himself led an assessment mission to Timor and released a damning report in May 2008 (UN Secretary-General 2008a; see also UNMIT Transition Team 2006), but the traditional barriers to change remained: many police officers whose language abilities were barely sufficient to communicate in English, let alone learn one of the local languages, most of whom had little

---

[45] Many police commissioners have also been quite openly opposed to receive guidance from the Police Division in New York, or even to release their senior associates to attend conferences. Interviews, DPKO police officials, May 2008, February 2010.

sense of how to manage or even change an organization, and little understanding of Timorese society and how the provision of order and justice could be made to work in that context.[46]

At the UN and in policy circles, the debate continues between those who argue that 'full-scale police reform is beyond the power of UN police' and their counterparts, who acknowledge its difficulty but retort that 'there is just no way around the fact that it is necessary from day one.' Both statements are probably true, and so the challenge remains for the Police Division to muddle through and try to leverage its slowly increasing muscle to learn from its own past experience as well as that of its partners in the UN system and beyond.

Conclusion

Of the three case studies of organizational learning in this chapter, the one on the creation of the SPC stands out as the only fully politically driven learning process. As a proposal that was going to cost money, if only little, to fund the first standing body of uniformed security forces, if only few in number and unarmed, the SPC needed a political push to overcome the hurdle of residual mistrust by member states. Savvy political management by the leadership of DPKO and the Police Division made that happen. After their success in advocacy, the substantial delay both in terms of funding, because of the duty station debate, and in terms of operational effectiveness, because of the UN's dysfunctional recruitment procedures, illustrate the level of political and structural impediments that continue to hamper every aspect of the secretariat's work, with little relief on the horizon. As a proposal for structural change at headquarters, the SPC depended on senior management and member states alone but required no institutional support for implementation in the field. As such, and despite the remaining obstacles, it was the least demanding lesson examined in this chapter.

The two case studies on constabulary police forces and institution-building share some key similarities. Quite fundamental in their ambitions – defining the role and limitations for a whole new kind of police with its own recruitment and compensation mechanisms, and recasting the organization's approach to police reform – both began as modest, infrastructure-driven processes of learning. Kicked off by knowledge acquired from the field at a time when DPKO's formal knowledge management procedures were not yet

---

[46] Interviews, senior UN police officials in Timor-Leste (November 2007), New York (May 2007, May 2008) and other missions (March 2008, April 2009), own observations in Timor-Leste, personal communication, international police expert in Timor-Leste, April 2010.

in place, they illustrate how personal networks occasionally did produce some sparks of learning and how even small investments into structures and resources can sustain such processes on a very modest level.

While the introduction of constabulary police was supported by senior management from the outset, the details of standard-setting and rules of engagement attracted little attention from DPKO's leadership. As it got entangled in working-level disputes, particularly with the Military Division of DPKO, even a modest piece of doctrine required a sprinkling of internal political support in terms of advocacy by the Police Adviser to get to the point of formal approval. Later, only a widespread sense of crisis forced the Police Division to allocate the level of resources required to fundamentally reevaluate the instrument of constabulary police units as it threatened to become the victim of its own success, and to develop the tools for actually institutionalizing its policies in practice.

The supporters of a more holistic and political approach to building police institutions had much less internal political support until 2005, and their advocacy efforts kept a low profile because of it. Only as part of Kroeker's agenda for his term as Police Adviser did the balance of internal debate tilt in favor of their ideas. The modest level of progress both in terms of advocacy for guidance development and in terms of institutionalizing the changes that had been formally made in the Policy Directive reflects not only the unresolved debate within the Police Division as to the merits of the new approach but also the inherent complexity of the challenge. Where the use of FPUs requires standards and common guidelines that work for dozens of contributing countries, training instruments, and ways of soft enforcement that are certainly complicated in their own right, the very cultural and political core of institution-building in a postwar society holds an even higher degree of complexity that defies simple standard operating procedures.

The failure of institutionalizing the early set of FPU standards or the principles of the new police building directive reflects the weak link in DPKO's learning infrastructure in its early years after its inception in 2005 (see Chapter 2). DPKO's own management review of the Police Division noted that 'the policy guidance available to police officers in the field is still based on traditional paradigms, with little direction on how to implement their interim law enforcement or police reform mandates. Thus, the Police Division must also urgently roll out existing doctrinal guidance and templates to the field so as to ensure uniformity of mission mandate implementation plans' (UN Secretary-General 2009: para. 117). Beyond the lack of effective means of training and evaluation, however, it also reflects systemic weaknesses of the UN police as a whole that largely remain unaddressed today: the bias toward sworn police officers rather than public managers as change agents in foreign police services, the lack of investment on the part of member states to provide and train appropriate personnel for international deployments, and the challenge of recruiting and preparing senior leaders for police missions who can fill the demanding roles of diplomat, change manager, and police commander with equal excellence.

5

Judicial Reform: Building Institutions for the Rule of Law

Over the past decade, the peace operations community has come to recognize that 'the consolidation of peace in the immediate post-conflict period, as well as the maintenance of peace in the long term, cannot be achieved unless the population is confident that redress for grievances can be obtained through legitimate structures for the peaceful settlement of disputes and the fair administration of justice' (UN Secretary-General 2004: 3). As the UN's former chief peacekeeper, Jean-Marie Guéhenno, told the Security Council in September 2003, rebuilding the judicial system 'may prove to be a more effective and efficient use of resources which, in the long run, does more to prevent relapse into conflict and saves both dollars and lives' (UN Security Council 2003a: 4). Yet, for a long time, peacekeeping all but ignored this task. Only in the late 1990s did the realization that sustainable peace requires an effective judicial system start to take root with the Security Council. Beginning with the transitional administrations in Kosovo and East Timor, the Council finally integrated judicial reform programs into new mission mandates as a core element of support for the rule of law, albeit often in a generic fashion. On the ground, UN peace operations have embarked on a wide array of activities to assist national actors in strengthening their judicial and legal systems, ranging from providing technical assistance and training to lawyers and judges, through restructuring justice institutions and drafting or revising laws, to rehabilitating infrastructure and improving access to justice.[1] Starting from scratch without any experience, doctrine, or guidance, the few pioneer lawyer-peacekeepers who were sent to Pristina and Dili had to make up their strategies on the fly in order to turn vague mandates into effective judicial reform strategies on the ground.

---

[1] While corrections or prisons issues are often also subsumed under the header of judicial reform, this chapter will solely focus on courts, prosecution, and the judicial process as such.

For the business of peace operations, engaging the justice sector (beyond the police) in states emerging from war is a fundamentally new activity. The Department of Peacekeeping Operations (DPKO) in particular had no experience in this field. Development organizations had run a few judicial reform programs before but this had not resulted in a shared global knowledge base on how to structure and facilitate the (re-)emergence of an effective judicial system. There is no coherent body of literature on judicial reform at a global or international level. Partly this is a reflection of the fact that judicial systems are highly culturally specific and that comparisons and generalizations are both challenging and contested. In fact, much of the broader 'rule of law' discourse, of which judicial reform is a key component, is seen in many developing countries as a mere extension of Western norms and values – a view that is shared in the self-styled 'critical' academic literature on the rule of law.[2] These perceptions are reflected in the considerable criticism within the UN system, especially on the part of some representatives of developing countries, about the ideological nature of the judicial reform agenda. As a result, any discussion of rule of law assistance at the UN takes place in a political minefield of normative disagreement. In this environment, every budgetary detail is contested. Indeed, so politicized is the atmosphere that UN officials frequently try to couch and camouflage the judicial reform agenda in technical language.

On the ground, UN officials grapple with the complexity of legal and political cultures that are ingrained in the very fabric of societies and make a mockery of any technical depictions of judicial reform. Peace operations officials quickly found out that there are no generic recipes for promoting 'the rule of law.' The extreme diversity of customary or tribal justice systems or dispute settlement mechanisms found in many post-conflict societies is a vivid example of the inherent cultural complexity of post-conflict judicial reform. Similar to other efforts at institutional-(re)building in post-conflict societies, interventions in this field are in constant need of local adaptation and contextualization. That is, experts have warned not only that 'no size fits all' but also that any application of general knowledge to judicial reform in a specific cultural context needs to be handled with exquisite care (Golub 2003; Sannerholm 2006).

As it began to deploy its first judicial advisers (which proved hard to identify and recruit) to such challenging environments, the peace operations bureaucracy was not in a position to provide guidance or conceptual support, not even of the generic kind against which experts had warned. Instead, it had little choice but to put its bets on the do-it-yourself skills of individuals who could draw on legal expertise, in the best of cases working as judges or

---

[2] A host of critical scholars see rule of law programming as an ideological extension of the 'liberal peacebuilding agenda.' For an overview of this strand of the literature, see Peterson (2009).

prosecutors, but had little, if any, experience in international and cross-cultural contexts. In 2000, when the first lawyer-peacekeepers were already operating in Kosovo and East Timor, the Brahimi report found that 'there is no unit within DPKO (or any other part of the United Nations system) that is responsible for planning and supporting the rule of law elements of an operation' (United Nations 2000: para. 179). Despite an unprecedented budget increase for the Secretariat, it took another three years until the nucleus of an organizational infrastructure for learning and guidance development on judicial reform was finally created. But with very limited resources, this Criminal Law Judicial Advisory Unit (CLJAU, later referred to as 'Judicial Unit') struggled for the greater part of the post-Brahimi decade to perform its basic functions to support missions under stress, let alone engage in reviewing experience and developing guidance.

Despite the Secretary-General's call in 2001 for half a dozen professionals to plan, support, and provide guidance to justice components of peace operations worldwide (UN Secretary-General 2001a), after two years of administrative pulling and hauling, member states in the General Assembly only accorded a single person for this massive task.[3] While judicial operations boomed, the personnel at this new Judicial Unit at headquarters increased only marginally in the first years of this decade. In the post-Brahimi years, the total number of judicial officers deployed in UN peace operations quickly rose to almost 200 field officers.[4] Experts familiar with the situation inside the bureaucracy thus readily acknowledge never to have seen situations 'where the headquarters-field ratio was so dramatic.'[5] Indeed, with such limited human resources, the mere task of recruiting field staff overwhelmed the capacities of the small Judicial Unit. Much needed work on the doctrine and guidance for judicial reform became close to impossible: 'between just two people, it basically came down to balancing priorities. Mission staffing and planning was number one. There is no point in doing policy and guidance if there is no time for getting missions going on the ground.'[6]

Aside from the critically underfunded and under-resourced headquarters capacity, another challenge for the organizational infrastructure for learning in judicial reform emanated from the fragmentation of responsibilities across the UN system. While DPKO is the central actor within the peace operations bureaucracy, the limited experience with judicial reform that existed lay with

---

[3] The CLJAU was initially authorized with two professional staff, with the second official covering prison support.

[4] Missions with judicial reform components include Kosovo (UNMIK), Timor-Leste (UNMIT), Sudan (UNMIS), Darfur (UNAMID), Côte d'Ivoire (UNOCI), Haiti (MINUSTAH), Central African Republic and Chad (MINURCAT), Liberia (UNMIL), Afghanistan (UNAMA), DR Congo (MONUC).

[5] Interview, UN consultant, September 2008 (telephone).

[6] Interview, DPKO official, November 2007 (telephone).

other UN departments. Consequently, in 2002, the UN leadership determined that the different UN actors would all support DPKO in devising strategies and guidelines for rule of law programs in peace operations.[7] But the mere task of bringing the different perspectives together overstretched the capacities of the Judicial Unit. With critically limited staff, the unit became caught up in an organizational dilemma: dependent on the different UN players' expertise and support, but lacking the resources to coordinate them. While this process consumed valuable time and resources, it did not effectively deliver the desired operational support in terms of setting up and guiding field missions in their rule of law activities.[8] At the same time, as the long-term nature of judicial reform became increasingly apparent, some practitioners and officials questioned whether DPKO should take the lead (at least in coordination) in the peace operations context or whether it should rather fall into the responsibility of the longer term players such as the UN Development Programme (UNDP).

But regardless of these debates about organizational competence and turf, for most of the early 2000s, none of the other UN actors were in a position to provide any further guidance themselves. As of the mid-2000s, this situation started to change with actors such as the Office of the High Commissioner for Human Rights (OHCHR), the UN Office on Drugs and Crime (UNODC), as well as UNDP beginning to build up their own capacities and guidance material on specific aspects of the rule of law.[9] Even so, senior officials still acknowledge the difficulty of their endeavor: 'we all don't know what we are doing and we have no skills in this.'[10] Most professionals working in this area, indeed, 'openly recognize and lament the fact that little really has been learned about rule of law assistance relative to the extensive amount of on-the-ground activity' (Carothers 2006: 5). Independent research on judicial reform in the post-conflict context is equally underdeveloped. As a result, despite a number of efforts tackling specific questions, outside actors such as think tanks and

---

[7] An internal expert task force composed of representatives from all UN departments and agencies with rule of law expertise recommended the creation of a so-called Focal Point Network spanning across the UN system in order to assist DPKO 'in developing rule of law strategies for new and existing operations' (UN ECPS 2002: para. 4).

[8] Key officials have attested the deficiencies of this institutional setup in terms of delivering concrete support and results (Interview, DPKO officials, May 2007, New York).

[9] As of 2003, OHCHR began to develop rule-of-law tools 'so as to ensure sustainable, long-term institutional capacity within United Nations missions and transitional administrations to respond to these demands. These rule-of-law tools will provide practical guidance to field missions and transitional administrations in critical transitional justice and rule of law-related areas' (UN OHCHR 2006b: v; see also UN OHCHR 2006a, 2006c, 2006d, 2006e, 2008a, 2008b). Similar initiatives have been undertaken by both UNODC (UNODC 2006) and UNDP (UNDP 2007b, 2009), pointing to the increased attention toward guidance development in this field.

[10] Interview, Secretariat official, May 2008 (New York).

academic experts have not been able to fill many gaps in the UN's own knowledge and resource repository.

As a consequence, building the nascent organizational infrastructure on judicial reform into an effective support capacity for doctrine development and learning in line with overall UN-wide policies proved a difficult and painstakingly slow process. Jean-Marie Guéhenno acknowledged as much in 2006 when he wrote that 'despite the importance of this aspect of peacekeeping, justice components of UN peace operations have long operated without significant operational guidance' (UN DPKO 2006: foreword). To address this problem despite the lack of resources, in 2005, officials of the Judicial Unit submitted a project proposal to the United Kingdom soliciting financial support for a systematic guidance development effort. Receptive and supportive of the broader rule of law agenda, the United Kingdom provided a grant to capture experience from the field in an extensive lessons learned study. The results of this study were also translated into a short introductory handbook or 'primer' for judicial field personnel (Carlson 2006; UN DPKO 2006). Now, with at least basic guidance in place, the organization achieved an important milestone in putting the UN's judicial reform practice in peace operations on more solid conceptual and institutional grounds.

At the same time, the UN leadership made steps to address the structural divisions hampering guidance development on UN rule of law efforts and to improve the institutional shortcomings in this field. In his 2006 report, the Secretary-General formally designated DPKO as the lead entity on strengthening legal and judicial institutions in peace operations settings, putting a formal end to the bureaucratic turf fights that affected much of the post-Brahimi debate on these issues (UN Secretary-General 2006*f*). In addition to that, in 2007, the incoming Secretary-General Ban Ki-moon upgraded DPKO's Judicial Unit by including it into the new Office of the Rule of Law and Security Institutions (OROLSI) as part of a larger restructuring of the peace operations bureaucracy. With a dedicated senior position at the level of Assistant-Secretary-General to promote rule of law issues both within the system and among member states, and with the additional resources of a dedicated office, the UN peace operations bureaucracy had given new momentum to the issue of judicial reform. Furthermore, in 2007, the Secretary-General launched a new high-level coordination mechanism presided over by the Deputy Secretary-General in order to instigate more structured UN system-wide coordination and guidance-development in this area. This Rule of Law Coordination and Resources Group (ROL CRG) comprises the heads of all the main UN departments and agencies that have rule of law functions[11] and is supported

---

[11] The following departments and agencies are represented in the ROL CRG: Department for Political Affairs (DPA), Department for Peacekeeping Operations (DPKO), Office of the High

by a dedicated secretariat called the Rule of Law Unit. As part of this overall process, both DPKO and UNDP have also significantly increased its policy-planning capacity in this area.

Compared to the situation when the UN first started to implement judicial reform programs in Kosovo and East Timor, the organization has thus come a long way, having established the basic infrastructure for supporting field components and gradually enhancing its conceptual capacity to guide their operational work. The resulting system-wide process of capacity and guidance development promises to significantly enhance the UN's ability to address rule of law challenges in peace operations in the future. However, this process remains incomplete at best as demonstrated in the following sections that address in more detail the three most important learning challenges that emerged from the field: rapidly addressing the rule of law vacuum in the post-conflict context; building sustainable justice institutions; and adapting programs to the local context, particularly with regards to traditional justice systems.

First, in the early days and weeks after the cessation of hostilities, there is a need to immediately reestablish basic justice mechanisms in order to contain crime and disorder and to win public confidence. This clashes with the long lead times for identifying and deploying suitable legal professionals. Beginning with the Brahimi report of August 2000, proposals emerged to address these challenges by creating UN rapid response teams of judicial experts. Adverse political pressure as well as bureaucratic politics among the different stakeholders within the UN system caused the learning process to stall for most of the immediate post-Brahimi period. As of 2005, an improved learning infrastructure within the department coupled with outside support by a UN member government helped to reinvigorate the advocacy stage for the learning process, which took another five years to clear internal and external obstacles.

Second, as part of the broader institution-building agenda, the UN bureaucracy was tasked to build or rebuild justice institutions guaranteeing the rule of law. For a while, efforts at institution-building were regarded as part of a technical assistance strategy. Then experts began to realize that the prevailing technical focus was insufficient to facilitate sustainable institution-building. This sparked a largely infrastructure-driven policy shift that culminated in new guidelines for a political approach to post-conflict judicial reform. However, changing organizational practice in the field proved a huge challenge

Commissioner for Human Rights (OHCHR), Office of Legal Affairs (OLA), UN Development Programme (UNDP), Office of the UN High Commissioner for Refugees (UNHCR), The United Nations Children's Fund (UNICEF), UN Development Fund for Women (UNIFEM), and UN Office on Drugs and Crime (UNODC).

with insufficient formal structures to support the full learning cycle and without supportive leadership or political pressure from the outside.

Third, many post-conflict societies practice diverse forms of informal or customary justice that are often unknown and appear suspicious to many UN professionals trained to operate in formal Western-style judicial systems. Since the beginning of the UN's involvement in post-conflict judicial reform, a slowly growing number of UN professionals and experts with field experience pointed to the need of engaging with these alternative forms of dispute resolution in addition to the more formal ones. But without political pressure from member states or effective leadership within the UN system, the over-stretched bureaucracy put this difficult and complex issue on the sidelines and prioritized more immediate operational needs, which caused the learning process to stall from its very inception.

Emergency Lawyers and Emergency Laws

The UN's experience with transitional administrations in both Kosovo and East Timor marked its baptism by fire in the field of judicial reform. Acting as the de facto government 'with overall responsibility for [...] the administration of justice' (UN Security Council 1999), as expressed in the mandate of the United Nations Transitional Administration in East Timor (UNTAET), key UN officials experienced firsthand the organization's inability to react swiftly to the sweeping rule of law vacuums that emerge in post-conflict settings.

When the UN start-up team arrived in Kosovo, in June 1999, they observed the complete collapse of the previous Serb-dominated judicial system: after the NATO air campaign had forced Belgrade to pull out of the province, most judges and prosecutors had followed suit. At the same time, the province witnessed a steep increase in revenge and retribution campaigns against the remaining Serb minority. Hundreds of murders took place, while looting, arson, forced expropriation, and abduction occurred on a daily basis. Organized crime also began to flourish as a result of the absence of law and order. When NATO troops started to detain criminals, jails quickly became overcrowded because there were no courts to provide swift trails or legal recourse against arbitrary arrest and detention. As the interim government of the territory, the UN could hardly just release any serious offenders and criminals. To avoid losing its legitimacy by compromising its own principles and standards in terms of due process and fair trials, the UN had to take quick and bold action.

The small UN start-up team that arrived in Pristina in the summer of 1999 had no previous experience to deal with any of these challenges. Never before had the UN taken on the tasks of kick-starting judicial proceedings, appointing judges, determining applicable law, and laying the foundations for judicial institution-building. At the time, the UN had no experienced lawyer-peacekeepers pre-trained for such situations, nor did it provide any instructions or guidelines for those pioneering officials that embarked on these tasks. Under such circumstances, the start-up phase in Kosovo was necessarily chaotic. Heading the UN team at the time, Sergio Vieira de Mello observed that 'the lack of personnel and essential start-up assets on standby for peace-building operations, means that the organization dedicates most of its energy and resources for the first six to twelve months of any such operation on establishing itself' (Vieira de Mello 2000: 17). Most people involved saw this lack of preparedness that was particularly pronounced in the judicial area as a key impediment with potentially critical consequences for the overall peace-building effort.[12] Not being able to establish a marked difference in the perception of justice-provision from the early days of the mission, therefore, was seen as undermining the very popular support that the UN depended upon in order to realize its broader peacebuilding goals.

* * *

Witnessing these enormous difficulties in Kosovo that a little later were repeated in East Timor, a number of UN officials with experience on the ground began to draw lessons and propose remedies. This marked the initiation of a long and arduous learning process that took more than ten years to gain traction within the organization. For those who lived through these experiences, the lessons from the field in Timor-Leste and Kosovo were clear: 'successful international intervention in the judicial arena should be immediate and bold, rather than incremental and crisis-driven' (Hartmann 2003: 2). One of the foremost early advocates of this lesson was Hansjoerg Strohmeyer, who served as legal adviser in both Kosovo and Timor. He argued that justice 'must be seen to be effective from the first days of an operation. The inability to react swiftly to crime and public unrest, particularly in post-conflict situations in which criminal activity tends to increase, and the failure to detain and convict suspected criminals promptly and fairly, can quickly erode the public's confidence in the United Nations. It is thus mandatory for the U.N., and the international community at large, to improve its rapid response capacity in this area' (Strohmeyer 2001a: 122). Equally clear to them was the necessary remedy: the establishment of substantial UN rapid response teams of judicial experts to avoid the kind of rule of law vacuums that had so far undermined the prospects of almost every multidimensional peace operation.

---

[12] For an overview on the broader mission challenges in Kosovo, see for example Dahrendorf et al. (2003) or Bull (2008). A more subjective but very insightful account is provided by King and Mason (2006).

In the summer of 2000, the Brahimi panel visited Kosovo in person and later received further direct input from officials in Timor as part of its review effort. The panel's report took up these suggestions from the field and developed concrete recommendations to significantly enhance the UN's capacity for addressing the challenges in the justice system. It advocated a two-pronged strategy to beef up the UN's rapid response capacity. First, the UN would need to develop a readily deployable team of lawyers and judges that could immediately kick-start court procedures and judicial processes in peace operations settings. Second, in addition to being readily deployable, officials would need to have an interim legal framework at hand that could be applied either temporarily pending the reestablishment of the domestic legal framework, or selectively in areas where domestic laws violated international standards. As the Brahimi panel argued, 'these missions' tasks would have been much easier if a common United Nations justice package had allowed them to apply an interim legal code to which mission personnel could have been pre-trained' (United Nations 2000: para. 81). Underscoring the urgency for such a capacity, Strohmeyer went so far as to argue that where the availability of civilian arrangements is lacking 'the quick deployment of units of military lawyers [. . .] could fill the vacuum until the U.N. is staffed and able to take over what is ultimately a civilian responsibility' (Strohmeyer 2001a: 122).

These bold 'Brahimi proposals' reflected the experience of key UN officials in the field with regards to the organization's lack of preparedness to deal with the challenges of judicial reform. But their initiative to sound the alarm bells about these problems and the Brahimi panel's political support in proposing remedies were just the first small steps into a long process of organizational learning. Whether an operational proposal would be developed, adopted, and implemented would depend on the higher echelons of the UN bureaucracy and, more importantly, member states heeding the call. Such far-reaching new tasks in the peace operations business naturally engendered interdepartmental turf fights, particularly with development agencies. Furthermore, a major investment such as a judicial deployable capacity and the adoption of an interim legal framework for post-conflict countries required the approval of the UN member states. Debate on this investment, however, generated anything but consensus.

The top echelons of the UN peace operations bureaucracy considered it more prudent to face these fights at a later stage with a more elaborate proposal that would clearly spell out the function of a beefed-up judicial deployable capacity within the framework of a broader UN rule of law strategy. There was no dedicated internal actor within the system to elaborate and pursue such a strategy, with elements of a learning infrastructure for judicial reform emerging only several years later. So the Secretary-General reported to the membership that 'further work needs to be undertaken on the broader issues related to the rule of law in peace operations in order to assist Member States in implementing this recommendation' and requested departments to draft 'guidelines covering the principles and practices of the rule of law sector of peace operations' (UN Secretary-General 2000: para. 102).

At this stage, a number of factors worked together to inhibit the learning process from moving forward. Conscious of the politicized nature of the 'Brahimi proposals,' senior officials had significant doubts about the prospects to reach agreement and, in anticipation of political resistance, moved the work on a conceptually richer proposal down the line of priorities. As a consequence, none of the detailed conceptual developments that the Secretary-General had called for took place, not even on the most basic and technical aspects of the proposals. The most ambitious suggestion to elaborate an interim legal code for judicial programs in peace operations fared even worse. An expert group appointed by the Secretary-General on rule of law policy concluded in 2001 'that it would not be desirable for the Secretariat to elaborate a model criminal code, given the diversity of country-specific legal traditions' (UN Secretary-General 2001b: para. 22.15). This effectively sealed the fate of the proposal to pre-train judicial experts according to a common UN legal standard in order to quickly react to rule of law challenges on the ground.

Without strong and purposeful leadership from the top, bureaucratic politics significantly inhibited the further development and deepening of the remaining Brahimi proposals throughout the critical advocacy phase. Indeed, the different UN departments and agencies approached the work for an overarching doctrinal framework for judicial reform components of peace operations very defensively. Naturally reluctant to assign the overall lead for such far-reaching doctrinal work to a single actor, the interagency task force set up by the Secretary-General to implement the Brahimi proposals on the rule of law argued that 'no single UN department or agency has the requisite expertise, experience, resources, or mandate to identify the priority rule of law issues in a peace operation' (UN ECPS 2002: 1). The task force also found that the individual agencies had already accumulated a significant amount of expertise on many of the rule of law aspects and decided that the organization's first priority should be to draw on this existing body of knowledge. It thus concluded that 'at this stage, no further action be undertaken or resources dedicated to draft overarching guidelines on "principles and practices of the rule of law sector of peace operations"' (UN ECPS 2002: 9). In the absence of strong pressure from the Secretary-General's office and the highest levels of the senior management team to produce substantive results, the interagency process degenerated into a peaceful delineation of turf that avoided open bureaucratic conflict at the expense of the substantive work at hand. The task force report resolved to establish a process of voluntary self-coordination and knowledge sharing among the different actors in the rule of law arena.

Given the UN's general difficulty with diverting limited resources from pressing operational demands to more long-term conceptual work, this process never took off. The bureaucracy failed to turn the Brahimi recommendations into a clear operational proposal, spelling out how the proposed judicial deployable capacity should operate and what exact tasks it should assume in situations where the UN does not have a full-fledged transitional administration mandate.

Much of this reluctance within the bureaucracy can be traced to the pressure senior UN officials received from the diplomatic realm, where agitation against the Brahimi proposals was rampant. Indeed, the Non-Aligned Movement (NAM) quickly came to question the intrusiveness of such a beefed-up judicial capacity. They argued that this would effectively give the Security Council too far-reaching means with which to intervene in the core areas of target countries' national sovereignty. Developing countries also feared that such an arrangement would be primarily composed of Western lawyers and promote Western legal standards, and in so doing 'use peacekeeping to sneak in through the backdoor and influence a state's domestic politics.'[13] Opponents in the developing world did not accept the supporters' argument that the proposal was a pragmatic response to very real challenges arising in the field. Rather they framed it as a deeply ideological project amounting to little less than Western imperialism in a new guise. In such a charged climate, the fundamental opposition of the NAM severely undercut the prospects of obtaining the necessary funding from UN member states for financing the judicial deployable capacity.

On a broader level, the Brahimi proposals on the judicial deployable capacity coincided with an ongoing shift in the peace operations debate toward increased 'local ownership' and 'light footprints.' In this context, the Secretary-General acknowledged a lesson from Kosovo and East Timor, contending that 'the international community has not always provided rule of law assistance that is appropriate to the country context. Too often, the emphasis has been on foreign experts, foreign models and foreign-conceived solutions to the detriment of durable improvements and sustainable capacity' thus calling on the UN to 'eschew one-size-fits-all formulas and the importation of foreign models' (UN Secretary-General 2004: 1, 6). This acknowledgment was reinforced by the arrival of a new series of missions with ambitious judicial reform mandates but limited UN executive powers. As the discussion shifted to putting a premium on local ownership from the start, the proposal for ready-made judicial reform packages came to be seen as an outdated attempt to find quick-fix solutions to complex social problems.

---

[13] Interview, UN Consultant, October 2007 (telephone).

A forceful advocacy campaign on the part of the UN Secretariat might have countered this perception. Yet, the senior leadership decided not to make advocacy for the judicial deployable capacity proposals a priority. It failed to translate the initial Brahimi proposals that were very much informed by the experience of full-fledged transitional administrations into the new realities of more limited mandates. At the same time, it did nothing to counter the claim that any investment into a UN judicial deployable capacity would necessarily imply imposing foreign judicial systems on post-conflict societies. The 2003 report on implementation of the Brahimi recommendations by the Secretary-General reflects this choice. It does not make reference to the dramatic staffing challenges for judicial tasks at the outset of UN peace operations highlighted by the Brahimi report. Rather, it contents itself with emphasizing the need for the United Nations 'to consult much more closely with local actors in the country concerned and engage them in a meaningful way in devising and undertaking rule of law initiatives in peace operations, so as not to impose a rule of law strategy on them' (UN Secretary-General 2003: para. 28).

Lacking any signs of leadership or supportive political pressure for the Brahimi proposals of judicial rapid response teams, by 2003 it was obvious that the process had faltered. In a context of deep internal bureaucratic divisions and political pressure from opposing fractions, the proposal fell prey to the accusations of a Western cultural bias. While those member states opposing a beefed-up judicial standby capacity were vociferous, countries supporting the proposals did not turn the issue into a cause worth fighting for – not least because they felt the bureaucracy did not provide them with the necessary conceptual and operational detail.[14] Lack of leadership, obstructive political pressure, and bureaucratic politics set the stage for a politically inhibited process from the very beginning. Progress on the ambitious Brahimi proposals therefore effectively stalled at the initial advocacy stage.

* * *

With such strong political pressure against the Brahimi proposals and quick progress on the full package of 'emergency lawyers and emergency laws' therefore unlikely, DPKO officials hoped for gradual infrastructure-driven improvements on the more technical part of the proposal and turned their attention to the small Judicial Unit that member states had agreed to fund. The 2002 interagency task force decided that the unit should improve staffing and recruitment mechanisms for judicial posts based on existing frameworks.[15] Working with the overall UN personnel recruitment system, the

---

[14] Interview, member state delegates, May 2008 (New York, telephone).

[15] See the final report of the ECPS Task Force for Development of Comprehensive Rule of Law Strategies for Peace Operations (UN ECPS 2002).

unit thus started to develop a roster of rule of law experts by filtering out suitable candidates from within the system, member states, and professional organizations such as the American Bar Association. This roster did not require formal member state approval and represented a working-level fix for the challenge of identifying qualified rule of law personnel at the start of a mission. Consisting of a list of professionals from various backgrounds and organizations that could potentially be deployed in missions for judicial and legal tasks, the roster did make the identification of potential mission person-nel much easier and swifter. Experts agree that the roster improved the orga-nization's ability to staff missions with qualified personnel faster than it was able to before, when it basically lacked any records on experts in this field. As an adviser to DPKO argues, 'at the very least, the roster helps us to ensure that the wrong people don't keep showing up in missions.'[16]

Yet, it is a far cry from the judicial deployable capacity put forward in the Brahimi report. Critically, the roster is no substitute for providing field per-sonnel with a clear career perspective in the peace operations community and to build a cadre of UN judicial experts that have a longer commitment to the organization than seconded national officials. Judges or prosecutors that trade their leafy national civil servant careers for a life within the UN system after a brief field assignment in a peace operation, such as former German trial judge Hansjörg Strohmeyer, are a rare breed. It is therefore only with different career incentives that the organization can expect its field staff to actively engage with its endeavor to enhance knowledge and expertise on judicial reform and to gradually improve practice through evaluation and training. Furthermore, the existence of the roster by no means implies that experts can always be deployed on short notice. DPKO officials readily admit that it remains a huge challenge to recruit and rapidly deploy justice experts to new peace opera-tions. This in turn may mean that the UN continues missing out on 'the honeymoon period immediately after the cessation of hostilities during which optimism and openness to change flourishes' (Pulver 2011: 85).

This became particularly apparent when, beginning in late 2003, a number of new multidimensional peace operations with limited executive mandates but far-reaching judicial reform goals had to be staffed. Despite the roster, rapid implementation of rule of law work continued to be hampered by staffing challenges at the beginning of a mission. Proponents of the ambitious Brahimi proposals can point to examples from virtually all post-2001 missions with judicial reform mandates to show that the operational problems that prompted the Brahimi proposals continue unabated. UN operations have continued to be exposed to failures of justice provision in the face of surging

---

[16] Interview, UN Consultant, October 2007 (telephone).

crime and often complex civil law disputes in post-conflict societies. Liberia, Haiti, and Côte d'Ivoire are all cases in point. In Liberia, a destroyed judicial infrastructure and a complete lack of public confidence in the judicial system, due to its past abuses, made the quick restoration of effective justice-provision an almost impossible task. The consequences in terms of rising crime and impunity seriously undermined the stabilization and reconstruction effort. Haiti is another striking example, where crime surged after former President Aristide's departure in 2004. The destruction of critical judicial infrastructure combined with dysfunctional institutions significantly slowed down justice-provision. As a result, prisons became overcrowded, some 96 percent of inmates had never been tried, and serious criminals could return to the streets emboldened by their apparent impunity.[17] The subsequent surge in gang crime brought the struggling UN mission close to the brink of failure.

While such problems are most obvious within the field of criminal justice, civil law questions have also been critical to the dynamics of conflict in the immediate reconstruction phase. In Côte d'Ivoire, for example, the question of *Ivoirité* – or in other words, who would be entitled to the rights of citizenship such as the right to vote – became an essential element of the civil war. Without legitimate judicial processes to address this delicate question, any attempts at stabilizing the country through elections and the establishment of a legitimate government were doomed to fail. While the planning team for the UN mission developed ideas for a rapid intervention package to resolve these citizenship issues with ready-made mobile courts provided by the UN, at the time, the organization was unable to implement this plan with its limited resources.[18] In retrospect, officials who had been involved in planning the mission's judicial strategy argue that the new outbreak of violence in January 2006 might have been avoided had the UN been able to provide quick and effective judicial solutions for the citizenship issue.[19]

For the first five years after the Brahimi report, most judicial reform efforts found themselves trapped in a cycle of failure. It hardly mattered how competent, dedicated, and hardworking the professionals on the ground were. They all too often deployed too slowly with few resources and little guidance on how to achieve the lofty mandates that the Security Council handed down to them. For the proponents of the ambitious Brahimi proposal for a beefed up deployable capacity, this only reinforced their view that the original 'lesson' was the right one.

* * *

[17] See for example International Crisis Group, ICG (2007).
[18] Interview, UN consultant, September 2008 (telephone).
[19] Interview, DPKO official, May 2007 (New York).

From 2005 onwards, the push for a judicial deployable capacity has slowly been reinvigorated in a largely infrastructure-driven process. The initial push toward renewing advocacy for such a capacity came when a strengthened DPKO Best Practices section prodded the Judicial Unit to focus on gathering lessons learned and developing guidance despite the operational pressures and shortage of resources. Best Practices also helped to secure financial support from the United Kingdom, a country that had established rule of law work as a priority of its foreign assistance and one of the few member states actively supporting this agenda in the peace operations context.

With these funds, an external consultant was hired in 2005 to undertake a lessons learned study of judicial reform programs in the field. This was the first study focusing on the broader experience of the UN in multidimensional peace operations beyond the confines of the Kosovo and Timor transitional administrations. One of the key conclusions was the UN's continued inability to react swiftly to judicial reform challenges in the field. The report highlighted the contrast between the police and judicial reform areas. It argued that while significant progress had been made in the area of police, the judicial area continued to lack operational capacities, holding that 'this more involved international role in the police area should be matched in the judicial system.' Furthermore, the study held: 'Though the axiom that each situation is unique is true, that fact should not stop the UN from developing a number of potential intervention templates, which could guide rapid assembly and deployment of resources tailored to the local circumstance' (Carlson 2006: 7).

The lessons learned study became the first internal document to highlight the continued need for a deployable judicial capacity. Reigniting the advocacy process for this lesson, it made clear that this need persisted in every multidimensional peace operation, reflecting the overall growth in judicial reform mandates. It therefore also made clear that the proposal was going well beyond the narrow context of the transitional administrations in Kosovo and Timor-Leste. However, there was again little follow-up to the study. While the British government extended its funding in order to turn the practical lessons from the field into an operational handbook for briefing mission personnel prior to deployment into judicial programs, there was no broader political follow-up. The UN Secretariat leadership did not take up the issue or push member states to support the implementation of a deployable judicial capacity. Neither did supportive member states engage in any substantial political advocacy on the study's recommendations.

With both the Secretariat leadership and member states on the sidelines, outside actors tried to fill the leadership gap and started to build momentum by advancing knowledge and debate on these issues. As early as 2001, the United States Institute for Peace (USIP) and other partners initiated a process taking on the Brahimi proposal to develop an interim legal framework for justice components of peace operations.[20] The original idea of the effort was to devise a comprehensive interim legal code for the immediate post-conflict phase of a peace operation. After half a decade of deliberations and consultations, the group settled for model criminal and procedure codes designed to support officials in advisory work on legal reform. The idea is to allow officials on the ground to draw on an internationally vetted body of law to guide and speed-up necessary reforms. The first volume of the model codes was published in 2007 and made available to UN personnel and mission planners. Given the early opposition to the idea of model codes, the UN apparatus would not have had the capacities to develop such a body of guidance, which proved to be resource and time intensive. By substituting with its own resources, USIP was able to contribute to the UN's knowledge base on this sensitive issue.

In a similar vein, the Henry L. Stimson Center, also based in the United States, put its efforts into spelling out the proposal of a judicial standing capacity in a politically acceptable manner. The Stimson Center's 2007 report described the need for a rapid deployment capacity of judicial experts as a logical extension of the Standing Police Capacity (see Chapter 4), a deliberate framing designed to leverage the much greater acceptance of police issues among member states as compared to the high degree of controversy surrounding the rule of law. The Stimson researchers made concrete proposals with regards to tasks, composition, and funding required for such a 'standing cadre of police and rule of law experts.' This cadre should be created 'to help plan, deploy, and fill key leadership posts of new missions in their critical first year and provide support to other, ongoing peacekeeping operations' (Smith et al. 2007: xiv). Such a standing rule of law capacity, or ROLCAP, the experts suggested, should be composed of roughly 400 personnel divided into eight teams of about fifty people each. 'One third of each team would address legal issues, prison support, and the judiciary' (ibid.: xiv). The report received a lot of attention both within the UN apparatus and among member states.

Toward the latter half of 2007, officials in a reinforced headquarters unit for the rule of law readily drew on this enhanced knowledge base from the outside to put the idea of a judicial deployable capacity back on the agenda. DPKO announced that its new OROLSI would make the development of such a capacity a priority issue. In doing so, officials underscored the need for matching judicial capacities to those in the police field where the Standing Police Capacity already started to improve the UN's ability to kick-start advisory and capacity-building programs in the field. As a nudge toward reluctant member

---

[20] The project was initiated by the United States Institute for Peace (USIP) in partnership with the Irish Center for Human Rights. See O'Connor (2005, 2006) as well as Rausch and O'Connor (2007).

states, officials argued in the 2008 Secretary-General report on the rule of law that 'the Organization has recognized that integrated criminal justice reform requires not only policing but also judicial and corrections assistance' and that 'more focus on security institutions must be coupled with equal emphasis on interlinked justice issues' (UN Secretary-General 2008b: para. 44). However, the Secretary-General`s report provided preciously little detail on implementing such a beefed-up capacity. While the overall advocacy process slowly gained traction with representatives in the budgetary committees in 2008, it still fell short of convincing the most reluctant member-state delegations with the power to veto the organization's budgets. As delegates from supportive Member States admit, their ability to shepherd this proposal through the budgetary processes and rally political support behind it has been 'hampered by the lack of concrete operational concepts coming from headquarters.'[21]

But the senior UN leadership continued pushing this renewed initiative, with the incoming head of DPKO, Alain le Roy, seeing the judicial capacity as one of the key priorities for the department. In October 2009, he affirmed that 'rapid deployment is critical to the early establishment of security and to the credibility of peacekeeping missions. As we have learned through the deployment of the Standing Police Capacity, rapidly deployable justice and corrections experts deployed alongside police capacities are essential to our effort to provide assistance to national rule of law institutions from the outset of a mission' (Le Roy 2009). Together with the explicit support of the United States for a standing judicial capacity under the Obama administration,[22] and dedicated officials at the working and mid-management level relentlessly steering the unwieldy budgetary processes, this advocacy process finally led to the adoption of the scaled down proposal. In June 2010, the Fifth Committee approved the 'Justice and Corrections Standing Capacity' with five international posts (UN General Assembly 2010). While the concrete implementation of this capacity and its impact on field performance remains to be seen, it definitely represents a watershed for the UN's judicial reform practice.

* * *

Taking more than a decade to reach formal adoption, the efforts at organizational learning to address the rule of law vacuum in the immediate post-conflict phase were anything but swift. Given the scope and the boldness of the initial proposal, it is not surprising that it took time to develop the sense that a judicial rapid response capacity is needed, and to develop member state commitment to pay. Without being embedded in a broader strategic framework for the rule of law and without clear delineations of bureaucratic

---

[21] Interview, member state delegates, May 2008 (New York, telephone).
[22] See for example Susan Rice (2010).

competence for such tasks, the initial Brahimi proposals proved to be vulnerable to charges of a Western and technocratic bias and therefore got easily entrenched in broader political conflicts among UN member states. Those charges, combined with reluctance on the part of the senior UN leadership to confront them, led to a politically inhibited process that essentially stalled at the very beginning of its advocacy phase. While the operational needs that prompted the initial proposals have anything but increased in recent years, the capacity will have to demonstrate its relevance in critical new and existing mission settings in a political environment that has significantly changed.

Beyond Technical Capacity-Building: A Political Approach to Institution-Building

When UN peace operations started to take over responsibilities for judicial systems during transitional administration in Kosovo and Timor, officials were primarily concerned with immediate law enforcement and justice provision. Long-term institution-building in the justice sector was not a priority for UN officials on the ground although this was part of the mandate. This quickly changed after the heyday of transitional administrations that was over in 2001. In new missions, the Security Council gave UN missions weaker executive mandates but tasked them with more and more ambitious institution-building tasks also in the judicial area. In Liberia, for example, the 2003 UN mission was mandated to 'assist the transitional government [...] in developing a strategy to consolidate governmental institutions, including a national legal framework and judicial and correctional institutions' (UN Security Council 2003b).

Many UN officials and experts argued that 'judicial reform' and institution-building were indispensable foundations of lasting peace (and therefore the UN's own exit strategy). Failing to do so could prove disastrous for the broader peacebuilding agenda – both for the civilians affected on the ground and the UN as a whole. The escalation of violence in eastern Democratic Republic of the Congo (DRC) four years into the deployment of UN peacekeepers is often seen as a case in point. The deficient judicial system in the Ituri region prevented villagers from seeking redress over prevailing land disputes between cattle owners and land owners, stirring up private revenge and retribution. In such a climate of impunity, it was all the easier for warlords to perpetuate a cycle of violence by mobilizing revenge-seeking civilians through the exploitation of preexisting ethnic and political divides.[23] The DRC is no exception.

[23] See, for example, Amnesty International (2003).

Experts agree that 'the culture of impunity marked by the lack of impartial institutions was a primary catalyst for the wars in Liberia, Sierra Leone, and Côte d'Ivoire' (ICG 2006: 1). What is particularly problematic in the goal of building lasting peace is that often judicial reform is not a priority issue for the elites in post-conflict states and therefore rigged judicial systems simply become carried into the new post-conflict political structures. Even after the peace agreement came into force in Liberia, the same judicial system that was used as a tool of abuse by previous governments became part of the new post-conflict order with much of the legal professional class remaining in power.

For the UN peace operations apparatus, building sustainable justice institutions required venturing into uncharted territory. Traditionally, institution-building was performed by development actors such as UNDP, which has also recently expanded its involvement in post-conflict judicial reform through its Bureau for Crisis Prevention and Recovery (BCPR).[24] Despite being the lead actor in countries with a peace operation, DPKO had no capacity and expertise in this field. Thus, when designing the headquarters' infrastructure for justice components of peace operations, peacekeeping officials turned to their counterparts in these agencies and drew on their established practices. In 2000, the Secretary-General argued: 'the Office of the High Commissioner for Human Rights and UNDP are engaged in institution and capacity-building programmes to strengthen rule of law institutions. They are the appropriate organizations for engaging in this kind of work' (UN Secretary-General 2000: para. 128). In this way, the UN decided not to build up entirely new structures within the peacekeeping department, instead forcing its new Judicial Unit to rely on the experience and approaches of the established UN actors in this field. As DPKO had no significant planning and programming capacities for justice components of peace operations, the Secretary-General's office saw this as a pragmatic decision to enable operational momentum in the field and to avoid potential turf fights within the system.

Initially, therefore, there was no attempt to develop guidance for judicial reform programs specifically for post-conflict contexts. The new Judicial Unit at DPKO operated with only two judicial officers who had to hit the ground running and meet operational demands as an immediate priority. Judicial programs had to be designed for a new surge of multidimensional peace operations in Liberia, Côte d'Ivoire, Haiti, and Burundi, all within the first year of the unit's existence. In this context, officials decided to essentially replicate the judicial reform programs operated by the UNDP or OHCHR in more long-term development settings: training individual lawyers, judges,

---

[24] In 2007, UNDP initiated the Global Programme on Strengthening the Rule of Law in Conflict and Post-Conflict Situations, complementing similar guidance development programs within DPKO and other parts of the UN system (UNDP 2007b, 2009).

and prosecutors and supporting courts and ministries of justice through technical assistance and colocation of international personnel. As a consequence, 'rule of law programs, regardless of where and at which stage of the conflict they are implemented, seem remarkably similar' (Hurwitz 2008: 291). What united these programs across the board was a focus on technical assistance and training, underscored by the idea that the fundamental role for international actors would be to effectively transfer the technical skills and knowledge of how to run an advanced judicial system to local actors.

* * *

Starting around 2003, practitioners began to question this focus as the fundamental shortcomings of the new judicial reform programs became apparent. In the politically charged post-civil war context, missions struggled to attract local government support for judicial reform, resulting in disappointing outcomes in terms of efficiency, effectiveness, or public perception of judicial systems. Such practical, if anecdotal, evidence from the field triggered the first steps of an organizational learning process on the reconfiguration of judicial reform strategies.

In hindsight, the former chair of the 2002 UN Task Force on the Rule of Law in Peacekeeping Operations argued: 'no UN agency developed experience or expertise in how to build adequate capacity for functional and effective rule of law institutions. To do so would require a transformation in the way the United Nations, across the board, has conducted business in this area' (O'Neill 2008: 103). The critics of the existing approach held that 'programs have typically focused on institutional objectives and formal legal structures without a nuanced understanding of the political and economic dynamics that prevented such structures from existing in the first place' (Samuels 2006: 17). The exclusively technical focus on assistance and training as well as a largely apolitical approach to building institutions came to be identified by experts as a huge shortcoming contributing to the failures in the field.[25] Critics argued that this resulted in 'shell-like institutions, un-enforced and poorly understood legislation, and judges and police with little commitment to the rights and values sought to be entrenched through the reform' (Samuels 2006: 18).

Faced with very limited progress in their operational work on the ground, it became increasingly accepted among practitioners that UN peace operations primarily needed to foster national reform constituencies both on the political stage and within the judiciary so as to support a political process facilitating the emergence of sustainable institutions. This is the approach that Lakhdar Brahimi, former head of the UN mission in Afghanistan, thinks he should

---

[25] See for example Pouligny (2003), Golub (2003), Sannerholm (2006), Stromseth et al. (2006), or Farrall (2007).

have pushed for much earlier: 'I often say that, if I could return to Afghanistan in the year 2001, one of the things I would do differently would be to place priority on strengthening the rule of law. What do I mean by that? Do I mean that we should have had more foreign experts focusing on rule-of-law issues, drafting laws and training judges? No; what we needed was better and more effective use of our political leverage on that issue. We should have played a stronger and a more proactive political facilitation role in uniting the various national actors behind a common vision and a national plan for strengthening the rule of law in the country' (UN Security Council 2008: 11).

When they started to recognize these challenges, officials began advocating more broadly for political considerations in judicial reform programs, setting off the advocacy phase for this learning process. Following an initiative by the United Kingdom, in early 2004, the Security Council requested the Secretary-General report on the UN's activities and needs with regards to the rule of law in post-conflict societies. This gave the internal advocates for change an opportunity to further develop these new ideas and strengthen their arguments in internal advocacy. Indeed, they wrote firm language into the Secretary-General's report, advocating nothing less than a full-fledged policy reversal in the peace operations apparatus: 'countless pre-designed or imported projects, however meticulously well-reasoned and elegantly packaged, have failed the test of justice sector reform' (UN Secretary-General 2004: para. 17). A paradigm shift was needed: 'While effective rule of law strategies necessarily focus on legal and institutional requirements, due attention must be paid to political elements as well.' The report also underlined that programs have to address 'as much political questions as technical ones' and that the international community has 'frequently underestimated the extent of political will necessary to support effective rule of law reform in post-conflict states' (UN Secretary-General 2004: paras. 19–20).

In shifting the terms of debate toward the newly proposed lesson, the 2004 report represented significant progress in terms of advocacy. But in terms of operational practice, it remained inconsequential. The UN's senior officials did not make judicial institution-building a priority and refrained from exercising effective leadership on the report's recommendations. They did not support judicial officials at headquarters in developing and implementing innovative operational designs taking into account the proposed political role and to test new approaches in the field. As a seemingly less threatening or imposing proposal than 'emergency lawyers and emergency laws,' advocacy for a political approach to judicial institution-building also did not arouse significant member state attention, neither supportive nor obstructive. At the same time, the learning infrastructure for the rule of law field in terms of formal structures and resources was still extremely weak. Indeed, DPKO's Judicial Unit was so overstretched with its role of recruiting and assisting mission personnel that it had to turn down friendly reminders by their colleagues from DPKO's Best Practices Section to engage in guidance development. Despite significant advocacy efforts, the initiative to introduce a political focus into judicial reform programs initially remained a largely infrastructure-inhibited process.

Further progress was only made once the resource base for judicial reform programming was temporarily increased in 2005, when the United Kingdom agreed to the Judicial Unit's request to fund a comprehensive lessons learned study. Released in early 2006, the study further developed the new political focus and advanced concrete proposals for implementing it in practice: senior leadership would need to make the rule of law part of their political dialogue with the host government, and use the political leverage of the Security Council mandate to press the government on progress in judicial reform. Arguing that 'often, where the technical fix is relatively easy or evident, the political will for reform is lacking' (Carlson 2006: 22), the study held that leadership in the field is a key factor to success. The Head of Mission and one of the deputies need to make judicial reform a priority issue in their interactions with the government and with the rest of the mission for it to have a chance to succeed. The report argued that Heads of Missions can use Security Council mandates to develop much more political leverage on judicial reform if they so choose. The study resulted in the previously mentioned 'primer' for judicial field personnel that echoed the new focus on the political dimension: 'Rule of law work is often more political than it is technical. Thus, the importance of incorporating rule of law concerns into the analysis of the conflict, political strategy development and political dialogue cannot be overstated. [. . .] If rule of law issues are not on the table of the international and national policy-makers, technical programmes and interventions will likely have minimal effect' (UN DPKO 2006: 9).

Officials in charge of planning and supporting judicial programs in the field were conscious of the fact that issuing nonbinding guidance documents for field personnel would not be sufficient to change the organization's practice and to assure the required leadership support. With system-wide action on judicial issues still inefficient and mired in turf fights, they convinced the Secretary-General to propose the creation of a high-level coordination mechanism on the rule of law, the ROL CRG, to lobby and press for more concerted action across the board (UN Secretary-General 2006f). Some of the long-term protagonists of judicial reform policy in the peace operations community joined the newly created secretariat of this group, the Rule of Law Unit, which became operational in 2007 as part of the Deputy Secretary-General's office. In light of the uncertainty created by the long-running policy debates about the fundamentals of UN rule of law assistance, their first priority was to clarify the organization's strategic approach in an authoritative way. The new team immediately started to develop an overarching guidance note on rule of law assistance, to be issued by the Secretary-General.

After being cleared by the senior management in early 2008, the new approach was codified at the highest level in the first overall rule of law guidance document to be formally approved by the UN system. It officially made 'the political context' one of the primary guiding principles for UN rule of law action. In particular, the note reinforced that 'rule of law assistance has often overemphasized technical questions and paid less attention to political and strategic considerations [. . .]. Senior UN representatives in the field need to understand the political nature of strengthening the rule of law, and dedicate attention to supporting both the political and institutional aspects of rule of law development. In cooperation with Headquarters and in partnership with the national political leadership and other stakeholders, UN leadership at the field level is responsible for fostering political space for reform and insulating the rule of law from inappropriate political influence or abuse' (UN Secretary-General 2008*a*: 3). In essence, the guidance note unambiguously acknowledged that the UN's assistance to often inherently flawed rule of law institutions in post-conflict countries will be ineffective if it is not underpinned by a concerted political engagement and strategy.

* * *

The official adoption of the guidance note marks the culmination of the learning process from viewing judicial reform as a purely technical exercise toward a more political approach. This infrastructure-driven process was facilitated by successive improvements in terms of resources and formal structures. However, promulgation of policy guidelines is not enough to complete the learning cycle. The new guidelines need to be implemented and, for a piece of doctrine at very high level of abstraction such as this note, complemented by concrete practical guidance to assist operational work in the field. The implementation also needs to be tracked and evaluated.

In this case, it is precisely the implementation of the newly adopted policy that has proven the toughest challenge to learning. One key reason for this is that the policy on the political approach to judicial reform – even though simple on paper – is extremely tough to implement in the field. It creates almost guaranteed resistance and push-back on the part of the government and the legal profession in the host country. As one UN official observes: 'former parties of the conflict often fear accountability and are not the best reform constituency as there are often remaining vested interests in the legal profession, making it very difficult to find willing reform partners.'[26] Examples abound. The UN peace operation's engagement with the judicial

---

[26] Interview, DPKO official, May 2007 (New York).

system in Haiti was strongly resisted by the local government on grounds of sovereignty, despite wide-ranging deficiencies and enormous public distrust in the judicial system. In Liberia, the strong national judicial and legal community even outlawed the work of foreigners in the national judicial system, providing significant problems for the UN operation's judicial reform program. These are just two examples of how the goal of 'fostering a political space for reform in partnership with the national political leadership' (as stipulated in the official guidance note) often runs into political opposition. The 'political space for reform' needs, therefore, to be actively pursued by the UN mission by dealing with opposition and using political leverage.

However, officials point to a widespread disinterest or unwillingness on behalf of the political leadership in UN peace operations on the ground to levy their political influence for judicial reform issues. Working-level officials of the justice components of a peace operation are unlikely to be able to make a difference in this regard as long as the senior mission leadership does not use its political leverage on these issues. As the Secretary-General argued in 2008, 'more needs to be done to ensure that United Nations leadership at the country level places the rule of law at the centre, rather than the periphery, of our initiatives in the field' (UN Secretary-General 2008b: para. 16). Indeed, well-placed insiders readily acknowledge that 'many ambassadors and SRSGs feel out of their element when asked to deal with judicial reform, which is perceived as technical and complex' (Pulver 2009: 24). Both Liberia and East Timor illustrate this dilemma. As early as 2003, when drafting the concept of operations for the justice component of the mission in Liberia, officials within DPKO's newly created Judicial Unit held that while the judicial program in Liberia 'should entail strong training, advising and monitoring programmes vis-à-vis all three branches of government,' the mission should also provide for 'diplomatic intervention' whenever such action is necessary.[27] But while the mission plan established dedicated personnel posts to perform the technical tasks at the working level, 'diplomatic intervention' was left as a vague commitment. Such operational designs left the lower level officers that perform the technical tasks without any procedures or instruments to 'effectively control and press mission leadership if not taking the rule of law as seriously as operationally required.'[28]

Timor-Leste is another example. Here, the failure of an entirely technical approach became clear when the crisis of 2006 exposed the shallowness of the rule of law in a country that had gained its independence under UN supervision. As a consequence, mission planners developed a new, more

---

[27] Concept of Operations for the UN Mission in Liberia (UNMIL); internal document (on file with the authors).

[28] Interview, UN consultant, September 2008 (telephone).

political concept of operations for the judicial affairs unit of the new UN peace operation. While technical assistance continued to be provided by development actors, 'the mission itself should have a small team to advise on assistance needed for the overall development of the judicial system' (UN Secretary-General 2006c: para. 90). It was the first time that a judicial unit of a peace operation was not modeled on the technical assistance approach, but rather exclusively focused on giving strategic advice to the host government. Yet, despite its formal setup, officials struggled with finding their exact role, especially with little high-level support by the senior mission leadership.[29]

These examples illustrate that the implementation challenges faced by the UN bureaucracy after successfully completing an infrastructure-driven guidance development process are indeed significant. On the one hand, this is linked to the weakness of formal structures to support the full chain of the learning cycle. The learning infrastructure remains insufficiently developed: enough for guidance development, but not for the full chain of the learning cycle including training and evaluation. The 2006 lessons learned study made concrete proposals for developing training programs for senior mission leadership in order to promote a better use of a mission's political channels to address judicial reform challenges. Nonetheless, at that time, the organization was still struggling to enact effective training, reporting, and evaluation schemes that could have helped the implementation of a more political approach to judicial reform. The limited resources and institutional capacity of the Judicial Unit at DPKO slowed down its capacity to actually translate these new polices into effective training programs. While significant progress has been made in the intervening years with regards to developing guidance on headquarters evaluations of justice components in field missions as well as new training programs for field officers (UN DPKO 2009), it is still unclear how this will enable the organization to implement a more political approach to judicial reform in the future.

On the other hand, this result also points to the fact that leadership is often a critical element for ensuring the full implementation of significant policy shifts. As key UN officials acknowledge, regardless of the guidance development process, some political actors in the Security Council as well as senior leaders on the ground continue to 'see judicial reform as purely technical or readily buy arguments of [national] sovereignty.'[30] In some cases, the mission leadership might have clear reasons for not exerting too much pressure on different factions of the host government on judicial reform. They might need the government's cooperation on other fronts and might not want to jeopardize political capital by focusing on judicial reform. At the very least,

---

[29] Interview, UNMIT official, November 2007 (Dili).
[30] Interview, DPKO official, May 2007 (New York).

however, they would need to justify their choice of priorities to headquarters and the Security Council, which is currently not required of them. Because it is often a difficult and frustrating undertaking in the field to press the host government on judicial matters, unambiguous leadership from headquarters or even the Security Council in support of the new political approach can go a long way in ensuring the effective implementation of the adopted policy.

In the same vein, headquarters officials need to invest even more in the development of clear accountability mechanisms, as implementation throughout all levels of the bureaucracy is critically dependent on clear lines of accountability. Only if there is a clear operational plan with inbuilt reporting requirements which field personnel are required to follow can implementation be achieved. Achieving this goal would require member states to be both ready and willing to scrutinize mission progress based on outcome indicators. Mission reporting in the public Secretary-General reports to the Security Council, however, continues to be primarily output-oriented, with a large focus on quantitative data such as numbers of legal officials trained or trials observed. These measures hardly allow scrutiny of the political successes and failures in judicial reform as a whole. Progress reports on the mission in Liberia, for example, have deplored that 'the judicial system is constrained by limited infrastructure, shortage of qualified personnel, lack of capacity to process cases, poor management and lack of *the necessary will to institute reforms*' (UN Secretary-General 2007*a*: para. 40, emphasis added). Reporting indicators, however, almost exclusively focus on quantitative outputs on the technical components of training and capacity-building, as is apparent from mission reports: the stipulation that 'since May 2006, 336 magistrates, 220 justices of the peace, 226 prosecutors, 147 magistrates' court clerks and 53 circuit and Supreme Court clerks have been trained' (UN Secretary-General 2007*a*: para. 43), as it appeared in the Secretary-General's report on Liberia, is a typical example. Appropriately designed reporting and evaluation systems are thus essential for the successful completion of this learning process.

While the UN's senior management is well aware of these challenges, it has been difficult to develop more suitable evaluation mechanisms and criteria. In 2008, the Secretary-General acknowledged that 'measuring our effectiveness is often hampered by incomplete baseline data and no system-wide arrangement exists on means to monitor and evaluate programming. Thus, rule of law practitioners have yet to move away from emphasizing quantitative data, such as the number of personnel trained, to understanding the actual impact of United Nations initiatives' (UN Secretary-General 2008*b*: para. 63). In this view, promising new initiatives have emerged from field practice, such as the use of contextual benchmarks in mission reports in Liberia aimed at including political and institutional developments into the analysis (Blume 2008). In a similar way, the UN Rule of Law Indicators Project, a joint initiative between DPKO and OHCHR, aims at developing a set of indicators that can be used to assess the functioning and transformation of the rule of law sector in a given country (UN DPKO 2010). However, the quality of these benchmarks and indicators, as well as the wider application of new reporting practices, is still unclear.

* * *

In overall terms, this case has demonstrated that improvements in both formal structures at headquarters and resources through limited member state support can promote a comparatively swift guidance development process. Despite starting off as an infrastructure-inhibited process, once improvements in resources and formal structures were made it took less than two years from a lessons learned study that promoted a new direction of judicial reform strategies to official guidance being approved by the Secretary-General. With internal and external political dynamics playing a neutral role, as neither the senior leadership team nor member states were overtly supportive or obstructive, these improvements were sufficient to spur an infrastructure-driven guidance development process. Nonetheless, with infrastructure components still lacking in terms of supporting the full learning cycle and only limited leadership in support for the new guidelines, full implementation of the adopted policy change continues to pose the greatest challenge to this learning process.

The Missing Anthropologists: Integrating Customary Justice Mechanisms into Reform Strategies

Building up a judicial deployable capacity and developing strategies for institution-building proved tough nuts to crack for the organization from a learning perspective. However, in the eyes of many observers, one challenge in post-conflict judicial reform stands out as the one for which officials in peace operations were least prepared: devising strategies to deal with informal mechanisms of justice, which are in widespread use in many post-conflict societies. Timor-Leste is a case in point, where different forms of traditional justice systems based on the authority of tribal elders and village chiefs had operated for centuries. Having survived the successive occupations by Portugal and Indonesia, customary justice mechanisms represented for much of the rural population both cultural and social continuity. In this context, formal courts based on foreign legal systems and proceedings conducted in a foreign language often merely appeared as illegitimate and predatory instruments of power imposed by the occupiers.

Some of these sentiments carried over to the new justice system that the UN and the new Timorese authorities began to set up after the referendum of 1999. Based on the Portuguese language and a formal body of laws inspired by modern international norms, the new system felt no less foreign to many than that of the Indonesian occupiers, despite the fact that it was legitimized by the support of Timor's independence leaders. One striking example of how formal mechanisms of justice often fail to reflect local perceptions of justice is the perception of punishment by detention in rural Timor-Leste: As a longstanding observer argues, 'where the majority of the population is involved in backbreaking subsistence agricultural work, the notion of being provided with free accommodation and three meals a day with no work requirement, albeit with the loss of liberty and separation from community, is sometimes considered a privilege, not punishment' (Graydon 2005: 33). Because of such divergent perceptions, the UN's attempt to build an inclusive locally owned court system did not change the rural population's habit to turn to their elders for community-based dispute resolution.

The UN's efforts in Timor-Leste provide an illustration of the difficulties the organization faced in tackling this challenge and to devise guidance and doctrine on how to engage customary justice mechanisms. In 2001, still in the early days of UNTAET, officials on the ground argued that the mission would need to develop strategies for integrating customary practices in their judicial reform efforts: 'It is indispensable for UNTAET to ensure that the new legal and judicial system of East Timor takes into account the important discussions within the East Timorese communities regarding the role of the notoriously variable and complex, but frequently significant, traditional or customary law' (Strohmeyer 2001b: 179). Despite this call for action, the successive UN missions in Timor failed to develop any concrete initiatives to address the informal justice system.[31] In 2006, six years after the UN had established its comprehensive presence to support the country's political transition, the incoming head of the judicial advisory section of the new UNMIT mission identified the divide between the formal and the informal judicial systems as one of the key impediments for justice sector reform in the country and pressed for UN action in this field. He quickly realized that 'the formal system was always foreign in Timor, and some 90 percent of people here use the traditional system because it is their own.'[32] The new head of the judicial reform unit found, however, that none of the successive missions had made this a priority for operational work. He tried to correct this by planning workshops and dialogues to develop concrete proposals for the government to engage with the customary judicial system. In this process, however, UN

---

[31] Interview, UNMIT official, November 2007 (Dili).
[32] Interview, UNMIT official, November 2007 (Dili).

headquarters officials 'did not provide any feedback or strategic advice' and effective operational work was clearly affected by a 'manifest lack of guidance on the combination of traditional and formal judicial systems.'[33]

Timor is no exception. Across the board, UN practice focuses almost exclusively on formal judicial institutions, with success of judicial programs being seen as solely dependent on the establishment of state-based judicial and law enforcement bodies. Customary justice systems have generally been outside the frame of reference of UN peace operations planners as well as of most officials on the ground.

* * *

In 2002, an internal assessment of the UN's capacities for rule of law assistance aimed at prioritizing areas for guidance development, in fact, singled out customary law as one of the areas where the UN system as a whole lacked expertise, strategies, and guidance.[34] This finding confirmed the arguments by the few practitioners and outside experts (Strohmeyer 2001b; Mani 2002) who argued for starting an organizational learning process to develop strategies on how to integrate customary mechanisms into the broader judicial reform effort within peace operations. But they were mostly lone voices and their advocacy was not strong enough to move the cause to the frontlines of the department's priorities. Senior officials did not consider customary law as a pressing issue for the nascent judicial reform practice in peace operations with its severely limited institutional capacities, effectively stalling the learning process even before it could gather broader institutional momentum. On its own, DPKO's Judicial Unit was far too overwhelmed with logistical and staffing challenges for the first couple of years of its existence to drive any learning process forward, let alone one fraught with so many conceptual difficulties.

While DPKO's Judicial Unit had no resources to spare for engaging in guidance development, officials did follow up on the advocacy process to raise awareness on these issues within the UN system and among member states. In early 2004, they wrote clear language into a thematic report of the Secretary-General on the rule of law, arguing that the UN necessarily had to 'focus on legal and institutional requirements,' while greater emphasis also needed to be given to include less formal mechanisms such as 'indigenous and informal traditions' (UN Secretary-General 2004: 8–12). However, this rhetorical recognition of a more comprehensive approach to judicial reform proved inconsequential for operational work. Officials, for example, failed to

---

[33] Ibid.
[34] Compilation of Available UN Expertise and Resources in core Rule of Law Areas, Final Report of the ECPS Task Force for Development of Comprehensive Rule of Law Strategies for Peace Operations (UN ECPS 2002: B-6).

solicit targeted donor support in order to close the internal resource limitations that prevented them from substantiating their calls for action.

Indeed, being stretched to the limit, DPKO's Judicial Unit was hesitant to engage with such complex and controversial issues. Seen from the field, 'headquarters strategies in the rule of law area generally focus on the technical issues because they are much easier to address.' Operational questions with political reach, such as how to deal with the customary legal system, have 'generally been left unaddressed by guidance and strategy development efforts.'[35] Senior officials within the Secretariat did nothing to remedy the lack of focus on the issue of informal justice systems. Additionally, DPKO officials considered the issue to be more of a development task and were therefore cautious not to infringe on UNDP's turf. This perspective was underscored by the Secretary General's decision in 2006 to assign the lead on guidance development for traditional justice strategies to UNDP, leaving a degree of ambiguity at the critical early phase of a peace operation where DPKO is fully in control and sets the direction for the entire transition process.

As a consequence, throughout most of the post-Brahimi decade, peace operations across the board did little to bridge the gap between formal and traditional justice mechanisms. While rhetorically admitting to the importance of this particular aspect of post-conflict judicial reform, headquarters effectively expected field personnel to deal with this challenge in an ad hoc fashion without any practical guidance. To square this circle, mission planners put their bets on the genius of individual peacekeeping personnel 'to rapidly integrate into a diverse range of legal, cultural, educational, and professional conditions' (UN DPKO 2006: 3), as the 2006 handbook for judicial field staff put it. However, with most judicial officers within peace operations lacking any specific regional or cultural knowledge as they are selected primarily for their legal qualifications, such calls did preciously little to improving the UN's capacity to engage with traditional justice systems.

Three underlying trends made the lesson to engage with non-statutory judicial systems a particularly tough one for the UN peace operations bureaucracy, significantly raising the threshold for any influence to have a supportive effect on this learning process. First, being mostly trained in Western-style legal systems, many UN officials are sceptical about the performance of less formalized legal and judicial systems. The modern state-building agenda has come to elevate the existence of functioning formal judicial institutions to a prerequisite for effective peacebuilding, seeing it as the only means to guarantee the respect of international human rights standards. Informal or traditional justice mechanisms are mostly viewed by the bureaucracy as

---

[35] Interview, UNMIT official, November 2007 (Dili).

'incompatible with Western liberal values' (Call 2007: 401) and lumped together with the pathological aspects of the previous local order that led to war and precipitated international intervention in the first place – a view shared by many important donors. Second, the exclusive focus on formal state-based judicial systems also corresponds to the preferences and priorities of local elites on whom UN peace operations staff depend for much of their information and the political willingness to implement their recommendations. In many situations, local political elites themselves proved unwilling to engage with informal structures. In Liberia, for example, the UN mission had foreseen a program in this area but 'did not succeed to get the government on board. It is impossible to start initiatives, such as training chiefs to respect basic human rights standards, if the government decides that it doesn't want this.'[36] Third, even if they were willing to tackle the informal justice system, UN peace operations generally lack the requisite cultural insight. Missions do not have access to in-depth anthropological knowledge of the different forms of customary legal systems in the various mission contexts that would be critical for designing effective operational strategies for engaging with them.

The isolated arguments about integrating traditional justice into DPKO's judicial reform approach were too weak to overcome these odds and to build political momentum behind proposals for integrating customary justice into the focus of the UN's work in peacebuilding. There was simply not enough advocacy weight behind the lesson. Without dedicated internal or external support, the strength of the learning infrastructure was insufficient to carry the lesson through to the point of formal acceptance and institutionalization.

Inaction has therefore been the prevalent consequence. Only a few isolated ad hoc initiatives emerged in field practice, none of which went beyond the stage of individual seminars or workshops for sharing knowledge among practitioners in the field. Field personnel have increasingly pointed to the shortcomings in addressing the customary system, bemoaning the widespread human rights abuses in such traditional practices as well as the fact that people in the countryside often have no choice but to rely on informal structures due to the centralization of the formal judicial system.[37] In Liberia, for example, reports on customary law endorsing extreme practices continue despite the UN peace operation's judicial reform efforts. Such practices include trial by ordeal, during which the accused is subjected to severe pain by being forced to jump into fire or to eat poisonous fruit, and the wounds incurred are interpreted as signs of guilt (ICG 2006). The UN mission on the ground did not

---

[36] Interview, UNMIL official, March 2008 (Monrovia).
[37] See for example successive progress reports of the Secretary-General on the UN Mission in Liberia (UN Secretary-General 2006e, 2007a, 2007b), as well as on Sierra Leone (UN Secretary-General 2006d), Sudan (UN Secretary-General 2006b), or Darfur (UN Secretary-General 2006a).

initiate any activities to engage the customary system, rather framing it as a capacity problem of the formal justice system: 'In some remote areas of the country, communities continued to practice trial by ordeal, in part owing to the absence of courts' (UN Secretary-General 2006e: para. 28).

The policy community and some practitioners have increasingly criticized this unidimensional focus on the formal judicial system, particularly in light of the expansion of multidimensional peace operations in Africa where informal mechanisms of justice are widely used. According to some accounts, up to 80 percent of all disputes on the African continent are not addressed through formal judicial institutions but rather through different forms of customary law.[38] Experts have come to bewail that 'the donor community places too much emphasis on the reform of rigid, formal structures that do not necessarily impact large segments of the population in question' (Hurwitz and Studdard 2005: 5). According to the critics, the exclusive focus on formal institutions is the wrong allocation of scarce donor resources: 'Formal institutions are expensive to build. Enforcement through formal institutions is complex. It requires the coordination of multiple agencies (e.g. judiciary, police, and prosecutor). Formal enforcement is also expensive' (Jensen 2008: 121). Furthermore, they hold, this focus leads to shell-like institutions that have often very little to do with the realities of the population, especially in the countryside. Hence, as one leading voice in the policy community puts it, 'the central governance dilemma is how to rely on traditional structures even while rejecting practices by local authorities that are antithetical to the principles of international organizations and donors' (Call 2007: 400).

But concrete proposals of how to overcome the widespread ignorance of traditional justice in post-conflict judicial reform programs are scarce and often contentious. Skeptics, for example, point to widespread human rights abuses and gender discrimination prevalent in customary systems to discredit approaches that rely at least in part on their practices. While experts converge around the argument that the UN's lack of engagement with the informal judicial system is detrimental to sustainable justice reform, they mostly fail to provide concrete operational strategies on how to tackle these challenges.

Some recent initiatives, however, are promising in this regard. Acknowledging the magnitude of the conceptual uncertainties, outside actors have started to work on more concrete proposals for integrating traditional justice mechanisms into judicial reform strategies. In 2007, the Rule of Law Program at the United States Institute of Peace (USIP) began an initiative to develop guidance to international and national policymakers on the potential role of customary justice systems in post-conflict environments. Within the UN

---

[38] See for example International Crisis Group, ICG (2006).

system, the lack of an overall strategy led to case-by-case experimentation in the field. In Afghanistan, for example, UNDP's BCPR developed concrete proposals for bridging the gap between formal and traditional justice systems. It suggested a clear division of labor between traditional justice mechanisms like the *jirgas* and *shuras* that are responsible for dealing with smaller incidents and are monitored by a semi-independent human rights body to ensure their compliance with basic standards (UNDP 2007*a*), and formal courts that are in charge of more severe crimes. A well-placed expert sees this pragmatic approach as a way forward for the UN's post-conflict judicial reform practice at large: 'Figure out what informal institutions are doing; which types of disputes are handled reasonably well by informal institutions and which are not; and tailor formal institution building to handle matters that are not being handled well by informal institutions' (Jensen 2008: 121).

But picking up these different elements of advocacy and fragmented practice in the field and integrating them into an overarching doctrine or guidance document for the UN's post-conflict judicial reform practice remains a tough challenge for the bureaucracy. Only through a marked increase of headquarters capacities for rule of law assistance in peace operations as of early 2007, could officials begin to put guidance development on traditional justice systems on the agenda.[39] Consequently, using the Secretary-General's 2008 rule of law report, they advocated bold action: 'The United Nations system requires clarity on how to address informal justice systems in the rule of law environments in which it works. We need to better understand how they function, their impact on individual rights [...] and perceptions of their fairness and effectiveness in order to consider a more thoughtful, coherent approach in our interventions' (UN Secretary-General 2008*b*: para. 40).

With improved infrastructure driving overall guidance development for justice components of peace operations, officials were able to draft elements of an emerging policy on traditional justice. The comprehensive policy note released in 2009 stipulates that 'justice components should consider assisting customary/traditional mechanisms in the development of policies and practices, for example, to help enhance their compliance with national laws and international human rights standards or to assist in resolving jurisdictional conflicts with formal justice institutions' (UN DPKO/DFS 2009: 9). Since then, UNDP as the official lead entity for traditional justice within the UN system has conducted several in-country studies on informal justice systems but they have not yet resulted in an overall policy or guidance on these issues (UNDP 2009). It remains to be seen to what extent the complexities and controversies which have stalled in-depth guidance development in this field for most of the

---

[39] Interview, DPKO official, May 2008 (New York).

post-Brahimi period can be overcome by these new initiatives and what difference they will make on the ground. Some experts remain pessimistic, holding that 'every time people look closer at the issue of customary law, it seems to become more complex.'[40]

In sum, while the challenge of traditional mechanisms of justice to the UN's judicial reform strategies in peace operations raised some flags early on among field personnel, the absence of strong advocacy support at headquarters stalled the process right from the beginning. Without being considered a priority issue by any significant stakeholders, neither internally within the UN system nor externally among member states and the donor community, the question fell prey to the general weakness of the learning infrastructure for rule of law programming. The complexity of the issue significantly raised the threshold for influences to have a promoting effect on the learning process, so that even the gradual improvements of both resources and formal structures for judicial reform programming was not enough to readily kick-start an infrastructure-driven guidance development process. Approaches to traditional forms of justice and potential ways of engagement with such mechanisms were (and remain) disputed, which explains why the very weak supportive influences on this learning process have so far failed to facilitate even the completion of the advocacy phase.

Conclusion

The three learning processes reviewed in this chapter all followed different patterns: The first case, the creation of justice packages with 'emergency lawyers and emergency laws,' was initially politically inhibited, but after shedding the most controversial part of the lesson, a strengthened infrastructure was enough to reinvigorate its advocacy phase and eventually led to adoption of a scaled-down version of the original proposal. The second case, the introduction of a political approach to judicial reform, appeared to go nowhere initially because of the weak learning infrastructure. The later buildup of such structures then supported a full infrastructure-driven guidance development process that finally stalled during institutionalization – still the weakest link of the learning infrastructure. The third case, dealing with traditional justice mechanisms, saw essentially no supportive influence high enough to overcome the significant contextual challenges that made this a particularly hard lesson for the UN bureaucracy. As a consequence, the process

---

[40] Interview, UN consultant, September 2008 (telephone).

stalled at the initial advocacy phase and, as of late 2010, detailed guidance on how to engage traditional justice systems is still lacking.

These patterns illustrate that in the field of judicial reform, we found very little supportive influences for learning in either of the two clusters of infrastructure and politics. A weak organizational infrastructure centered on a small (and only slowly growing) Judicial Unit that was often unable to compensate for the high degree of conceptual ambiguity and lack of knowledge in this field accounts for the high number of infrastructure-inhibited processes – especially in the first half of the post-Brahimi decade. Capacity overstretch was a limiting factor in all three cases. Even incremental improvements in the resource base for learning support increased the chances for learning to succeed, as several critical steps forward in the learning processes followed the creation of new posts or units. While overstretch and crisis-driven working modes are general features of the UN bureaucracy, compared with the magnitude of tasks assigned to it, the judicial reform area has been particularly poorly endowed with both formal structures and resources to support learning. The unclear internal distribution of competences such as for the question of institution-building, traditional justice, and guidance development more generally, further accentuated this weakness. Both the general improvement of the learning infrastructure within the department as well as the specific strengthening of the rule of law headquarters capacity have provided the basis for initiating or reinforcing advocacy on all three learning processes discussed.

At the same time, these infrastructure reinforcements were insufficient to successfully support any of our judicial cases all the way through the learning cycle. To a greater or lesser extent in each case, the perception of ambiguity and political risk involved with each of the proposed lessons created high opportunity costs for leaders to spend political capital on these issues as well as high levels of politicization or even outright adverse political pressure. Despite their origins in pressing operational demands in the field, none of the three learning processes examined in this chapter received any significant support from senior leaders or member states. In other words, none of the processes were markedly politically driven. Under conditions of a learning infrastructure that remains weak in terms of support for institutionalization, the lack of dedicated leadership support made full implementation of any lesson slow and difficult even when guidance was adopted. As a result, even an infrastructure-driven process such as the paradigm shift from technical assistance to political support for judicial institution-building had difficulties getting fully institutionalized. In this case, without leadership support and without aligned incentive and accountability structures, even the adoption of operational guidance did not translate into a change of behavior in practice and the completion of the learning cycle.

Outside actors can contribute to both infrastructure and politics, by either providing resources or influencing the priorities of the bureaucracy. Member states can fill some of the capacity gaps of an overstretched bureaucracy with targeted grants, such as the UK-funded lessons learned study and primer handbook for rule of law professionals. Other actors such as think tanks, research institutes, or NGOs can provide remedies for weak internal capacity to develop solutions for complex issues, such as the model codes, the standing capacity, and guidelines on customary law. With limited staff and resources, the organization has, inevitably, turned to such non-UN actors for assistance. But, as underlined by the Secretary-General, this also bears dangers for the organization as a whole: 'Though external expertise is extremely valuable, chronic outsourcing undermines any attempt at building and retaining institutional memory and dedicated expertise within the United Nations' (UN Secretary-General 2006f: 2). Even more importantly, member states can shape the agenda of senior officials by formally or informally promoting their 'pet issues' even outside the budgetary process, by requesting reports (such as the Secretary-General's first comprehensive report on the Rule of Law, which had been initiated by the United Kingdom and formally requested by the Security Council), and tying grants or in-kind assistance to work being advanced on certain issues.

Each of our three cases of judicial reform lessons reached a different stage of the learning cycle and demanded a different degree of change. While top-level guidance on the political dimension of institution-building was finally approved, incomplete implementation makes it premature to call this a full-scale success – in fact, recent advances on the rather technical ROLCAP proposal might turn out to be more rapidly implemented than either the approved guidance on institution-building or the stalled lessons on traditional justice. What the 'emergency lawyers' case has clearly demonstrated, however, is that learning processes that directly depend on budgetary decisions by member states might easily get caught up in broader political disputes, and are therefore more likely to degenerate into politically inhibited processes.

This politicization was also exacerbated by the ambiguous and often contested knowledge base. The lack of consensus on many of the key questions within the broader rule of law context significantly influenced the trajectory of new concepts and ideas within the UN system. Even though all the initiatives and ideas arose from operational needs in the field, the lack of conceptual certainty made it extremely difficult to frame proposals as pragmatic improvements rather than the reflection of specific normative agendas – a sure recipe for disaster in the policy process. Furthermore, at the working level, even in the relatively more supportive learning environment that emerged after 2006, learning processes easily stalled due to the significant costs for the bureaucracy to advance knowledge in unclear territory. As showcased by the fate of the debate on integrating traditional justice into reform initiatives, the complexity of many of these judicial reform questions, combined with a lack of active support from senior leaders, provided a clear disincentive for working level officials to pursue these questions, especially while being faced with other pressing operational demands.

* * *

As World Bank experts put it, 'less overall progress has been made in judicial reform and strengthening than in almost any other area of policy or institutional reform in transition countries since 1990' (Anderson, Bernstein and Gray 2005: 57). While to date there is no comprehensive study of the post-conflict context, there is little indication that this finding does not apply to judicial reform in countries with UN peace operations. Experts are quick to volunteer the reasons for failure: 'We expect too much, too soon, with too little money, too much emphasis on technical precision, and too little on the embedded political, economic, and cultural dynamics that surround institutional change' (Jensen 2008: 120). They argue that in the complex interplay between the internal politics of the UN family and other donors with the politics of domestic institution-building, 'both of which discourage critical learning and response – we waste scarce international assistance resources. More importantly, purported beneficiaries of rule of law projects lose security, opportunities, and hope' (Jensen 2008: 137).

In order to prevent this dark picture from dominating future reality on the ground, serious investments in the UN's learning capacity with regard to judicial reform continue to be required. As the experience of the three cases portrayed in this chapter show, dedicated institutional capacity is a critical determinant of learning. That is why it is a positive sign that in 2007 the UN managed to establish a more firm institutional anchor for judicial reform within the broader peace operations bureaucracy: it reorganized police, justice, and disarmament functions together with a new security-sector reform team into the new high-level OROLSI, headed by an Assistant Secretary-General. While this has facilitated a more advanced organizational posture, it still remains incomplete with still very limited capacity for training and implementation. However, as the Secretary-General has highlighted in 2008, 'guidance without training and implementation is hollow.' To really improve the quality of judicial reform assistance provided by the UN, 'the Organization requires a stronger cadre of professional and well-trained personnel' (UN Secretary-General 2008b: para. 53). So far, the UN's haphazard stumble toward organizational learning has fallen far short from meeting the enormous challenges of judicial reform – challenges for which the organization has proven utterly unprepared.

6

Reintegration: From Quick Fixes to Sustainable Social Rehabilitation

Between late 2002 and early 2003, several thousand ex-combatants from Sierra Leone, mostly of the Revolutionary United Front (RUF) rebel group, left the country to fight in the final phase of the civil war in neighboring Liberia. Recruited to support the embattled forces of Liberia's dictator Charles Taylor in their final campaign to stave off defeat, they looted villages and terrorized civilians. Many of these fighters had been subject to efforts by the United Nations Assistance Mission in Sierra Leone (UNAMSIL) to disarm the militias and reintegrate their members into their home communities. Initially, the UN's disarmament, demobilization, and reintegration (DDR) process in Sierra Leone had taken a good course. In early 2002, fighters swiftly surrendered their arms to the blue helmets and formally left their militia groups. Yet, in contrast to the relatively smooth disarmament and demobilization process, reintegration was beset with challenges. Many ex-combatants had to wait for over a year before being able to enter training programs or receive benefits for economic reintegration.

The UN mission was unprepared for the unexpectedly high turnout at disarmament sites and the initial policies for disarmament and demobilization overwhelmed the financial and logistical capacity for the successive reintegration program. As a consequence, ex-combatants lingered near disarmament centers instead of returning to their home communities. In some districts they even linked up with their former units in the bush. In the absence of government and international support, their fellow rebels were their only reliable support group. Having committed atrocities against their own people during the war, many of the former fighters feared retribution and were hesitant to return home. With the UN's reintegration support lacking, these fighters were easy prey for Charles Taylor's recruiters when they searched for support in Sierra Leone. All recruiters had to offer ex-combatants was the prospect of returning to their former occupation and make a living as fighters in the civil war in neighboring Liberia. For ex-combatants this was a lucrative offer: it gave them economic opportunity through the prospect of pay and loot, as well as a way to escape the feared stigmatization and revenge from local communities. The UN's DDR failed to give any substantial or similarly lucrative offer, which saw ex-combatants answer to the recruiter's calls. The result was tragic: the UN's failed reintegration effort in Sierra Leone enabled further brutalities in Liberia.[1]

* * *

Three years before these dramatic developments in Sierra Leone, the 2000 Brahimi report warned that 'the basic objective of disarmament, demobilization and reintegration is not met unless all three elements of the programme are implemented. Demobilized fighters (who almost never fully disarm) will tend to return to a life of violence if they find no legitimate livelihood, that is, if they are not "reintegrated" into the local economy' (United Nations 2000: para. 42). At the same time, as the Brahimi report noted, to fully implement the ambitious goals of ex-combatants' economic and social reintegration has proven tremendously difficult for the UN peace operations apparatus. Indeed, reintegration is one of the most long-term and multifaceted aspects of the post-conflict transformation agenda undertaken by contemporary peace operations. It is also the one furthest removed from the Department of Peacekeeping Operations (DPKO)'s core strengths. In order to provide lasting reintegration perspectives to former combatants, UN peace operations and their partners from UN agencies set themselves a daunting task: to go beyond short-term fixes and tackle the long-term socioeconomic development of the host country. In doing so, they find themselves in a tough spot: not only do dire poverty and lack of opportunity often fuel the war in the first place but they also pose some of the most formidable barriers to sustainable peace.

Reintegration programs involve a great variety of initiatives such as training for income generation, vocational training, labor-intensive public works, healthcare, cash payments, in-kind compensation, as well as psychosocial counseling. None of these tasks relate closely to the security-focused expertise at the DPKO. As a consequence, reintegration programs are carried out by a multiagency network mainly composed of development players. More than a dozen different UN organizations including UNDP, ILO, UNICEF, UNIFEM, and the World Bank, as well as bilateral donors and NGOs, fund and implement these programs.

With all of these actors implementing DDR programs across the world since the early 1990s, by the time of the Brahimi report the UN system had acquired an extensive amount of experience. While anecdotal evidence and cursory

---

[1] See International Crisis Group (ICG 2003) for an in-depth discussion of cross-border recruitment of ex-combatants from Sierra Leone for the war in Liberia.

reviews regarded programs in places such as Mozambique and Central America as successful, neither the UN Secretariat nor other agencies across the UN system undertook any systematic efforts to document these experiences. Instead, a small group of DDR experts within the different agencies harbored their individual expertise while the UN as a whole raced along the tunnel of path-dependency, designing each program based on the template of the previous one. There was little critical review and exchange between the different actors involved. Instead of coming to terms with different mindsets and jointly reviewing lessons across departmental boundaries, silo thinking and turf wars characterized the UN reintegration community.[2]

Indeed, conceptual discrepancies between the vastly different actors of the peace operations bureaucracy are possibly most extreme with regard to reintegration (compared to other activities). DPKO's security focused mindset puts a premium on collecting weapons and demobilizing fighters quickly to remove them from the immediate control of their commanders. In the face of pressing security concerns and often fickle attention by the Security Council, DPKO officials often had little patience with attempts to conceive the DDR not only as an end in itself but also as an opportunity for advancing a broader development agenda. In contrast, development actors argued for exactly that: steering DDR activities toward the more long-term goal of preventing ex-combatants from turning into a social underclass that threatens to hold back the broader long-term development of a country. Both mindsets hardly ever met in practice.

As early as 1999, the Security Council had advocated an integrated security and development perspective on DDR. It highlighted that 'disarmament, demobilization and reintegration cannot be seen in isolation but rather as a continuous process which is rooted in and feeds into a broader search for peace, stability and development' (UN Security Council 1999: 1). But on the ground, this integrated perspective did not take root easily. As long-time observers argue, the result of this discrepancy has been a rhetoric of transformation that stands in stark contrast to the capacity of peace operations to achieve its goals, namely: 'DDR should produce robust change in the role of combatants and change in the political, social and economic environment. However, in project implementation there tends to be tensions between, on the one hand, DDR as a more narrow/minimum effort of security promotion, preventing war re-onset and keeping ex-combatants busy and, on the other hand, DDR as broader/maximum effort of furthering large-scale societal change and fundamentally transforming the conditions and status of combatants' (Torjesen 2009: 417). These discrepancies between UN peace operations,

---

[2] Interview, UNDP official, July 2009.

agencies, funds, and programs have often rendered planning and implementation of reintegration programs a difficult, if not impossible, balancing act. Analysts therefore concur that DDR operations have often fallen short of their expectations – sometimes with disastrous consequences as the Sierra Leone example demonstrates.[3]

* * *

Guidance development and learning on reintegration in DDR programs took place in this context of conceptual and institutional divisions. In terms of institutional capacity, DPKO was not very well placed to drive guidance development and learning in this field. For most of the past two decades, DPKO did not have a dedicated headquarters capacity to steer and orient DDR programs in the field and to coordinate the various multilateral and bilateral actors contributing to these efforts. In fact, the entire UN system lacked such an institutional focal point for DDR at headquarters, leaving officials on the ground without doctrine, knowledge repositories, or guidance. The Brahimi report was first to draw policymakers' attention to this deficiency: 'Because so many actors are involved in planning or supporting disarmament, demobilization and reintegration, it lacks a designated focal point within the United Nations system' (United Nations 2000: para. 43). When asked by the members of the Security Council to assess the UN's performance in this field, the Secretary-General thus had to admit, in early 2000, that 'in view of the extensive engagement of peacekeeping operations in disarmament, demobilization and reintegration, the creation within the Department of Peacekeeping Operations of dedicated capacity for these issues could favour greater effectiveness, enhanced communication, and the development of essential institutional knowledge' (UN Secretary-General 2000: para. 102). But in the wake of the Brahimi report, DPKO created only an embryonic capacity of one professional officer to cover the entire DDR spectrum. With such limited capacity, DPKO was unprepared to drive learning processes for an issue area as far removed from its core business as reintegration among the vast range of actors with widely divergent interests and mindsets.

In this context, only small-scale advances on guidance development and learning took place. In 1999, the Security Council tasked DPKO for the first time to draw up a more institutionalized knowledge base on DDR programming. Without any specialized in-house capacity, the Best Practices Unit commissioned two external consultants to develop a DDR handbook capturing best practices from the first decade of experience in the field (UN DPKO 1999). Yet, as seasoned practitioners readily admit, the resulting handbook

---

[3] For critical reviews of DDR operations, see Muggah (2005, 2006), Ball (2006), and Colletta and Muggah (2009).

was 'nothing that would have made planning on the ground any easier.'[4] As a mere description of existing practice, the manual did not address the underlying conceptual fault lines between the different perspectives on what could and should be achieved by the reintegration component of DDR programs on the ground. The following years saw little progress toward joint efforts at guidance development and learning. Only an egregious failure on the ground in Liberia, a high-profile mission for senior leaders of the two main institutional players DPKO and UNDP (United Nations Development Programme), triggered a large-scale coordination and guidance development process.

On December 7, 2003, the UN Mission in Liberia (UNMIL) launched the first stage of its DDR program at the former rebel holdout Camp Schieffelin near Monrovia. Rushed into the launch of the program without the requisite planning, the mission failed to communicate the details of the DDR process ahead of time and severely underestimated the number of ex-combatants to show up, resulting in the prepared facilities being far too small. Overrun with fighters who expected immediate cash payments in exchange for their weapons, UNMIL quickly lost control of the crowd. As a consequence, 'when frustrated ex-combatants fired shots and took over the disarmament site, it became clear that preparations were woefully inadequate' (Nichols 2005: 110). Looting and chaos on the streets continued for three consecutive days and led to a dozen casualties.[5]

In response to this incident, the mission and UNDP conducted a joint inquiry into what had gone wrong. One of its key conclusions was that mission managers needed clear guidance on DDR programs, based on which they could also be held accountable. A member of the evaluation team who opposed the mission's cash-for-arms approach, for example, stated that headquarters needed the ability 'to smash a guidance booklet on their heads and say "you don't do arms buy-backs!"'[6] In the same vein, pointing to the fact that initial actions of the mission – such as setting the standards for who is entitled to receive reintegration funding – have far-reaching implications for the work of the more long-term development actors, the evaluation underscored the need for joint and fully integrated planning.

The Liberia experience fed into and reinforced informal discussions at headquarters to develop a common body of policy guidance on DDR. In a pioneering interagency process that started in early 2004, formally endorsed as the Inter-Agency Working Group on DDR (IAWG), DPKO and UNDP steered the entire UN system to jointly develop high-level policy guidance based on the experience of all the involved UN actors. The resulting 700-page

---

[4] Interview, DPKO official, May 2009.
[5] For a broader discussion of DDR in Liberia, see Paes (2005) and Jennings (2007, 2008a, 2008b).
[6] Interview, UNDP official, July 2009.

strong Integrated Disarmament, Demobilization, and Reintegration Standards (IDDRS) represent one of the most ambitious and far-reaching guidance development processes within the entire UN peace operations system (United Nations 2006). In conjunction with these advances to standardize DDR practice at the policy level, DPKO and UNDP also gradually beefed up and professionalized their headquarters capacities to adequately reflect both security and development priorities. Since 2005, staff numbers at DPKO's DDR unit have increased from one to five professional officers, significantly boosting the department's capacity to review experience and serve as a focal point for guidance to activity in the field. This nascent capacity allowed the UN peace operations apparatus to engage in the first sustained efforts at developing guidance and learning lessons on the reintegration component in DDR programs.

* * *

This chapter reviews the experience with learning on three key issues: securing long-term funding for reintegration programs, facilitating community-based reintegration to take into account more complex conflict environments, and integrating gender into reintegration programming.

First, while the disarmament and demobilization components of DDR were mostly part of peace operations assessed budgets, reintegration had to rely on unpredictable voluntary funding. Officials on the ground have criticized the resulting delays in program implementation, spurring calls for bringing the entire breadth of DDR tasks into missions' assessed budgets. Practical constraints in terms of shifting programming responsibilities away from agencies, as well as bureaucratic resistance to such a far-reaching step, essentially stalled this learning process for much of the post-Brahimi decade. Effective political bargaining by the reinforced DDR section at headquarters facilitated a compromise through the inclusion of a short-term reinsertion component into the assessed budgets, while longer term efforts still depend on unpredictable voluntary funding.

Second, whereas early reintegration programs have focused exclusively on individual combatants and followed a rigid top-down model, practitioners alerted the need to extend programs to entire communities in order to facilitate economic and social reintegration and to take account of more complex conflict environments. This led to the increasing popularity of the 'community-based approach' in the UN's rhetoric on reintegration. However, again, specifying what this new approach means and implementing it has proven the hardest challenge for the organization, particularly given the underlying contentious conceptual questions about the ends and goals of reintegration that this learning process forcefully highlighted.

Third, DDR programs have traditionally equated combatants with able-bodied male adults. Experts have held that the neglect of women and girls involved in or associated with fighting forces significantly undermined the overall effectiveness and sustainability of DDR programs, particularly the reintegration component. Supported by UN-wide advocacy by women groups for integrating gender concerns into program planning, as well as the supportive environment of the IDDRS process, this assessment led to an unprecedentedly swift guidance development process for gender-sensitive DDR programs. But implementing the ambitious targets set out in Security Council Resolutions and the IDDRS guidance proved a much tougher challenge for the organization.

Overcoming Ad Hocism: Securing Predictable Long-term Funding

Following the conclusion of peace negotiations between the Liberian conflict parties in Accra in early 2003, the Security Council mandated the UNMIL to 'develop, as soon as possible, [...] an action plan for the overall implementation of a disarmament, demobilization, reintegration, and repatriation (DDRR) program for all armed parties' (UN Security Council 2003: para. 3f). With its clear focus on getting fighters off the streets, however, UNMIL's DDR budget covered only the initial disarmament and demobilization phases and left a significant gap until other agencies could raise funds for reintegration efforts. At the same time, contrary to initial mission plans, the vast increase in program beneficiaries resulting from the initial disarmament and demobilization process significantly raised the funding requirements for reintegration. With clear caps on the mission's assessed budget, 'voluntary contributions had to pick up the slack' (Ball and Hendrickson 2005b: 32) which made the fate of these program components uncertain and unpredictable.

In contrast to the guaranteed assessed mission budgets that are available for standard mission tasks including disarmament and most demobilization components of DDR, reintegration has always been undertaken by development and relief agencies that lack access to mission budgets and instead raise voluntary contributions from donor countries. To design projects, produce detailed cost estimates, and to find interested donors take much more time than the budget process for peace operations. Donors are often less than enthusiastic to help former fighters, who are often linked to gross human rights violations, when they could be building schools instead. As a result, funds have often been massively delayed and insufficient as compared to the need for effective and sustainable reintegration of ex-combatants.

In practice, this has often made program implementation extremely difficult. By default, the activities pursued to facilitate ex-combatant reintegration are more long-term in nature and often dependent on a continuous flow of money. Analysts hold, for example, that activities such as creating business opportunities for ex-combatants require several years of ongoing financial support in order to reach a basic level of sustainability. Delays and interruptions in such programs often have such a detrimental effect that, far beyond the damage to individual opportunity and prosperity, they affect the entire peace process by leaving ex-combatants desperate, broke, and ready to be recruited to take part in renewed violence. The earlier example of Sierra Leoneans fighting in Liberia is a case in point.

* * *

Already in the 1990s, many UN bureaucrats and other practitioners held the view that predictable long-term funding for the entire DDR process was a prerequisite for a successful transition from war to peace (Boutros-Ghali 1995: para. 50).[7] When DPKO began implementing such programs on a larger scale, officials were concerned about recurrent funding-related gaps in implementation which they felt were often severely hindering the peace process. While in individual cases mission planners occasionally managed to scramble together funding for reintegration activities through peace operations budgets, there was no clear and predictable rule on how to secure the funds for reintegration programs. The Brahimi panel summed up these concerns in 2000, arguing that since 'the reintegration element of disarmament, demobilization and reintegration is voluntarily funded [...], funding has sometimes badly lagged behind requirements' (United Nations 2000: para. 42).

For DPKO officials who were charged with implementing these programs in the field, the budgetary separation between the different DDR components as well as the resulting administrative differences in terms of procurement policies did not make any operational sense.[8] The Brahimi report gave them the opportunity to voice their demands for expanding the scope of UN peace operations budgets to include reintegration, since these budgets offer a reliable and comparatively swift source of funding, drawing on member state's assessed contributions. This, they argued, would be crucial to get the reintegration component off to a running start rather than having it lag behind the other DDR components. Translating these demands into its policy recommendations, the Brahimi panel suggested that 'the legislative bodies [should] consider bringing demobilization and reintegration programmes into the assessed budgets of complex peace operations for the first phase of an

---

[7] Interview, DPKO official, December 2009.
[8] Interview, DPKO official, December 2009.

operation in order to facilitate the rapid disassembly of fighting factions and reduce the likelihood of resumed conflict' (United Nations 2000: para. 47c).

The Brahimi proposal sparked immediate political resistance from member states. While the lesson did not appear as particularly controversial or conceptually challenging to its proponents, member state diplomats received it as yet another potentially bottomless pit of funding demands. Without a clear limit to the price tag for those new reintegration funds and in the context of already rising peace operations budgets, key funders immediately opposed the proposal. Assessed contributions are linked to overall economic prosperity, so the bulk of the peace operations budget is supplied by only a few countries, above all the United States, Japan, Germany, and the United Kingdom. With a 'general lack of understanding at the policy level of what precisely reintegration should achieve and accordingly a lack of certainty about the spending limits,'[9] these member states were not ready to hand out a blank check for including such programs into their assessed contributions. While developing and beneficiary countries were generally supportive of an expansion of assessed contributions, they have comparatively little weight in the budgetary committees. The funders' political resistance thus inhibited the learning process from its very inception.

At the same time, even though far less significant than the political resistance of member states, DPKO officials also found that other UN agencies tried to resist the attempt to change the budgetary rules of the game. As close observers put it, 'issues of institutional and personal turf continue to affect external support for DDR processes. The question of which body is best suited to manage DDR resources has not been systematically explored' (Ball and Hendrickson 2005b: viii). Agencies such as UNDP put forward arguments against the peace operations taking on overall control over budgets. They pointed to the agencies' extensive expertise in recovery and development. Fearing that with a move to assessed funds, planning might be monopolized by mission staff with none of the agencies' socioeconomic experience, some argued that 'the multidisciplinary nature of DDR processes militates strongly against any one type of organization (development, peace support, diplomatic) being able to manage all the necessary functions' (Ball and Hendrickson 2005a: 18). UNDP in particular also cautioned that assessed budgets allow for almost no host country participation, being entirely controlled by the mission. An extension of the mission's assessed budget to the entire reintegration phase would therefore also imply that the entire process would yield very limited national ownership.[10]

---

[9] Interview, UNDP official, September 2008.
[10] Interview, UNDP official, September 2008.

As a consequence, the Brahimi proposal to include reintegration in peace operations budgets faced resistance at both the interbureaucratic and the intergovernmental level. With the debate in New York largely stalled, missions had to continue to muddle through with the existing budgetary constraints. To ease that challenge, officials in the field came up with a way to use Quick Impact Projects (QIPs) to implement smaller reintegration efforts in the short term. QIPs are a small-scale flexible funding instrument provided under the assessed mission budget. Tapping into these funds, they developed dedicated stop-gap projects to bridge demobilization and reintegration. Foreseen as short-term interventions to ease the transition from demobilization to reintegration, this field-based innovation allowed officials to divert some of the more stable mission funds to small projects to improve the short-term economic well-being of ex-combatants. In Sierra Leone, for example, the mission managed to employ several thousand ex-combatants in short-term infrastructure reconstruction and agricultural development projects. A UNDP DDR practice note also officially acknowledged the utility of such projects highlighting that they 'can help reintegrate ex-combatants into the community by creating short-term jobs, whilst they wait to enter longer-term reintegration programmes' (UNDP 2005: 49).

While seen as effective if well managed, not even opponents of the assessed funding proposal saw QIPs as an effective substitute for a real solution of the funding gap between demobilization and reintegration. In early 2005, the reinforced DDR team at DPKO launched a new attempt to broker an agreement with member states on more reliable funding mechanisms. Conscious of the political minefield they were about to enter, the DPKO team decided to take an incremental approach and abandoned the Brahimi report's original suggestion to include the entire reintegration stage into the assessed budgets of peace operations. Instead, they used a part of the Secretary-General's annual budget proposal to develop new definitions for each step of the DDR process. As part of these definitions, they proposed adding an intermediary category between demobilization and reintegration: reinsertion or the 'assistance offered to ex-combatants during demobilization but prior to the longer-term process of reintegration.' They went on specifying that 'while reintegration is a long-term, continuous social and economic process of development, reinsertion is a short-term material and/or financial assistance to meet immediate needs, and can last up to a year,' and stressed that 'financial support for reintegration will continue to be resourced through voluntary contributions and managed by the appropriate agencies, funds and programmes' (UN Secretary-General 2005a). By endorsing these new definitions, member states implicitly agreed to include a reinsertion period of one year in the assessed mission budgets (UN General Assembly 2005).

DPKO officials had to skillfully maneuver through the budgetary process to secure this deal. With general support for DDR within the budgetary committees relatively high, the officials now had a good case to make.[11] Much of the initial reluctance on the part of member states to simply extend assessed funding to the reintegration phase was not based on substantive opposition to the need for more predictable funding for reintegration, but rather to the lack of clarity about when reintegration ends and where funding would end if they were signing on to full assessed coverage of these programs. The reinsertion formula helped to establish that clarity and, at the same time, also limited the duration of funding to one year. Concerns of a seemingly endless commitment to pay for what was essentially seen as development assistance were therefore laid to rest, which paved the way for an agreement with member states.

* * *

Above all, it was the improved headquarters capacity that reignited the previously stalled learning process and facilitated comparatively swift adoption of a modified version of the initial lesson. Only the existence of a dedicated unit of experts allowed the issues behind the initial political resistance on the part of member states to be identified and solutions to be pursued with the kind of persistence that only a genuine bureaucratic 'owner' of an issue can bring to bear. This was particularly important since there was little senior leadership attention to this process, both on the bureaucratic level within the UN and on the diplomatic level in embassies. Once the reinforced DDR team had developed the compromise formula that addressed member states' concerns, institutionalization followed swiftly. In this case, improved headquarters capacities were critical because they allowed a few politically savvy DDR officials to effectively steer a scaled-down proposal of the original lessons through the diplomatic and bureaucratic processes of decision-making.

For a number of observers, though, the adoption of the compromise formula leaves many questions open that were raised by advocates of the original lesson on the need for sustained and predictable funding for reintegration activities. They point to the fact that the question of how to link the one-year insertion measures to long-term, development-oriented reintegration programs that continue to be voluntarily funded has largely remained unanswered. Some experts have even argued to fully abandon reintegration as a goal of DDR: 'Given the political and security objectives of DDR, it might make more sense to redefine the "R" portion of DDR as "reinsertion," [. . .] and to identify ways in which longer-term assistance can be used to support the

---

[11] Interview, DPKO official, December 2009.

reintegration of former combatants and their dependents into civilian life without overly privileging them compared to other war-affected populations' (Ball and Hendrickson 2005a: 22). While organizationally delinking the process of disarming and demobilizing combatants from that of planning and delivering reintegration support is precisely what the proponents of the initial lesson wanted to avoid, 'there continues to be debate among policy-makers on what can be expected from the R-phase [i.e. reintegration] as part of DDR processes and on which activities should instead be part of wider recovery programmes' (Specker 2008: 3). Whether it is called reintegration or recovery, however, the need for sustainable funding and delivery after the first year remains unaddressed. As senior UNDP official Jordan Ryan puts it, despite these achievements 'the shape, scope and sustainability of reintegration is [still] too often determined by the availability of resources, rather than the reintegration requirements coming from thorough assessments' (Ryan 2009). As the following case highlights, part of this challenge is linked to broader conceptual disagreements about what can and should be expected from reintegration programs.

More Than Individual Combatants: Extending Reintegration Assistance to Communities

When the UNMIL started granting cash and employment benefits to former fighters in order to facilitate their economic and social reintegration into civilian livelihoods, parts of the receiving communities reacted with strong resentment. People who did not take up arms during decades of civil war had little understanding for rewarding the perpetrators of extreme atrocities with money and exclusive economic opportunities. Analysts highlighted that it was indeed a 'common perception [in Liberia] that civilians are excluded from benefits and perpetrators are rewarded for atrocities' (Willibald 2006: 326). Resentment was so severe that some feared for the long-term reintegration perspectives of the former combatants if communities were antagonized from the outset of the program. Reports quoted civilians as complaining that the UN's practice was like offering people jobs because they had done something wrong and not considering those they had done wrong to (Crawley 2004). The consequences of such sentiments were evident in Sierra Leone, where the UN had to admit in 2003 that 'the targeted reinsertion benefits were sometimes perceived as rewarding perpetrators of violence and atrocities and often led to increased tensions between host communities and ex-combatants rather than an investment in peace and reconciliation' (UN DPKO/PBPU 2003: 27).

For a long time, most UN officials and the institution as a whole did not recognize this tension. By design, DDR programs focused on individual combatants. The immediate security imperative of removing combatants from their former fighting roles and reintegrating them into an emerging post-conflict society required specific benefits and entitlements in order to ease the transition of a uniquely dangerous part of the population into civilian livelihoods – not just for their own benefit but for the sake of society at large. This is part and parcel of the security mindset that informs much of early programming in DDR. Initially, officials were thus less concerned about the long-term perspectives of these fighters within the societies and communities into which they were supposed to reintegrate. Neither did they recognize what analysts later pointed to as two main obstacles to sustainable reintegration: first, the fact that many ex-combatants had committed crimes against their very own communities who are therefore very reluctant to take them back into their midst, and second, the breakdown of the labor market and most of the economy that severely constrains any kind of economic activity and, if not addressed, also dooms any efforts to get ex-combatants into jobs.

Practitioners on the ground were first to point out that the sole focus on individual fighters in DDR programs had the potential to significantly under-mine the long-term success of such interventions. If, for example, the stipends received by ex-combatants were higher than the average salary of community members, the returning fighters were likely to be viewed with jealousy by the community and discriminated against when it comes to employment or other economic opportunities. The exclusive focus on soldiers, these observers held, can therefore make it difficult to successfully reinsert and reintegrate ex-combatants. It is within communities that ex-combatants ultimately need to forge new livelihoods. Further developing these initial observations by practitioners, scholars have started to advocate community-based reinte-gration as an alternative or complementary model to traditional individual-focused approaches: 'Community security mechanisms tend to adopt area-based approaches, endorse collective incentives to enhance compliance and community participation, and harness the influence of indigenous power-brokers and agents of change' (Colletta and Muggah 2009: 444).[12]

* * *

A few individual UN officials recognized this challenge early on. In a 1999 practice note on DDR, DPKO officials argued that 'community-based pro-grammes are particularly successful in bringing about social reintegration and durable reconciliation and should be encouraged' (UN DPKO 1999: 81). DPKO at large, however, did nothing to pick up on the proposed lesson. Neither did it make the community focus a programmatic priority or develop the requisite policy guidance for field personnel or review existing approaches

[12] See also Body (2005) and Kingma and Muggah (2009).

158

to better facilitate community-based integration. As a result, missions continued with business as usual: whether or not their reintegration plans would feature some sort of community focus would largely depend on the experience and initiative of individual officers on the ground. In some missions, pragmatic officials implemented innovative community-based programs, as was the case in Sierra Leone. In an early evaluation of UNAMSIL, DPKO's nascent Best Practices Unit found in 2003 – again – that 'the success of reintegration programs depends crucially on the degree to which ex-combatants are accepted by the receiving communities' (UN DPKO/PBPU 2003: 27). UNAMSIL implemented community-based stop-gap projects that included intense consultations with community members in deciding on specific reintegration measures for returning ex-combatants. These projects were largely hailed as a success (Berman and Labonte 2006). But such initiatives remained the exception rather than the rule.

DPKO was at great pains to fully embrace a community focus because it counteracted its institutional identity as a security actor implementing short-term measures to create breathing space for political progress and not long-term, sustainable programs of socioeconomic transformation. Community-based reintegration was much closer to the long-term approach practiced by development actors and would require a fundamentally different operational logic. UNDP, on the other hand, recognized the 'fit' with its own paradigm and stepped up its advocacy for a community-based approach to reintegration. In a practice note on DDR programming released in early 2005, UNDP argued that 'many DDR interventions have in the past failed because of their narrow focus and short-term approach. A well-designed DDR programme will not only enhance basic security but also support wider recovery and development' efforts (UNDP 2005: 18). Officials made it clear that while much of the focus of DDR programs has to be on ex-combatants, 'the main beneficiaries of the programme should ultimately be the wider community' (ibid.: 11). Hence, DDR activities should ideally link 'disarmament and demobilization directly into a wider community-based recovery strategy' which also implies that 'ex-combatants are not specifically targeted for livelihood support' (ibid.: 55). UNDP officials suggested striking a balance between supporting the specific needs of ex-combatants and the needs of the wider community in order to prevent resentment and assure the sustainable integration of former combatants into communities.

This conflict played out in Haiti, where DKPO and UNDP started an integrated DDR program as part of the MINUSTAH mission that was deployed in 2004. While the initial mission plan featured a community-based reintegration strategy, disagreements between the two institutions prevented them from implementing this common approach (Muggah 2007). The DPKO component essentially reverted to individually based reintegration while UNDP officials started promoting community-based violence-reduction programs as an alternative to the DPKO-dominated DDR process. As a well-placed expert highlights, 'the integrated DDR Section was thus effectively administering at least two separate programmes' (Muggah 2007).

The disjointed Haiti experience also featured at the higher policy level in New York and Geneva. When the IDDRS process was established in 2004, it offered DPKO and UNDP a framework for discussing and aligning their approaches to reintegration. But rather than facilitating debate and the development of common solutions, the process led to cementing the often-rehearsed opposing arguments. As close observers report, 'the IDDRS basically allowed everyone involved in the DDR business to bring in and codify their pet projects and their individual perspectives.'[13] As such, the IDDRS features language on community-based reintegration, largely mirroring UNDP's approach. But the IDDRS documents do not address the tension with other approaches or at least a consolidated discussion of the different approaches. Rather than giving practical instructions when or in what cases to implement a community-based approach or how to reconcile it with more traditional reintegration efforts, the IDDRS merely provided a definition of what community-based reintegration means: 'to support ex-combatant reintegration as component of wider, community focused reconciliation, and recovery programs' (United Nations 2006: 4.3). As a DDR expert from UNDP underlines, there are thus 'no signs that the divergence between development actors and DPKO would have been resolved by the IDDRS process. The module on reintegration is helpful to a certain extent; it clarifies a few things and features language on community-based reintegration, but still does not provide any guidance on what precisely should be achieved or how long the support should be.'[14]

Critics of the IDDRS hold that the entire process avoided this fundamental conceptual question. They argue that the consultative process between the different departments, funds, and agencies merely provided for the parallel accumulation of different perspectives and did not address widespread conceptual fault lines regarding what DDR should be about and what UN peace operations should achieve and prioritize.[15] The broad and encompassing language of the IDDRS represents the continuum between a security-oriented (improving security in the short term) to a development-oriented (as an opportunity for development) interpretation of DDR, represented by DPKO and UNDP, respectively. The standards did not resolve the underlying conflict over whether reintegration programs should be placed on the continuum,

---

[13] Interview, DPKO official, May 2009.
[14] Interview, UNDP official, September 2008.
[15] Interview, UN consultant, May 2009.

severely undermining coherent program planning and implementation. Insiders therefore lament that 'there appears to be comparatively little consensus on how integration should be defined, or how it can be operationalized,' leading to the conclusion that 'despite optimism among diplomats and senior UN officials in New York and Geneva, there are growing concerns on the ground that "integrated" DDR missions are in fact "disintegrating"' (Muggah 2007).

In this context, where the learning process was stalled at the official level because of these broader normative disagreements among the different bureaucratic actors, pragmatic security and development practitioners on the ground and in specialized think tanks continued experimenting with and promoting community-based reintegration efforts. As close observers put it, 'a growing number of security promotion interventions are purposefully reducing incoherence and competitive friction ("turf battles") among implementing agencies by developing collaborative and inter-sector planning and implementation strategies' that follow a community-based pattern (Colletta and Muggah 2009: 437). In Haiti, for example, as a reaction to the difficulties encountered by the formal integrated DDR program, UN agencies as of 2007 started to develop community-based violence-reduction to achieve the same goals. Similarly in Liberia, the UN mission used information collected through community 'hot-spot' assessments developed by the Joint Mission Analysis Center (JMAC) in the design of targeted reintegration programs. To its promoters in the field, what such new approaches allowed was deviation from rigid DDR programming in order to provide early economic interventions with long-term development goals and immediate security benefits (Colletta and Muggah 2009).

Officials at headquarters recognized these field-based innovations, and, through the process of updating the IDDRS standards three years after their initial publication, started to put community-based reintegration more firmly on the policy-development agenda.[16] In this context, DPKO commissioned a study on such new innovations on DDR practiced in the field with the aim of trying to integrate them into the UN's guidance on DDR. The paper emerged out of the assessment that 'the complexity of the environments in which [peace operations] operate could potentially be addressed by the emergence of a new set of options, often developed in response to localized needs and that can be mixed and matched to meet current contexts' (UN DPKO 2010: 30). As the report highlights, 'whereas traditional DDR focuses mainly on combatants that are present within military structures, the focus of Second Generation programmes shifts away from military structures towards the larger

---

[16] Interview, DPKO official, December 2009.

communities that are affected by armed violence. [...] Instead of implementing relevant provisions of a peace agreement, Second Generation activities are programmed locally using an evidence-based approach. These efforts, reinforced by regular assessments, enable practitioners to more effectively and quickly adapt to new developments' (UN DPKO 2010: 3).

While not featuring any entirely new approaches, this report represents the first official policy document published by DPKO that gives a detailed account of what constituted community based reintegration and how concretely it can be implemented in the field. As the report argues, 'while these stop-gap measures are not new, the new focus on these issues within peacekeeping (Liberia, Côte d'Ivoire, Haiti, and, increasingly, Afghanistan) is generally being welcomed by stakeholders as having considerable potential to fill a problematic gap between the demobilization and reintegration phases of traditional DDR processes' (UN DPKO 2010: 4–5). In view of bridging the gap between development actors and peace operation actors that has for a long time hindered progress on these more integrated approaches to DDR, the authors of the report took pains to highlight the unique advantage of peace missions in setting the stage for effective reintegration: 'Peacekeeping missions have an important role to play since they have access to: (1) assessed funds (which are therefore potentially accessible early on in the process); (2) well-placed and competent staff across the mission area; logistical capacity (including equipment, vehicles and military engineers when available); and (3) considerable capacity for national public information or sensitization campaigns' (UN DPKO 2010: 23). In essence, what these new approaches promise is to ensure that reintegration programs are better linked to broader peacebuilding strategies – the key stumbling block for reintegration programming in peace operations from the very beginning. To achieve their goals, reintegration programs need to provide a flexible and effective link between exit strategies of missions and the development programming undertaken by development actors, bilateral donors, and host governments.

While the publication of a formal report on these new approaches to reintegration comes close to promulgating official DPKO policy, it is clear that more work will be required to develop a clear implementation strategy based on the comparative advantages of all actors. As DPKO formalizes these practices into official guidance and works toward institutionalization, it will be crucial to do so in collaboration with development partners and national donors in order to achieve greater cohesion between the different perspectives of security, recovery, and rehabilitation.

* * *

The lesson to open up reintegration programs to communities rather than merely to individual combatants was initially the sole initiative of individual practitioners in the field. It was difficult for DPKO in particular to come to terms with such a new approach as it exposed broader conceptual discrepancies between the main UN peace operations actors about what should be achieved by reintegration programs. The learning process was therefore politically inhibited from the very beginning. Yet, the general move toward integrated DDR operations in the field, supported by the broader IDDRS process and forceful advocacy from the specialized think tank community gradually led to an implicit adoption of the development approach. For the lesson to be fully implemented, however, the organization needs to develop more specific guidance and provide the requisite mechanisms for ensuring its application and evaluation across the board.

Beyond Male Fighters: Gendering Reintegration Programs

When the LURD[17] rebel outfit took on the fight against Liberian President Charles Taylor from 1999 to 2003, women and girls were active members of the fighting forces on all sides. The same holds true for MODEL fighters[18] who joined the war at a later stage in 2003. Some experts have put the number of female combatants in Liberia's civil war at more than one-third of the entire combatant population (UNIFEM 2004). Some were forced to support male rebels as cooks or sex slaves while others joined the ranks of the rebel outfits in order to escape from and seek revenge for the atrocities committed by government soldiers. Only a minority of women and girls attached to the combatant groups were actively fighting or in possession of arms, but all played a significant role in supporting fighters and running camps and operations bases. However, when the UNMIL started to disarm and demobilize the former combatants after the peace agreement in 2003, a mere 7 percent of program beneficiaries were women (ibid.). Stigmatized by their own communities and mostly unable to return to their traditional gender roles while the lack of education and wealth foreclosed other opportunities, many of them were forced into poverty, exclusion, and deprivation.

Far from being an exception in the way the UN implements DDR programs in peace operations, the case of Liberia underlines how women and girls were neglected as targets of DDR programs across the board. UN peace operations mostly failed to develop dedicated strategies for dealing with women and girl combatants. Throughout much of the 1990s, when the DDR concept was developed and implemented in missions across the world, female combatants and women associated with fighting forces were not on the radar screens of

---

[17] Liberians United for Reconciliation and Democracy.
[18] Movement for Democracy in Liberia.

mission planners and UN officials. The sole aim of these programs was to increase security by disarming male belligerents, and women or girls were mostly not regarded as posing significant security threats. Confronted with scarce resources, mission planners pragmatically focused their DDR efforts on what they perceived as the 'real' and most immediate problem: disarming fighters with guns and removing them from the streets by finding them new livelihoods. These fighters were supposed to be adult males – and so reintegration packages rarely addressed the specific needs of women and girls.

* * *

Toward the end of the 1990s, women's groups started to advocate systematically for women in conflict and post-conflict situations. Their campaign forced DPKO officials to recognize their lack of engagement with gender-specific needs in the DDR process. Key actors in this process were women's NGOs that came together in the NGO Working Group on Women, International Peace and Security, specialized UN agencies (such as UNIFEM), as well as individual member states such as Canada and Germany. Their concerted advocacy led to the negotiation of UN Security Council Resolution 1325 on Women, Peace and Security, passed on October 31, 2000. In it, the Security Council not only requested the Secretary-General to provide 'training guidelines and materials on the protection, rights and the particular needs of women as well as on the importance of involving women in all peacekeeping and peace-building measures,' but also specifically encouraged 'all those involved in the planning for disarmament, demobilization and reintegration to consider the different needs of female and male ex-combatants and to take into account the needs of their dependents' (UN Security Council 2000: paras. 6, 13).

Women's groups hailed Resolution 1325 as an outstanding achievement, representing the first element of international law that recognized women as both victims and subjects of international peace and security. However, its abstract language on gender and DDR still needed to be translated into concrete operational guidance. A high-level expert panel on 'Women, Peace and Security' acknowledged as much in a follow-up report on the resolution. The panel emphasized that a key constraint in the implementation of gender perspectives in peace operations was the fact 'that many managers and professional staff are still uncertain what relevant gender perspectives are in their areas of work and how they should integrate these perspectives in different areas of peacekeeping work' (UN Secretary-General 2002: 77). More concrete guidance would therefore be required to help peace operations officials mainstream gender perspectives into the daily work of all mission components. But, as the panel acknowledged in 2002, DPKO 'currently lacks the human and financial resources necessary to effectively promote gender mainstreaming and provide backup to the field' (ibid.: 77).

Without more detailed guidelines on how to implement the political commitments of Resolution 1325, reintegration programs in the field continued unchanged. Only the language of the Security Council mandates was slightly adapted to reflect the new gender commitment. Liberia is a telling example. When laying out the Secretariat's operational recommendations for the newly authorized UNMIL on September 11, 2003, the Secretary-General suggested that 'special measures and programmes should address the gender-specific needs of female ex-combatants' (UN Secretary-General 2003: para. 46). Mirroring this call and in line with the demands of then Council members such as Germany, the Security Council authorized the mission on September 19 with a specific reaffirmation of 'the importance of a gender perspective in peacekeeping operations [...] in accordance with resolution 1325' (UN Security Council 2003: para. 11).

On the ground, however, the mission launched its DDR program without any specific gender elements (Jennings 2009). Only when reconfiguring the program after the initial blow-up referred to at the beginning of this chapter, UNMIL articulated specific provisions and services to be made available to women and girls in the DDR process. In collaboration with the newly created gender unit in New York, DDR officers in UNMIL broadened the benefits scheme to target both women who engaged in active combat as well as women and girls who played support roles as cooks, sex slaves, and porters during the war. In the same vein, the mission also launched an information campaign in order to encourage women and girls to participate (UN DPKO 2005). But notwithstanding these efforts, women's activists argue that the results were rather disappointing. 'Despite gender-sensitive mandates, language and targets, women and girls are not participating in the DDR process in proportion to their participation in the actual fighting' (UNIFEM 2004: 9). Other missions fared even worse. As a DPKO practice review acknowledged, 'in MONUC and ONUB, advocacy efforts by the gender units and partners to include women associated with fighting forces as part of the DDR programme achieved limited success' – polite UN language for falling far short of the intended goals (UN DPKO 2005).

The difficulty of implementing the commitment to gender mainstreaming on the ground has exposed significant discrepancies between declared policies and operational practice. As one UNIFEM Executive Director put it, 'while "getting it right" in terms of mandate and institutional scope are necessary prerequisites, "getting it right" does not automatically translate into "doing it right"' (UNIFEM 2004: 9). The translation into practice is indeed where much of the gender advocacy hits operational limits. It often proves much easier to claim the need to consider women's needs in DDR programs than it is to actually design specific programs and implement them effectively. Indeed, the 'acknowledgement on paper of gender dimensions in all these modalities is common, but implementation of genuinely gender appropriate modalities often remains problematic' (Barré 2004: 16).

In order to bridge these deficiencies, a group of young and entrepreneurial UNIFEM officials took on the recommendations of the 'Women, Peace and Security' panel and started to develop a ground-breaking report on women and DDR with specific reviews of best practice from the field. Against the backdrop of emerging discussions at headquarters to initiate a large-scale process of formalizing the UN's DDR practice (which became the Integrated DDR Standards project, IDDRS), they saw an opportunity to establish their agenda at the core of the policy debate. In doing so, they could also draw on an increasing amount of studies on gender and DDR that had been produced in the ensuing years by the wider expert community (Farr 2002; Watteville 2002; McKay and Mazurana 2004).[19] To them, it seemed reasonable 'to develop a specific input into the DDR guidance development debate at a time when a major exercise of codification and professionalization of DDR practice was underway.'[20] As such, they saw the coincidental timing of these advocacy efforts and the emerging discussions about DDR guidance development as a 'window of opportunity to replace *ad hoc* measures and one-off projects with routine consideration of the different needs and capacities of women and men' (UNIFEM 2004: 3).

While this initiative to develop a best practices review on gender and DDR came from within UNIFEM in pursuit of its own strategic goal of bolstering its relevance within the broader peace operations system, DPKO was very open to the initiative. Under heavy pressure from women's groups and select member states to take gender issues more seriously, DPKO was actually 'craving expertise on these issues and turning to UNIFEM for advice.'[21] While DPKO had established a post for a gender adviser in 2003 as a response to the pressure from advocacy groups, it took over a year for this post to be filled. Furthermore, guidance development for gender perspectives on the various substantive areas of peace operations practice was not an immediate priority for the incumbent. The operational demands of recruiting, coordinating, and supporting more than a dozen gender advisers in all field missions virtually exhausted her limited capacities.[22] Guidance development on women's issues in DDR programming thus had to draw its substance from outside the department. Yet, officials were also keenly aware that implementation would depend on more explicit support by the UN's senior management team. The UNIFEM report thus recommended that the Secretary General issue high-level policy

---

[19] For a later assessment, see also Jennings (2009).
[20] Interview, UNIFEM official, November 2009.
[21] Interview, UNIFEM official, November 2009.
[22] Since 1999, DPKO has gradually established gender advisers in all new and existing peace operations in the field.

guidance in order to 'provide SRSGs and DPKO with optimal sample language for the negotiation of gender issues into DDR packages and processes' (UNIFEM 2004).

With UNIFEM filling the gap in its own knowledge base and a constant string of setbacks in DDR programs due to insufficient considerations of women's needs, pressure was mounting on DPKO to change course. In late 2004, for example, experts argued that in Sierra Leone women and girls were sometimes the leaders of protests among ex-combatants against the delays that occurred in disbursing their reintegration benefits, protests that often erupted into violence and civil disorder. 'Without support or care from their former "parents" or "husbands" [in the rebel group], their own families, the community, or the state, many of the young women – particularly those with children born as a result of their captivity – resorted to civil unrest as a means of accessing basic goods for the survival of their children. For these young women and girls, the stakes are, in effect, greater than for some of the men and boys' (Mazurana and Carlson 2004: 26).[23]

Scholars and practitioners increasingly started to underline that traditional DDR programming does not sufficiently provide for the needs and requirements of these specific groups of combatants. Women and girl combatants, they held, often end up marginalized at the fringes of society with much worse perspectives for economic and social integration than their male counterparts. Economic reintegration is generally complicated for all combatants by the general lack of opportunities in post-conflict situations. Employment opportunities are often limited, skills are lacking and educational systems severely underdeveloped, and land for subsistence farming is often unavailable or unevenly distributed between different groups. All these factors are generally more difficult for female soldiers as they are expected to revert to pre-conflict labor patterns, face legal restrictions on land ownership and inheritance, or have limited mobility, especially if they are responsible for children and other dependents (Bouta 2005; Bouta et al. 2005).

As the Executive Director of UNIFEM put it in her foreword to the 2004 practice review on gender and DDR, 'the terrible irony is that women and girls are not invisible to armed groups, who see them as essential, accessible – and often expendable – military assets. Yet having survived the devastating experiences of war as combatants, sexual captives or military "wives" and slave or willing labourers in the conflict period, these women and girls often become invisible when DDR planning begins.' Equally clear to hear was the 'depth of change – in procedure, assessment, delivery, attitudes and habits' –

---

[23] A USIP survey of ex-combatants in Liberia also underlined that women combatants were more likely than their male counterparts to return to violence as a means of income generation (Hill et al. 2008).

that would be necessary to implement more gender-sensitive procedures across the UN system (UNIFEM 2004: 1). For this to happen, officials would need clear and unambiguous practical guidance for their operational work and leaders would need to be held accountable for delivering on these issues, requiring both doctrine and specific progress benchmarks.

This is precisely what European member states pressed for at the Security Council in October 2004, when they initiated a Presidential Statement that requested the Secretary-General to submit an action plan on the implementation of Resolution 1325. In doing so, they effectively created a mechanism for accountability at the highest level. In response, the Inter-Agency Task Force on Women, Peace and Security started consultations and prepared an encompassing Secretary-General's report that was released in October 2005. This report acknowledged that information on gender aspects in progress reports on UN peace operations was sparse and did not allow for effective monitoring and evaluation of the UN's gender-related benchmarks and targets. In order to improve the UN's performance in this field, the Secretary-General's report announced that the broader IDDRS process would include a module on women and gender as well as for DPKO to create guidance on gender-responsive DDR programming (UN Secretary-General 2005b). The IDDRS working group on gender, driven by the same UNIFEM officials, then endorsed the provisions set out in the earlier report, codifying the best practices put forward by UNIFEM and including them in this large-scale interagency guidance document (United Nations 2006: sect. 5.10). Reinforcing these specific provisions, only three months after the publication of the IDDRS, DPKO also issued a policy directive on gender equality in UN peace operations that also stressed the need to integrate gender perspectives in DDR programs (UN DPKO 2006).

* * *

In contrast to other cases in which we found guidance development to be painstakingly slow due to genuine knowledge gaps or deep controversy about policy, gender-sensitive DDR programming is an example for swift guidance development. Within the matter of a few years, the organization was able to tackle an obvious blind spot in its policy. This process was triggered by external advocacy groups putting pressure on the UN peace operations bureaucracy and the Security Council to mainstream overlooked gender concerns into their operations. The advocacy movement turned key member states such as Canada, Germany, and the Scandinavian countries into supporters of the cause. A high-level policy decision from the Security Council codified the lesson that had yet to be operationalized into concrete guidance for use in the field. For this step, an actor from within the UN system but outside the immediate peace operations proved critical. UNIFEM was the only actor with a claim to substantive expertise on how to operationalize gender-sensitive programming in peace operations. Given the strong support by key member states, the wider gender movement had created such strong momentum in the Secretariat that other players in the IDDRS process did not oppose UNIFEM's suggestions and best.[24] As a consequence, the UNIFEM officials were able to take the lead in drafting the entire IDDRS gender module. Their original suggestions were quickly adopted as official high-level guidance for the entire UN system.

However, as many of the individuals involved acknowledge, the real challenge in this field lies in changing operational practice and thereby effectively improving the life of women on the ground. The mere inclusion of gender-sensitized guidance in the overall IDDRS process does not in and of itself produce the successful implementation of these provisions on the ground. As one of the top UNDP officials puts it, 'the launch of the UN integrated DDR standards in December 2006 provided detailed gender-sensitive policies on DDR, but we still need to translate the policies into gender-responsive DDR programmes' (Ryan 2009). Officials involved in the guidance development process argue that with the IDDRS they had set out an extremely ambitious agenda that is 'beautiful on paper, but extremely hard to implement at the field level.'[25] While the basic challenge of making the organization and its senior leadership aware of these issues in order to enact appropriate policies had worked exceptionally smoothly, officials contend that when it comes to actual program implementation, 'a lot continues to depend on the sensitivities of individual actors in the field.'[26]

Officials in the field are cautiously optimistic about the gradual organization-wide traction of the gender-sensitive DDR guidance. In Haiti, for example, an official argued that with the availability of the UNIFEM practice review and some first informal drafts of the IDDRS module on gender at the time of the inception of the DDR program on the ground, 'officials looked at gender aspects very carefully in program planning and conceived of dedicated projects for women associated with armed groups.'[27] In Sudan, the existence of embedded gender officers was seen as 'a critical success factor not only in terms of having the right expertise on hand but also in terms of ensuring there is accountability on gender mainstreaming within the unit.'[28] At the same time, however, officials are doubtful whether the existing guidance and associated training efforts are already strong enough to root gender-sensitive programming in more hostile circumstances. Effective implementation of these ambitious targets still depends on the right people, and officials are

[24] Interview, UNIFEM official, November 2009.
[25] Interview, UNMIS official, November 2009.
[26] Interview, MINUSTAH official, November 2009.
[27] Interview, MINUSTAH official, November 2009.
[28] Interview, UNMIS official, November 2009.

clear about the fact that the few reported success stories usually coincide with officials on the ground that have previously been exposed to issues of gender programming or awareness-raising.[29] At the very least, however, as a senior UNDP official argues, 'we know that women and girls can no longer be considered an afterthought' (Ryan 2009).

Conclusion

The three cases reviewed in this chapter all took different paths moving from knowledge acquisition to advocacy and eventually institutionalization. The suggestion to include reintegration programs in the assessed peace operations budget was, in principle, not a conceptually difficult lesson. It emanated from the operational challenge of dealing with often unreliable voluntary contributions. But touching on the core of power and institutional interests as well as on practical divisions of competence between peace operations and the different UN agencies, the learning process was politically inhibited from the beginning. The Brahimi proposal did not only encroach on the established division of labor between peace operations and UN agencies but also would have required such a massive shift of donor contributions and budgetary control and oversight that it was essentially doomed to fail from the start. Only the creation of a new unit with the subject matter expertise and bureaucratic ownership of the DDR issue allowed its officials to untie the Gordian Knot that reintegration funding had become, drop those parts of the Brahimi proposal that met principled opposition, and broker a compromise that split the difference between assessed funding for short-term reinsertion and continued voluntary funding for the rest of reintegration. Ultimately, the learning process was completed with what many would regard a watered down lesson because of improvements in the organizational infrastructure and effective working-level leadership exercised by the new DDR team.

The lesson to target reintegration programs to communities rather than individual combatants was politically inhibited by an interdepartmental conflict between UNDP and DPKO about the basic character of these programs. Several times, the lesson emerged from field experience and was put on the agenda at headquarters level inside DPKO. Despite supportive infrastructure conditions provided by the IDDRS process, the positions were too deeply entrenched to allow for a cohesive new approach taking into account the lesson on community-based approaches. Unlike some of the lessons on mission integration as a whole (see Chapter 7), there was no additional senior-

---

[29] Interview, UNMIS official, November 2009.

level leadership support available. It took continued advocacy from field practitioners and the expert community to achieve a gradual rethink in DPKO's official approach. However, this rethink still has to effectively take root within organizational practice (including evaluation).

In contrast, the lesson to include a gender perspective in reintegration programming is an example for a clearly politically driven process. The strong support from women's groups and the absence of any internal or external political opposition coinciding with the existence of an established high-level guidance development process made this a clear success story in terms of guidance development. At the same time, it also demonstrated the limitations of high-level policy guidance when it actually comes to changing organizational practice which, in many cases, requires broad training and sensitization efforts. As a learning process, it faced its biggest challenge at the level of institutionalization.

These learning processes highlight several underlying commonalities of the field of reintegration: At the time of the Brahimi report, there was already a substantive amount of knowledge and experience available on DDR programming due to the relatively long history of UN DDR efforts in various settings across the world. Despite this comparatively long horizon of experience, headquarters officials largely avoided the broader conceptual questions about the exact ends and means of DDR – in part due to limited personnel capacities. The most important political factor was bureaucratic politics: different departments fighting for 'their' interpretation of reintegration (either coming from a security or a development mindset). At the same time, there was little member state resistance to the substantive policies or lessons emerging from the field. Overall, member states were either supportive or in benevolent indifference about policy initiatives emerging out of field practice and none of the cases caused or suffered from broader political controversies. Even the controversial question of funding for reintegration could be resolved relatively smoothly through a compromise proposal, as initial opposition from member states was not principled but rather due to the lack of conceptual clarity and unspecified financial risks.

But the three learning processes also exemplify the point that full implementation of the learning cycle often remains challenging even in the context of some structural, procedural, and financial learning support within a partly professionalized, more or less enabling organizational culture. As the debate on community-based reintegration demonstrated, the existence of an overarching guidance development process supported by an effective learning infrastructure does not guarantee the resolution of interdepartmental conflicts nor does it in and of itself secure a change in organizational practice – particularly if the effectiveness of the learning infrastructure remains limited to guidance development and there is little, if any, effective support for training and evaluation. The various learning processes have shown that implementation is often where processes stall, even if they were quickly debated and codified in formal guidance. Therefore, as the former head of DPKO puts it, 'developing a culture of evidence will be crucial for improving DDR and peace-keeping practice in the twenty-first century' (Guéhenno 2009: xvi).

7

Mission Integration: Bridging the Gaps between Security, Relief, and Development

For the UN peace operations community, the memory of the civil war in Sierra Leone and the UN's tragic role that culminated in the hostage crisis of May 2000 was one of the strongest points of reference throughout the past decade. Many officials mentioned it in our interviews, almost every time without prompting. It signifies not only the hostage incident and its immediate causes but also the larger failure to communicate and collaborate effectively across organizational and cultural barriers that came to a head during this crisis. This painful and embarrassing experience was a clear demonstration of the failure to institutionalize earlier integration efforts that began in the Balkans and Haiti during the 1990s. As such, it sparked a lot of soul-searching in the Department of Peacekeeping Operations (DPKO), both internally and in terms of coordinating with the UN partner organizations.

The regionalized civil war in Sierra Leone foreshadowed many of the trends that came to define UN peace operations in the decade that followed (see Chapter 2). Since the outbreak of fighting in 1991, the West African country had been locked in a vicious cycle of violence and foreign interventions. A host of aid organizations provided humanitarian relief and also documented and campaigned against human rights abuses, diamond and arms trafficking, and the use of child soldiers. In 1999, the UN Assistance Mission to Sierra Leone (UNAMSIL) was deployed to help implement the Lomé peace agreement, a flimsy deal between the exiled government and a fractious group of rebels that would soon collapse.

Each time the crisis intensified and security conditions deteriorated tensions between the peace operations and the humanitarian community rose. To maintain access to all vulnerable populations in the country, humanitarian agencies sought to uphold the image of absolute neutrality, even in the eyes of the most vicious and violent rebels. Yet at the same time, the state-based nature of the UN, the imperatives of international law, and the pressure of major donors dictated that the diplomatic wing of the UN maintain privileged relations with the government, even when the latter was in exile. While humanitarians saw their already complicated and sensitive work made harder by the local perception of 'the UN' being too close to the government, political staff and bilateral donors were concerned about prolonging the war and suffering by allowing aid deliveries to be diverted to the various rebel groups by way of 'road taxes' and similar means.

This vicious cycle of mistrust came to a head during the May 2000 hostage crisis. As the UN's own 'lessons learned' report on the mission acknowledged, the 'United Nations Mission in Sierra Leone (UNAMSIL) was being humiliated by a rebel army of young thugs called the Revolutionary United Front (RUF), led by Corporal Foday Sankoh. Hundreds of UN peacekeepers were taken hostage, disarmed and even disrobed by the RUF' (UN DPKO/PBPU 2003: 3). Following an aggressive (and successful) intervention by British paratroopers the hostages were released, while the UN and member states finally managed to reinforce their blue helmets. Alan Doss, at the time the UN Development Programme (UNDP) resident representative in Sierra Leone, recounted how '[t]he implications of a more robust UN military presence mandated to re-establish government authority throughout the country raised fundamental issues for the humanitarian community. Although they were no longer operating in RUF held areas for security reasons, both UN agencies and NGOs were concerned that the new UN rules of engagement would lead to open conflict between the RUF and UN forces which would make access even more difficult and dangerous and, in the case of UN agencies, would compromise their neutrality by association' (Doss 2003).

In a desperate attempt to distinguish themselves from the 'military UN,' the agencies went as far as to change the color of UN logos on their vehicles from black to blue. One day 'in early May, during the height of the crisis,' as one agency representative told a visiting researcher, the agencies' security officer was even 'thrown out of UNAMSIL security meetings' – apparently for fear that he would leak sensitive information to rebel groups (quoted in Porter 2003: 38). Unsurprisingly, an attempt to develop a 'strategic framework' to coordinate the UN's work and avoid gaps and overlap quickly fell victim to the high level of tension within the UN.

* * *

Born out of the practical challenges of operations such as the one in Sierra Leone, a tenuous alliance of reformers and partisans for the primacy of the peacekeeping paradigm together led by Secretary-General Kofi Annan launched their agenda to better integrate the work of the many agencies deployed under the blue flag. Their rationale was straightforward: in a politically volatile and residually violent situation, uncoordinated interventions by many different foreign actors with often overlapping priorities waste scarce resources, duplicate effort, and create gaps in coverage. If even a residual level of organized violence remains, the lack of information about what others do and about the observations they make also puts the lives of mission personnel at risk, civilian and military alike. Worst of all, if shrewd warlords and criminals are given contradictory signals or adverse incentives to exploit divisions within the international community, the mere lack of coordination can easily become a serious threat to the common goal of stabilization and sustainable peace.

The major trends driving the evolution of peace operations in the decade since 2000 made coordination harder and increased the costs of failure. The paradigm of peacebuilding as institution-building drew many new actors into the peace operations fold, which created much of the coordination challenge in the first place. The trend toward more complex, less settled, and therefore more violent 'post-conflict' situations raised the stakes from dollars and euros wasted to lives put at risk. Already by 2000, following the initial quantitative growth in peace operations, many of the institutional gaps that, a decade earlier, a couple of smart, flexible senior officials managed to bridge on account of their individual creativity and strong personal networks, now dearly required institutional solutions.

In the public debate and in member state politics, it is the peace operations bureaucracy that is held accountable for the disjointed actions of the system as a whole, because peacekeeping is the public face of the 'post-conflict UN.' Fueled by the constant prodding of diplomats and experts as well as the dedication of UN officials in the field to overcome the daily frustrations of collaboration in a stove-piped system, Annan's first reform plan (1997b) unleashed more than a decade of bureaucratic tinkering to produce more effective integration. Integration, coordination, and coherence became buzzwords that often meant different things to different people while there was almost no policy paper, planning document, or best practices report whose author could afford not to pay tribute to the imperative to improve integration everywhere and at all levels. Secretaries-General and high-level member state initiatives have repeatedly taken up the issue (United Nations 2000; Eide et al. 2005; Challenges Project 2006).

From the outset, two approaches emerged within the UN on how to improve integration in practice. Following the explicit premise of the Brahimi report 'to build the United Nations capacity to contribute to peace-building...in a genuinely integrated manner' (United Nations 2000: 1), Kofi Annan tried to subordinate the other UN agencies to his Special Representatives at the top of the peace operation in each country. By means of a 'note of guidance,' he assigned his heads of mission the responsibility 'for giving political guidance to the overall UN presence' and 'to chair a senior management team in country' (UN Secretary-General 2000: 2; Jones 2001). In the extreme, the result would be 'structural integration' where the mission absorbs the agencies' strategic (and occasionally operational) roles, staff, and offices.

The alternative approach was outlined at a conference on field leadership in July 1998, which about two dozen senior mission leaders and UN officials attended. Their deliberations began with the opposite premise that all heads of agencies would report to their respective headquarters and depend on them for promotions and other benefits. As a result, participants argued that 'the SRSG cannot expect to enjoy a greater degree of authority in the mission area than the Secretariat strains to exercise throughout the entire system' (Taylor and Hooper 1999: 43) and the effective mission leader should take a 'service-oriented approach' and become a coordinator among equals (Taylor and Hooper 1999: 47). His or her challenge would be to find a practical mix of incentives to make integration attractive for the agencies and to adopt a coordinating role that they would accept despite DPKO's and the missions' status and reputation as the biggest 'agency' by far and the occasional classroom bully. Years later, its proponents termed this approach 'strategic integration.'

A decade of trial and error followed to determine which way or mix of ways would be more effective to implement the call of the Brahimi panel. It quickly became apparent that the panel's case in favor of integration was only one side of the coin. Not only did integration come with a price tag in terms of transaction costs. Some also felt that the practice of integration systematically compromised their organizations' core values. In a number of instances, humanitarians felt that their highest principles of helping according to need and acting in a neutral way toward all parties to a violent conflict were in danger of being subordinated to a political logic of intervention. The learning efforts in our case studies were fundamentally shaped by these tensions. The bar for learning on integration was high: for learning on integration to take place, it is not enough for DPKO, the focal organization of our book, to learn. The whole family of organizations within the broader peace operations universe needs to agree on the same lesson – a process which is fraught with difficulties given the manifold obstacles to integration.

The basic challenge for integration is that the peace operations bureaucracy operates within a political context defined by the fragmentation of mandates and constituencies among UN agencies as well as within national governments themselves. Ultimately, the root causes of fragmentation in peace operations are located in the capitals of member states, in Washington, Berlin, and Beijing, far from the mission planner in New York or the Special Representative of the Secretary-General (SRSG) in Khartoum or Kinshasa. Functional differentiation in modern societies has created an intentional division of political agendas between ministries and government departments at the national level, each of which presses its particular agenda and that of its particular political constituency in international forums such the governing boards of UN agencies.

Nonetheless, there is significant variation in terms of how coherent 'the UN' is acting at each level along the chain of command from member state capitals through diplomats and the Secretariat in New York to senior managers in the field. The need for compromise between states, the lack of detailed information about conditions on the ground, and the fluidity of events over time creates often large areas of ambiguity in missions' and agencies' mandates. These ambiguities translate into political space for individual initiative (or lack thereof) on the part of senior officials on the ground. Testament to the fragility of these field-based UN bureaucracies, personal inclinations and personalities often make a large difference in what priorities are pursued, at what pace, and in what kind of relationship to other UN actors. In the past, this has been both an opportunity for personal leadership in favor of pragmatic collaboration and integration as well as an obstacle for the implementation of agreed upon goals. These unintended sources of political leeway are rarely matched by similar opportunities to allocate administrative resources freely in support of a mission's or agency's assigned goals. Instead, trying to compensate for the lack of overt political direction and responding to cases of waste and abuse, member states have long curtailed the bureaucracy's operational discretion in terms of budget and personnel.

Boxed in between their own reporting chains and administrative straight-jackets, DPKO's senior managers find themselves in a challenging position from which to engage their humanitarian and development partners. Each of which, in turn, faces equally complex but markedly different political and organizational constraints itself. From DPKO's perspective, its relative bureaucratic power and the nature of its relationships with its partners in the UN system vary significantly. Within the Secretariat, the Secretary-General is the ultimate authority in disputes between DPKO and the Department of Political Affairs (DPA) or the Office for the Coordination of Humanitarian Affairs (OCHA), even if he would rarely exercise that authority. In contrast, the Secretary-General's day-to-day influence over agencies such as UNDP, the World Food Programme (WFP), or the UN High Commissioner for Refugees (UNHCR) is extremely limited.

As a result, the obstacles to organizational learning on integration are much the same as those to integration itself. Every organization creates its own budgetary rules, standard operating procedures, and, ultimately, cultures. In practice, these translate into different time horizons and political constraints for funding, different administrative and security regulations governing everything from the use of equipment to the mobility of personnel, as well as positive or negative cultural reflexes toward other actors. Much can be traced back to the structural setup of the UN: different funding sources create different channels for member states to exert power, which in turn shapes different accountability mechanisms and incentives for each organization.

One of the most important obstacles to integration is the bifurcated funding scheme for peace operations and other post-conflict activities at the UN. There are two basic funding arrangements: assessed contributions and voluntary contributions. Assessed contributions are exclusively available to DPKO-run peace operations and mostly limited to military expenses, staff, and equipment costs, but with a few rare exceptions they cannot be used for project implementation. These funds are quickly available and dependable within their annual budget cycles. Voluntary contributions pay for everything outside the peacekeeping mission, in particular for the emergency aid and development agencies. Before they are able to get going, they need to appeal for aid money or apply for project funding with donors. In the crucial early weeks and months after the Security Council mandate, the agencies are therefore much less agile than the mission. In the long run, however, they usually have access to project funds and expertise at a higher scale and over longer timelines.

Another fundamental issue is the fragmentation of reporting and oversight mechanisms among the different parts of the UN peace operations bureaucracy. For peace operations themselves and DPKO in particular, the crucial member state constituencies are the main funders and the major troop and police contributors, while the agencies are often much closer tied to their donors. Over many decades, these relationships have sparked their own pathologies in each sphere, similar to the administrative micromanagement on the part of the budget committees for peace operations which is seen in member states as one of their few levers over an overly independent and wasteful Secretariat. Just as the peace operations apparatus and the agencies cater to different constituencies of states, the reporting lines of military peacekeepers, political experts, and development agents end in very different parts of those Western capitals, in particular, which exert the most influence as big donors. Through this link, the partly systemic but often petty rivalries between ministries of foreign affairs, aid agencies and the military are transmitted and even amplified on the international level.

Cataloguing the resulting cleavages, it becomes clear that while each one goes back to a divergence in material interests and constraints, they have over time been overlaid by clashing organizational cultures. Whether the distinction between a 'black' (peacekeeping mission) and a 'blue' (aid and development) UN, between strict neutrality vis-à-vis the state and its violent competitors on the part of humanitarians and the imperative of local (state) ownership held by development agencies, between 'emergency' and 'sustainability' approaches, military and civilian mindsets, or 'field-driven' and 'headquarters-based' organizations, each of these shifting boundaries carries at least as much cultural significance as it reflects material priorities and constraints. In that climate, specific attempts to increase integration were either limited to common-sense communication and conflict avoidance mechanisms on the working level, or they were rapidly politicized when powerful parts of the UN saw their independent survival threatened by subordination, or when the pretext of integration was used to further a politically contested agenda.

On top of these inter-bureaucratic cleavages, each organization has developed its own learning infrastructure of structural characteristics, procedures, human resource systems, material resources, and cultural attitudes to learning. These learning infrastructures developed along very different trajectories in each organization, which makes it more difficult – if not impossible – to synchronize a genuinely common learning process across bureaucratic boundaries. A few governments, particularly those of Norway and Sweden, have made tremendous strides in the past few years to fill those gaps in some organization's learning infrastructures and, even more importantly, to bridge the political divides among member states and overcome the coordination failures between different diplomatic committees. Individual governments can play a role in organizational learning on mission integration that is both crucial and, frustratingly for many reformers, limited. They can provide resources for studies and conferences to spread best practices and raise the prestige of innovators and reformers. More importantly, they can use their convening power as states to set agendas and raise awareness among their peers. If they are comparatively small players at the UN, such as the Nordics, they cannot realign the priorities of their bigger peers all by themselves – and if they are bigger players with their own well-known interests in the integration arena, such as a major financial contributor or a permanent member of the Security Council, any policy initiative would be tainted by association.

An additional constraint on the UN's ability to integrate and to learn to integrate in recent years is linked to a gap between research and practice that is wider than in many other fields. In contrast to many other areas of peace-building practice and many other case studies in this book, there was no lack of good scholarship. Unlike building effective and legitimate justice systems, for example, the problem of organizational fragmentation, its causes, and possible solutions are well understood in the theoretical realm (Lipson 2007; Herrhausen 2009). Unfortunately, the present state of organization theory provides little of practical value to the manager struggling with integration challenges in the field. Only with the infusion of Nordic political interest and money in the last five years did a cottage industry of think tanks and academics begin to form that is helping the UN along on the bumpy road toward implementation.

* * *

In the following sections we examine three of the most fundamental and prominent learning challenges that the UN identified as part of its post-2000 integration agenda. The *first case* looks at the evolution of leadership structures in the field as reformers tried to resolve the dilemmas between the political, humanitarian, and development mandates of the UN by tasking a single manager with creating coherence in implementation. Having caught on at headquarters as part of Secretary-General Annan's drive for full-scale structural integration, form quickly displaced function. In response, the process faced significant resistance from the humanitarian community which sparked a rethink of the concept and its application.

The *second case* examines one out of a series of attempts that continues to the present day and seeks to develop a participatory framework for common planning between peace operations and their humanitarian and development partners in the UN system. Sparked by the failure of both bottom-up coordination in the 1990s and top-down structural integration in the early 2000s, redesigning and trying to implement the Integrated Mission Planning Process (IMPP) in 2005–8 became a prime example for the complexity of the integration challenge as a whole: to create incentives for effective collaboration while acknowledging the existing fragmentation of power in the UN.

The *third case* moves to information and analysis, another key area where fragmented communication and reporting between military, political, and humanitarian actors has long been the norm, often with devastating effects. As peace operations faced new threats and new tasks that exposed them to greater risk, a group of military officers proposed to introduce integrated information gathering and analysis in Joint Mission Analysis Centres (JMACs) that would draw on civilian reporting and open-source intelligence – long a toxic word in the UN lexicon.

Structuring Integrated Leadership in the Field

In the fall of 2000, shortly after the Brahimi report had called for greater integration between peace operations and UN agencies working in the same country under a development or humanitarian mandate (United Nations 2000), Secretary-General Kofi Annan began to establish the 'structural' approach to integration. Under the new rules his Special Representative had 'the authority and the responsibility to . . . provide overarching leadership' and 'give political guidance' to the other UN agencies, whose humanitarian and development coordinator (in one person) would be 'triple-hatted' as a deputy to the DPKO-appointed SRSG (UN Secretary-General 2000). Three years later, the new UN Mission in Liberia (UNMIL) stretched the meaning of the Secretary-General's ambiguous language to the limit.

For the first time, UNMIL was designed to structurally absorb the function of humanitarian coordination rather than coordinating with or overseeing an OCHA field presence, which had otherwise been the rule. Even before the mission deployed in September 2003, its budget was set up to provide a rump Humanitarian Coordination and NGO Liaison section of two staff and one UN volunteer, to be complemented by OCHA field staff already on the ground (UN Secretary-General 2003: para. 70).

When UNMIL arrived in Monrovia, irreconcilable differences of policy and principle emerged between the forceful SRSG Jacques Klein and his DSRSG/HC/RC, a development official, on the one hand, and the head of the existing OCHA office and most of the humanitarian community on the other. Klein's combative personal style played a role, as did a number of specific incidents. In one instance, against the advice of his humanitarian team, he 'encouraged . . . refugees to return to ill-prepared home areas so that they could vote in mission-supported elections' – effectively misleading them into risking their lives or health for the electoral process, as the humanitarians saw it (Eide et al. 2005: 30). Another source of conflict was his uncompromising behavior toward rebel groups with whom some of the aid agencies had had to cooperate and expected to have to continue to cooperate in the future to support populations in need. By trying to cut off uncooperative rebel groups from their incomes from 'taxing' aid supplies, OCHA and the humanitarian community felt that Klein and his deputy tried to politicize access to aid, a violation of the principles of humanitarianism. After nine months of resistance, OCHA headquarters gave in, removed their head of office, and allowed their staff to be integrated into UNMIL's humanitarian coordination unit. Five months later, almost all international staff had left in protest, and the mission had to rebuild the entire function from scratch with a new head who arrived in February 2005 (Zeebroek 2006: 21).

* * *

The events in Liberia and the controversy around Klein reverberated far beyond the policy decisions and leadership style of a single senior official. The crisis in Liberia became a beacon of outrage to all, particularly the humanitarian community, who criticized the reigning agenda of structural integration for absorbing their political leadership (the humanitarian coordinator) and their operational capacity (the OCHA office) into a military-dominated mission that was bound to become a party to the conflict rather than a neutral actor. The original idea to create a structural link between the peacekeeping operation that was created, funded, and managed by DPKO for the duration of its Security Council mandate and the various UN agencies that had been on the ground before the mission began and would remain after the mission closed emerged much earlier. In 1995, SRSG Lakhdar Brahimi in Haiti had come up with the arrangement to bring the humanitarian and development coordinator at the time, Cristiàn Ossa, closer into the mission's information and decision-making structures. Initially a one-off experiment sparked by Brahimi's high regard for Ossa,[1] in a reversal of cause and effect, it was the setup rather than the team that acquired a reputation for success (Maguire 1996: 107).

It was picked up at a July 1998 seminar in which UN Secretariat officials, recent Special Representatives, and a few participants from the key agencies such as UNDP came together to discuss key leadership challenges in peace operations. In general terms, the workshop rapporteurs Mark Taylor and Rick Hooper collected all the principles that should later define success in mission leadership vis-à-vis the UN country team: a 'service-oriented approach' to coordinating the agencies as largely independent entities. Rather than inventing hierarchical subordination were none existed, their principles honored the agencies' fiduciary responsibilities toward their donors and the humanitarian principles binding relief agencies as well as the ultimate need to hand over to them when a peace operation left the country. Ultimately, the greatest leverage for creating operational coherence would probably come from establishing joint working groups and forums between UN agencies, other donors, and local political actors because such organizational tools would favor the SRSG's coordinating role (Taylor and Hooper 1999: 47). The latter point would be the one common feature about the strategies of successful integrative mission leaders such as Alan Doss in Sierra Leone and Liberia, Jordan Ryan also in Liberia, or Ross Mountain in the Congo, besides the 'personality factor': their ability to build complex webs of coordinating bodies that worked, often by leveraging the legitimacy of local political leaders to set priorities with themselves, providing much needed technical support and direction.[2]

A considerable part of the discussion at the forum was directed at exploring options to improve the relationship between the SRSG and the key officials from the UN development and humanitarian agencies, the Resident Coordinator (RC) and Humanitarian Coordinator (HC), respectively. The head of UNDP at the time, a US political appointee named James G. Speth, suggested that 'in circumstances where an SRSG has responsibility for a wide range of assistance activities as well as a peace-keeping mission, it may be useful to consider a new command-oriented (*sic!*) organizational pattern within which the Resident Coordinator also functions as Deputy to the SRSG' (Taylor and Hooper 1999: 48). It was a rare case of a bureaucrat asking for his agency to be

---

[1] Interview, senior UN official, May 2008.
[2] Interviews with UN officials in Monrovia (March 2008), Dili (November 2007), Port-au-Prince (April 2009), and New York (May 2008).

subordinated to another's authority. As resident and humanitarian coordinators had long been double-hatted in conflict areas already, his intervention did not only affect UNDP and the recovery part of the UN family but also the humanitarian agencies who felt that they had much more to lose in a 'command-oriented' relationship with the SRSG.

Alternative options were discussed, as well, including that of attaching the HC/RC to the mission as an additional Deputy SRSG for UN coordination while leaving the regular deputy in charge of day-to-day mission management – Brahimi's model in Haiti. Ultimately, the conference participants recommended a review. That review was set in motion even before the conference report had been published, and its ultimate result was the Secretary-General's Note of Guidance (2000) on which SRSG Klein in Liberia would base his authority. Its language veered much more toward the command relationship suggested by Speth than the pragmatic service orientation advocated by Taylor and Hooper's report.

* * *

As the situation between the 'integrated' peace operation in Liberia and the humanitarian agencies and NGOs deteriorated into open conflict, their parent departments at headquarters in New York realized the need to find a more effective way of integration than the one practiced in Liberia. In mid-2004, the political and peace operations departments joined hands with the humanitarian agencies to commission 'a joint lesson learning review ... with the aim of defining the overarching issues of concern to the respective humanitarian, development and peacekeeping constituencies regarding the question of integration of humanitarian and development coordination and operational responsibilities into multi-dimensional peacekeeping operations' (Eide et al. 2005: 46). The review was conducted by consultants from the Norwegian Institute of International Affairs in Oslo and King's College in London.

At the same time, next door to Liberia in Sierra Leone, a much different model of integration was practiced that showed that the UN had not entirely forgotten Brahimi's innovation from Haiti and the lessons of the Taylor/Hooper report. Before the 2000 hostage crisis, the Sierra Leone mission had gained notoriety in UN circles as one where political and peacekeeping officials were in an open state of war with their humanitarian colleagues (Porter 2003: 20–2). After the crisis, as part of a general move toward 'triple-hatted DSRSGs' in 2001, headquarters sent Alan Doss to Sierra Leone as deputy SRSG, humanitarian coordinator, and resident coordinator. Doss managed not only to overcome the intense enmity among the different UN actors but also quickly made a name for himself and the UN country team in Sierra Leone as an example of pragmatic coordination. In January 2003, months before the decision was taken to design the new mission in Liberia so as to structurally absorb the humanitarian unit on the ground, Doss (2003) wrote a memo to argue for patient, participatory approaches rather than 'forcing the pace' of coordination. His paper had no effect on the Liberia planning effort, but became prominent in UN circles nonetheless.

The independent Norwegian review served as a third party that most officials on either side of the debate regarded as trusted and neutral – a position that owed much to the long-standing role of Norway as a major donor to humanitarian aid and champion of humanitarian principles while, at the same time, having always supported peace operations and the goal of better integration.[3] That pivotal role gave the study team the space and also the obligation to criticize openly when they found integration efforts to fail or create negative consequences, but always in a way that would not throw the baby of integration as a goal out with the bathwater of its current ways of implementation. Based on evidence from Liberia and Afghanistan, among other cases, the report argued that the structural innovation of the triple-hatted DSRSG alone was insufficient to bridge the gap between the priorities of conflict management and humanitarian aid. Ultimately, further attempts at integration should uphold the rule that 'form follows function,' that is, that activities should only be integrated if and to the degree to which they need to be integrated to build sustainable peace. Specifically, along with many other suggestions, the report recommended against structural integration of humanitarian offices while supporting the direct link through their head, the triple-hatted DSRSG (Eide et al. 2005).

The review was the turning point from a trend of increasing formal and structural top-down integration that had reached its peak in Liberia in 2003–4 to a new pragmatism that allowed for diverse institutional arrangements in the service of the greater goal of 'strategic integration.'[4] For the Secretariat and DPKO, as its driving force on the integration agenda, this change was certainly due to the recognition that overly or solely formal–structural tools were not only insufficient but also could be massively counterproductive, as exemplified by the Liberia episode and analytically confirmed by the Norwegian study. At the same time, officials saw that cultural change was taking place among the entire field-based UN as the original cause for integration became more widely understood and its promise appreciated.[5] To be forced into a common organizational structure, while creating much resentment, may also have contributed to overcoming some of the engrained cultural gaps between UN agencies rooted in different professional communities. After that process

---

[3] Interviews, DPKO and OCHA officials, national diplomats, May 2007 and May 2008.
[4] Interviews, UN OCHA and DPKO officials, May 2007 and May 2008.
[5] Interviews, UN OCHA, DPKO, UNMIT, UNMIL, and MINUSTAH officials, May and November 2007, February and May 2008, April 2009.

of increasing cultural openness for collaboration within the UN system had taken hold, it became easier – perhaps even just possible – to promote more effective functional rather than structural integration.

* * *

The fundamental framing of the lesson had not changed from the one that had been available to the organization at least since the Taylor and Hooper report of 1999. Rediscovered in the interdepartmental feud about Liberia, the idea of functional, bottom-up rather than hierarchical, top-down models of integration now got traction because of the high-profile failures on the ground and the advocacy support provided by the independent study. In 2005, when the study was delivered, Jean-Marie Guéhenno, the head of DPKO, and Jan Egeland, the OCHA head and Emergency Relief Coordinator for the UN system, agreed to revisit their integration doctrine to institutionalize the new consensus in a way that would provide practical guidance and bureaucratic cover for their field officials.[6]

At the level of doctrine, two major documents reflect the change. In January 2006, Secretary-General Annan issued a new 'Note of Guidance' to supersede the previous one. Drafted by a committee led by DPKO but including officials from OCHA and other agencies, the note retained its emphasis on the political role of the SRSG as integrator-in-chief vis-à-vis the UN family in country. In so doing, however, it explicitly instructed the SRSG to 'uphold humanitarian principles' and use existing coordination arrangements among the agencies while directing all UN actors to conduct their work 'in a manner that does not undermine the mandate of the mission' (UN Secretary-General 2006b). Providing an explicit mechanism of recourse to resolve conflicts, the new note was slightly less vague than the previous one; but more importantly, it set a new tone as the document that formally recognized the lesson of the independent review as the new guiding principle.

The second major document is DPKO's 'Principles and Guidelines for UN Peace Operations,' also called the capstone doctrine. Issued in February 2008, it sets out the fundamentals of UN peace operations at a policy level. On integration, it minces no words in its departure from older statements and practice: 'integration among the members of the broader United Nations family cannot simply be imposed by edict from above, and can only be achieved through a constant process of dialogue and negotiation between the actors concerned' (UN DPKO/DFS 2008). In a rare case of learning from the field, the text picks up a concept of graduated scope and depth of integration that was developed in MONUC by Lise Grande and Ross Mountain, and

---

[6] Interview, OCHA official, May 2008.

entered the capstone doctrine through a consultative conference in April 2007 (Detzel 2008: 67; see also Campbell 2007; Campbell and Kaspersen 2008).[7]

In practice, trial and error in the field produced several new ways of coordinating with various forms of structural integration. Far from a simple reversal of the previously dominating trend, peace operations in the Congo, Timor, and Liberia (after a change at the top, with Alan Doss coming it to take over) invented their own ways of improving coherence. In a telling example that bucked the new trend, when the UN reopened its mission in Timor-Leste after a breakdown in the peace consolidation process in 2006, it created another structurally integrated humanitarian office, like it did in Congo. This time, it worked. And in Sudan, the mission gave itself a 'unified' rather than an 'integrated' structure which allowed the different components greater autonomy in their day-to-day actions.

* * *

With the doctrinal revisions of 2006–8 and the emergence of a variety of organizational structures in the field, this learning process was completed. It was the second major iteration of the learning cycle in terms of organizing the UN's field leadership in peace operations. It became necessary after the previous learning cycle had introduced the concept of integration and the triple-hatted deputy as its structural implementation, but too many in the peace operations bureaucracy mistook the outward form on their new organizational charts for the solution of the underlying functional problem.

Sparked not by complaints or suggestions from the field – although plenty of these were voiced – but by a major leadership crisis in one of its most prominent missions at the time in Liberia, the new learning process still proceeded more smoothly and more quickly than many for a number of reasons. First, the top managers of both of the key organizational stakeholders quickly took charge and steered, what began as an insurrection in the UN humanitarian community against the very idea of integration as they understood it – that is, as being subordinated to the political–military mandate of the Security Council and DPKO – into the calmer waters of how to integrate effectively while respecting both sets of principles. Pragmatic progress on integration was driven relentlessly from the top to the point where officials in every department complained what a sacred cow it had become.[8] Only an exceptional level of leadership was able to hold the centrifugal forces of bureaucratic politics in check and to overcome the lack of established

---

[7] Lise Grande was the head of MONUC's integrated office supporting Ross Mountain, the mission's DSRSG/HC/RC as well as UNDP's resident representative for the DR Congo.

[8] This was a common theme in many of our interviews at the working level in 2007–8, across agency and departmental borders.

procedures for learning across the UN system, though at a significant cost in terms of senior management time and attention.

Second, financial as well as troop contributors supported integration in principle. Some governments leaned more toward DPKO's view and others more toward OCHA's, and none would have considered to address the fundamental institutional fissures they had built into the UN system in the first place. Generally, however, they presented a closed front in support of integration as such: because there were different ideas about the specifics, they came together on the lowest common denominator of supporting any kind of integration that would be effective. Taken together, member states were too diverse in their priorities to drive the specifics of integration but they did nothing to undermine the learning process that Guéhenno and Egeland drove forward. A few member states such as Australia, Norway, Sweden, the United Kingdom, and the United States provided additional support by funding the independent study, hosting workshops, and greasing the wheels of the learning process in a way that helped to compensate for the lack of a UN-wide learning infrastructure and the weakness of most existing infrastructures in the individual departments and agencies.

The Quest for Integrated and Strategic Planning

In the spring of 2006, six years after the crisis in Sierra Leone, DPKO was again tasked to prepare plans for a mission that would further stretch the capacity of the peace operations apparatus. Partly because of the advocacy of high-profile celebrities, the complex civil war in the Western Sudanese province of Darfur that had sparked a massive campaign of ethnic cleansing or even genocide was high on the political agenda. Due to the size of the country and its geography, the logistics of deployment and supply alone were a nightmare, compounded by the huge scale of soldiers, police, and everything else that would be required to provide any sort of meaningful protection to settlements and refugee camps. An African Union mission, woefully underequipped on every level, had been trying in vain to provide a minimum of protection and was desperately calling for the UN to take over.

The call for a mission to Darfur reached the Secretariat when the advocates of integration were just recovering from a double hangover, having found voluntary self-coordination to have failed in the 1990s and seen the attempt to impose hierarchy to fare no better in the 2004 fallout in Liberia. As a consequence of the latter and the subsequent Norwegian study on integration, DPKO's senior management turned away from the paradigm of full structural integration. The new learning challenge was now to create a process in which all relevant actors would benefit from sharing their plans early on and incentivize them to use whatever leeway they had in their own organizations in support of a more coherent UN effort. To do that in a way that acknowledged the existing fragmentation of power in the UN was to take a 'service-oriented approach' to integrated planning, just like the one that the 1998 leadership workshop had found necessary for field-level coordination (Taylor and Hooper 1999: 47).

In this context, Darfur represented an opportunity as well as a potential nightmare: on the one hand, the logistical challenges and the political attention from key member states provided external incentives for every agency to collaborate. On the other hand, without a comprehensive, sustainable political settlement, the UN would intervene into a lingering multiparty civil war. With the overwhelming resources and military footprint of a peace operation descending on their already tough operating environment, humanitarian agencies saw their independence and security threatened. In addition, as in every new mission area, relief organizations already worked according to previously developed and funded needs assessments, while development agencies were tied to assistance frameworks agreed years before with the local government. In any case, a new integrated planning framework to harmonize all of these disparate elements needed to be field-tested, and not just under fair-weather conditions. Under-Secretary-General Guéhenno ordered the full Integrated Mission Planning Process (IMPP) to be put into action.

At this point, the IMPP as a set of formally defined procedures existed in its second major revision, after an earlier version had failed to win any support both within the peace operations bureaucracy and beyond. As a formal procedure, it attempted to define a comprehensive yet practical way of incorporating UN partners into DPKO's way of launching new missions. On paper, the IMPP was a well-organized procedure in which one stage neatly informed the next: through a common 'strategic assessment,' all actors would come up with a common analysis of the Darfur situation and the strategic objectives of the UN as a whole, on the basis of which a 'technical assessment' would determine the practical needs of the mission to fulfill its mandate (in terms of facilities, equipment, outline of tasks, staff, etc.). A draft mission plan would then inform the Secretary-General's report to the Security Council, which would be followed by mandate authorization, budget approval, and deployment. At this point, mission staff on the ground would take over, finalize the mission plan, and conduct periodical revisions as required.

In practice, it remained unclear which office would conduct the strategic assessment, and there was little guidance on how to do so. Time was short, and the strategic assessment was not part of the 'hard' requirements handed down to DPKO officials by their budget committees and the Security Council, so it was quickly skipped. For the technical assessment mission, thirty-four officials from almost as many agencies were dispatched to Sudan from June 9 to 23, 2006.

Few had any previous exposure to peace operations; naturally, most had never done a DPKO technical assessment before. Written guidance did not exist, nor were there enough helicopter seats to take anybody from DPKO's IMPP development team along to explain. UNDP, at least, managed to send as their representative the person who had participated in the IMPP working group.[9]

When short timelines and limited resources met vastly different levels of experience and planning cultures, a rift opened up. Soon during the trip, the technical assessment began to get bogged down between the very specific and comprehensive requirements of the formal procedure, the unresolved basics of strategy, and the unwieldy structure of the thirty-four-strong, extremely heterogeneous assessment team. Despite the strong backing for integrated planning on Guéhenno's part at the top of the peace operations bureaucracy, participants and other officials agree that some of the crucial second and third tier managers within DPKO were not committed to the idea. Two of the most powerful people in DPKO after Guéhenno, the Assistant-Secretary-General for Operations and the Africa Director, regarded the travails of integrated planning as a dangerous distraction in a situation that was already fraught with political risks for the UN. From the perspective of one DPKO mission planner, the exercise 'became a problem when IMPP became the object in itself rather than a means to achieve integrated planning.'[10] This person's superiors expected a rapidly delivered technical assessment that would meet the requirements of the budget committees and Security Council members; everything else – including integration – was dispensable. On the agency side, most organizations had been contacted at the headquarters level and consequently sent generalists, some of whom had never taken part in a field-level planning process before. As a result, when it became clear that a few more days and perhaps additional consultations would be required to deliver a truly joint technical assessment report, the DPKO core team was forced by its own superiors to hole up in a hotel room in Khartoum over the weekend and write up the report on its own. In the words of one participant, 'IMPP requirements were a fair weather set of objectives – they clearly did not have the status of results-based budgeting in terms of [political] backing or member state cover.'[11] The result was a rushed technical assessment report that satisfied neither the IMPP developers nor the agencies.

Within little more than two months, a mission plan was drafted, cost estimates produced, and, on August 31, 2006, a Security Council mandate obtained – for a mission that was never deployed. After more than six months

---

[9] Interviews with DPKO officials, May 2008.
[10] Interview, DPKO official, May 2008.
[11] Interview, DPKO official, May 2008.

of stalling by the Government of Sudan, the UN found a compromise with Khartoum and created a 'hybrid mission' with the African Union. When the decision came down to DPKO to cobble together the first ever joint peace operation with another body, in this case with an extremely weak African Union Secretariat in Addis Abeba, DPKO fell back to its cultural default mechanism: UNAMID, the United Nations-African Union Mission in Darfur, was drawn up in an ad hoc fashion entirely by DPKO itself.

* * *

In 2000, the Brahimi report had already raised joint planning as a challenge for the peace operations community. Following its prescriptions, the first attempt at implementation envisaged the so-called Integrated Mission Task Forces (IMTF) as the core structure of integrated planning and subsequent mission management. Within an IMTF, middle managers with substantial political leeway and delegated decision-making authority from DPKO and their other home agencies would work full-time together in a common location in New York to plan and deploy a new mission (United Nations 2000). By that definition, IMTFs were never put into practice. Two attempts in 2001 (for the mission to Afghanistan) and 2003 (Liberia) failed for insufficient buy-in and mistrust on the part of senior mission leaders and agency managers (Durch et al. 2003: 47–50). For the stalwarts of integration, it had become clear that an IMTF alone would neither be sufficiently integrated into their home organizations nor staffed at the rank required to take decisions to set the parameters for planning.

In February 2002, riding on a political wave of support for integrated and strategic planning from a Security Council debate and a Secretary-General's report (2001) on 'No Exit without Strategy,' peacekeeping chief Guéhenno launched a review of the department's planning process 'to make it more integrated and responsive to the growing complexity of peacekeeping operations' (UN DPKO 2005: 1). As a result, DPKO created an Integrated Mission Planning Process (IMPP) that would incorporate outreach to UN agencies into its internal planning procedures. The result was driven by DPKO's military planners and shaped by political incentives that privileged the established requirements of the Security Council and budget committees over the demands of effective integration. Approved in 2004, the first IMPP doctrine failed even more miserably than the original IMTF concept. Amid a number of clashes in the field between 'overbearing' peacekeeping officials and 'uncooperative' agency representatives, all sides regarded IMPP as a bureaucratic monster that demanded too much and delivered too little for everyone – an impression confirmed in a survey run by DPKO among officials of five key agencies.[12]

---

[12] DPKO documents on file with authors, Interview, DPKO official, May 2008.

In July 2005, the Secretary-General's Policy Committee mandated a fresh start, benefiting from renewed agency buy-in that resulted from the survey and the high-level agreement between Guéhenno and Egeland after the Norwegian review.[13] Despite improved interagency participation in the drafting group and a significant investment of staff time that yielded many technical improvements of the IMPP's quality as a professional planning tool even in the eyes of its critics,[14] the results of 'IMPP 2.0' still fell significantly short as exemplified by the Darfur trial in 2006.

These early failures of the IMTF and IMPP show how, compared to other fields of integration and the two other case studies in this chapter, the obstacles to integration were strongest in the realm of planning. Unlike day-to-day management in the field, planning is tightly controlled in every UN agency by strict procedures that reflect the politics among member states in oversight bodies rather than the needs of the mandate or people on the ground. In planning, the power of the purse – ultimately wielded by member states but conveyed by budget departments at headquarters – has the most direct impact on outcomes, while the peacekeepers' argument of the Security Council mandate's legal and political precedence, bolstered by the Secretary-General's political clout, is least influential with regard to other agencies.

As a result, there are three entirely separate funding and reporting frameworks for integrated missions, each operating to its own time line and political logic. First, humanitarian aid funds are generated through Consolidated Appeals, basically lists of requirements based on rapid needs and capacity assessments by many different UN agencies and some NGOs, coordinated by OCHA. Based on these appeals, each aid agency collects donor funds for a few months or at most one year at a time. These funds come with tight constraints as to their use. For example, any kind of support to conflict parties is prohibited.

Second, recovery and development funds take much longer to raise and require some involvement of the host country government to ensure local ownership and sustainability of what are often multiyear programs. This is hard to ensure in the immediate post-conflict phase where the only indigenous authority is often a barely legitimate transitional government. In addition, the voluntary nature of donor contributions to recovery funds allows donors to pick and choose among possible projects. The effect is an often massive imbalance in funding according to donor priorities: 'everybody wants schools, nobody wants prisons,' as one UN official on the ground told us.[15]

---

[13] Decision of the Policy Committee on a Review of the Integrated Mission Planning Process, July 19, 2005; Interviews, DPKO, UNDP, and OCHA officials, May 2008.

[14] Interviews, DPKO officials, May 2008.

[15] Interview, UN official, May 2007.

Third, there are the peace operations' own budgets. They have the advantage of being funded by mandatory contributions of member states which makes the flow of money much more predictable – once the budget is approved by the General Assembly. The Assembly's powerful budget committees insist on a Results-Based Budgeting framework (RBB) which governs the funds and assets of peace operations. In the absence of useful strategic guidance and realistic time lines from the Security Council, the RBB has deteriorated into a hugely complex and distracting exercise that measures only outputs rather than the eponymous 'results.' Because of its simplistic insistence on quantifiable indicators and the political dangers of being caught by the powerful Advisory Committee on Administrative and Budgetary Questions (ACABQ), Secretariat bureaucrats systematically commit only to output objectives – numbers of human rights seminars held or police officers trained – rather than meaningful outcome indicators about improved capacity or public safety. In sum, none of the individual planning and funding mechanisms involved in integrated missions are strategic in nature, as the UN's own internal watchdogs regularly complain (UN JIU 2005; UN OIOS 2006, 2007). Hardly could the integrated whole be expected to be much more strategic than its parts.

* * *

The integrated planning procedures used and then cut short in Darfur in 2006 ('IMPP 2.0') went back to the scathing indictment of the UN's record in joint planning that the Norwegian 'Report on Integrated Missions' had delivered in 2005. Key decisions on organizational design, the authors argued, reflected the 'predilections of senior mission management, with little if any substantive reference to best practices, concepts of integration or modern management practices' (Eide et al. 2005: 18), planning was 'reactive rather than proactive' (ibid.: 21), did 'not reflect an overall strategic vision' (ibid.: 22), and 'departmental or agency perspectives and interests tend to overshadow the need for more holistic approaches' (ibid.: 21). The new IMPP that had its first field test in Darfur was meant as a tool to overcome at least some of these problems.

To the supporters of IMPP in the peacekeeping department, the Darfur test run was a mixed success: after all, six years after Brahimi's call for integrated planning and four years after Guéhenno had initiated policy development, a partly inclusive process guided by the IMPP template had taken place and agency buy-in had largely survived the negative aspects of the experience. For reasons outside the scope of IMPP, the overall climate for integration had definitely improved and the IMPP guidelines had become a little simpler and more realistic without needlessly reinventing the wheel. Certainly, the new version still had its flaws. Unlike one contributor to the preceding review in whose view the 'silly parts' were only the result of parochial agency interests, many DPKO and agency officials recognized other shortcomings as well.

For one, the IMPP's fundamental first step, the strategic assessment, remained ill-defined. The only formally agreed piece of doctrine described it in as little as one paragraph and five bullet points, providing little clarity on either methodology or objective. Its very ambition to describe the common objectives for the UN's intervention in a country, based on a shared conflict analysis, and its baseline role within the overall framework made the strategic assessment pivotal for subsequent planning stages. Yet even in the final version of the IMPP doctrine approved by the Secretary-General, it remained open if the lead role in writing a strategic assessment would be assigned to the Department of Political Affairs (DPA) or the Peacebuilding Support Office (PBSO). The Darfur technical assessment had also shown that the new IMPP was a tool for professional planners, but barely any participant could call on previous planning experience. Finally, despite strong support from the very top of the peace operations bureaucracy as well as the key partner organizations on headquarters level, it was clear that crucial middle and senior managers continued to oppose the concept.

Doctrine development on the IMPP continued to be run through an interagency working group convened by DPKO and led by an experienced official out of the Best Practices Section, by now the department's in-house think tank. As a first step, the existing package had to be made more usable. The interagency group proceeded to develop four guidance documents to tackle challenges it had identified. On the strategic assessment question, its approach was to substitute working-level guidance for a political decision that was not likely to come down any time soon. If the respective roles of DPA and PBSO could be pragmatically defined and knowledge gaps covered with explanatory notes, the results in future planning scenarios would improve and internal skeptics brought around. This time, the guidance development process got off to an energetic start. Within a few months, the group developed first drafts of each note – helped by the fact that the humanitarian and development communities were finally allowed and funded by member states to each put a full-time IMPP liaison officer in place. Both OCHA and the Development Group Office (after 2008: Development Operations Coordination Office, DOCO) had tried to get those positions for more than two years and repeatedly been rebuffed by member states who underestimated the challenge of integration and the need for resources to address it.[16]

In the summer of 2007, the four drafts were put out for system-wide consultations which culminated in a workshop in August. At the meeting, the

---

[16] Interview, member state diplomat, October 2010.

fundamental unresolved tensions came out again and the process got bogged down in 'turf-driven negotiations,' according to one UN diplomat. As a result, scores of reservations, many from the side of humanitarian agencies, turned the drafts into unwieldy, overly abstract documents that had little utility for guiding an already complex planning exercise.

Why the breakdown? What became apparent amid mutual recriminations was that for all the work done on planning tools the motivations of each bureaucratic actor for pursuing integration remained unchanged and incompatible. In the words of one well-placed observer, 'DPKO wanted more control, others wanted DPKO to have less control, the Department of Political Affairs wanted out and others wanted them to take responsibility.'[17] The strategic assessment, as the foundation for any common planning and the topic of one of the guidance notes, was a crucial example. From the perspective of a senior OCHA official, the humanitarian office saw itself on the losing side of a genuine political conflict. By the natural ways of bureaucracy, the strategic assessment was going to be assigned to the office with the best claim to the relevant expertise: the Department of Political Affairs (DPA). DPA is the UN's 'foreign ministry' and carries the image of diplomats and mediators, with the mandate and institutional culture of cutting deals and hammering out peace agreements even at the expense of lofty humanitarian principles. From OCHA's perspective, DPA was an unlikely honest broker in a process that would pit the humanitarian perspective against that of 'the political side.' Instead, OCHA favored the recently established Peacebuilding Support Office (PBSO), a weak entity without an agenda of its own, as the shepherd of the strategic assessment process.[18] Others argued that PBSO has little capacity to effectively fulfill such a demanding task, particularly since the 'lead department' would also be expected to fill in for the lack of planning and political analysis capacity on the part of humanitarian and development agencies in the field (Gowan 2008).

This basic conflict derailed the whole process. Over the months that followed, little progress was made and the four drafts became more and more bloated as every organization had its pet issues and reservations included. During that time, a new opportunity presented itself in late 2007 to field-test the key element by conducting a strategic assessment for a possible integrated mission to Somalia. A number of important Security Council members, particularly the United States, were pushing for the deployment of a peace operation even without a viable political process in place to end the long-running civil war in the East African country. In a large exercise involving a field trip and many meetings between November 2007 and March 2008, the

---

[17] Interview, member state diplomat, October 2010.
[18] Interview, senior OCHA official, May 2008.

Somalia Integrated Task Force tried to create a common strategic assessment by the IMPP book. At the end, according to participants, there was little commonality about strategy. Fundamental unresolved questions were kicked up to the level of agency principals.[19]

In terms of learning to plan jointly, the Somalia assessment only underscored the depth of the gap – as did complaints about the low rank of participants and the little political leeway some were given by their home organizations. The attempt to have basic contradictions between the political mandates of their whole agencies pragmatically resolved by junior officials on the working level did not generate sufficient trust in the OCHA participants that their vital concerns would be preserved. Thus, a typical solution out of the experienced peacekeeper's playbook – the same which had been used for years by DPKO's regional directors and senior officials in the field to constructively work around the crippling gaps and contradictions in Security Council mandates – proved insufficient, at least at a time of high tensions.

By the spring of 2008, most members and close observers of the interagency group agreed that the working-level process had exhausted itself. Organizational learning on integrated planning, reenergized in 2005 by the Norwegian Report on Integrated Missions and top-level leadership in the two most important departments, had stalled.

* * *

The post-2005 attempt to make mission planning more integrated and strategic suffered from the lack of a system-wide learning infrastructure across different agencies, internal resistance within DPKO and its partners, and a legacy of assumptions and procedures brought along from the history of IMTF and the first IMPP framework that many agency representatives saw as exclusively tied to DPKO's priorities. The most important obstacle, however, and the one at the root of the conflict about the strategic assessment, was the unresolved political question about the purpose and the consequences of integrating at the bureaucratic level as long as deep fragmentation continued to dominate the political level of the UN, to which each part of the bureaucracy continued to be individually accountable (Gowan 2008). As a result, when in June 2006 Kofi Annan formally approved the third new integrated planning framework since 2000, it immediately stalled and was not put into practice. The process remained incomplete until another fresh start in June 2008 with a Policy Committee debate and subsequent decision by Ban Ki-moon that reaffirmed the shift from structural to strategic coordination and launched a new Integration Steering Group to drive the next learning cycle.

[19] Interviews, various UN officials at DPKO and OCHA, May 2008.

In the 2005–8 period, IMPP development and advocacy was still hampered by the fact that while DPKO's individual learning infrastructure just came into its own, the UN had no system-wide, interagency learning infrastructure to support guidance development and implementation at all, let alone at the scale of the revolutionary change that Annan and the early advocates of integration sought. While even the most advanced players such as DPKO, OCHA, and UNDP acquired some learning capacity in this period, smaller agencies always found ways of stalling the process when they felt steamrolled by their bigger cousins. Even after the high-level rapport between the heads of OCHA and DPKO in 2005 sparked a new level of interagency leadership support for the IMPP process, internal opposition was sufficiently entrenched at the middle-management level to throw up the occasional roadblock or obstruct a field trial such as that in Darfur. By that time, the various IMPP working groups – long led by DPKO alone because key agency partners had not effectively participated – had dug themselves deeply into formal technical planning procedures that privileged DPKO's needs over anybody else's. As long as the ever-present threat of subordination under a 'political' logic of engagement with local actors hung over the humanitarians, however, they continued to carve out exceptions and veto opportunities for themselves in order to protect their mandate. The Somalia assessment showed that all the work since Darfur had done little to bridge that underlying gap, leaving the learning process incomplete at best.

By 2008, the attempt to establish the IMPP as a set of operating procedures for integrated strategic planning had fizzled out at the headquarters level. Regardless of this failure at a doctrinal level, in the field mission managers from Monrovia to Kinshasa came up with their own innovative planning procedures. This development was greatly facilitated by a shift of attitudes toward integration. Officials on the ground were now much more supportive of integration in principle. What began in 2000 as a headquarters-driven effort to impose some kind of formal structure was taking root in the field – albeit in an independent manner as missions developed planning systems tailored to local conditions. This trend has fed into the next learning cycle – now under the label of an 'Integrated Strategic Framework' – that appears to have incorporated more of these lessons from the field and provides a more flexible framework than the ultimately ill-fated IMPP. It remains to be seen, however, how the doctrinal turn toward a less ambitious and more service-oriented model of integration will fare in practice.

Integrating Information and Analysis for Strategic Decision-Making on the Ground

On June 2, 2004, UN blue helmets evacuated Bukavu, a town in the eastern DR Congo, in the face of an advancing rebel force led by Laurent Nkunda who came to support a renegade army unit led by Jules Mutebutsi in its fight with troops loyal to the Kinshasa government. After a week of fighting between different armed factions in the area and several UN-mediated ceasefires in which MONUC headquarters in Kinshasa had on multiple occasions withdrawn commitments and threats made by the senior UN commander on scene, the blue helmets had lost any credibility with the rebel forces.

For months, MONUC staff in the eastern Congo had reported the signs of an impending crisis that were ignored by the senior leadership of the mission, whose cables to UN headquarters in New York did not even acknowledge the potential crisis. When the fighting finally broke out, it came as such a surprise that it produced a chaotic, pathological dynamic of crisis decision-making among a small, informal group of senior executives who excluded key colleagues of their own senior management team, regularly ignored information from their field offices and military headquarters on site, and micromanaged the crisis from 1,500 km away. The results were devastating. 'During the days that followed,' reports the UN's internal lessons learned study, 'heavy looting and violence, including rape, took place in Bukavu ... [Congolese army] troops had retreated south to Walungu where they too carried out pillaging in the town. Military and civilian casualties in Bukavu were estimated at more than 100 persons. These casualties were largely the victims of troops belonging to Mutebutsi and Nkunda' (UN DPKO/PBPU 2005: 7). The fall of Bukavu and the atrocities committed there also had severe repercussions on Congolese politics and a catastrophic effect on MONUC's credibility (ICG 2004).

Among a number of causes that explain the failure of MONUC to manage this crisis more successfully, an internal review carried out between the mission and DPKO identified shortcomings in information collection and analysis as one of the most important factors. This part of the review is worth quoting at length:

> MONUC offices in Bukavu and Goma had frequently warned of the increasing volatility of the situation in the Kivus. Nevertheless, despite having staff on the ground with access to germane information, the June events took the Mission's senior leadership by surprise, denoting failure on its part to analyse and use the information gathered, detect underlying tensions, assess the situation in the Kivus from both the political and military perspectives and develop a political-military strategic plan accordingly.
>
> ... [T]he daily reports sent to UNHQ provided little or no indication that tensions were rising in the Kivus, creating the misguided impression that the

transitional process was healthy and moving forward, albeit slowly, when in fact it was not. At the same time, little effort was made to develop a deeper understanding of the dynamics of the situation itself. For example, at no point prior to or during the crisis was the task given to produce a concrete political or military assessment of Laurent Nkunda's capabilities, intentions, or actions. A profile of Nkunda and his strengths would not have been difficult to obtain with the collaborative efforts of military and civilian staff in the Kivus who had their local networks and access to verifiable information. Such a profile would certainly have improved the Mission's ability to deal with Nkunda, thus likely weakening the impact of the crisis in Bukavu. (UN DPKO/PBPU 2005: 11–12)

Ultimately, the Secretariat concluded in its first post-Bukavu report on the Congo operation, 'there is an urgent need to establish a civilian-military joint mission analysis cell, established at all levels, capable of accurately analysing information, distinguishing real threats and anticipating crises before they occur' (UN Secretary-General 2004c: para. 98).

* * *

At DPKO in New York, the call from Bukavu fell on fertile ground. The UN's top peacekeeper, Jean-Marie Guéhenno, had just returned from a visit to the Eastern Congo a week before the crisis broke out, where he had reviewed the plans and preparations of local MONUC officials for just such an event – only to see them countermanded and micromanaged from a mission headquarters in Kinshasa that had ignored their warnings for months. Dismayed by the failure of MONUC's core mission leadership, the senior management team also realized that Bukavu provided a perfect example to make their case for the concept of a "Joint Mission Analysis Centre" (JMAC) that had just gotten stuck in budgetary negotiations with member states.

Until less than a year earlier, the discussion about information and analysis capabilities for peace operations had been subdued by the traditional allergic reactions that had surrounded any proposal that the UN engage in intelligence for decades, since the UN's first Congo operation in 1960–4 (Dorn and Bell 1995; Chesterman 2006). The lack of adequate information and analysis reemerged on the agenda with the growing challenges of peace enforcement in the 1990s (Dorn 1999). The debate proceeded unevenly along three different tracks, on each of which the UN's own experts had time and again identified the need for better information and analysis: intelligence for tactical operations (such as moving its troops or securing a weapons cache), intelligence for force or mission protection, and intelligence for strategic and integrated mandate implementation.[20]

---

[20] These labels follow the categories introduced by Shetler-Jones (2008: 518) whose analysis informs most of this paragraph.

Force commanders in the field and troop-contributing countries mostly worried about the first and second types of intelligence. Largely to protect their own, major and middle powers such as France, the United Kingdom, and Canada began to assign intelligence personnel to high-profile hotspots such as Croatia, Bosnia, Kosovo, Iraq, Haiti, and Somalia where they had put sizable numbers of their own troops in the line of fire (Villeneuve and Lefebvre 1996; Dorn 1999: 428).

The third type of intelligence went beyond the tactical, day-to-day needs of military components or security teams. This was about analytically enriched information to support strategic decisions with regard to the local environment: if and how to react to a provocation, which political figures to engage and how, and to what extent to trust local partners with sensitive information – things that senior civilian leaders need to know to implement their mandate effectively. A lot of that information was available from open sources, from the myriad of UN reports including those of humanitarian staff who were often much more widely deployed across a mission area than the blue helmets or political staff – and even, on occasion, from secret sources by way of a friendly government. However, the UN lacked the expertise to analyze such information professionally. Its political officers were already overworked in their day-to-day reporting, planning, and support to mission management and unable to focus on longer term trends and issues.

In the 1990s, this strategic-level intelligence gap was understood as an institutional shortcoming of DPKO which needed an appropriate intelligence staff at its headquarters in New York. Top officials made that case to the membership, to little avail. In a 1997 internal report, Under-Secretary-General Marrack Goulding proposed a strategic analysis unit that failed right away and failed a second time three years later after being briefly resurrected as part of the Brahimi recommendations (Durch et al. 2003: 38). Meanwhile, the Secretariat built a tiny 'Information and Research Unit' as part of DPKO's Situation Centre. Starting with one US analyst in 1994, by 1999 it had grown to include four seconded officers from four of the five permanent members of the Security Council (without China), each of whom brought some access to their national intelligence communities to the table (Dorn 1999: 433). However, with the enforced departure of military personnel provided to the UN free of charge by its Western members, these officers had to leave – and the Brahimi panel's recommended replacement never overcame the resistance from member states. It took several years until the Situation Centre was able to rebuild a tiny 'Research and Liaison Unit,' now staffed solely with UN civil servants.

The single-minded focus of senior officials on the headquarters level lasted until the August 2003 terrorist attack on the mission headquarters in Baghdad that claimed the lives of dozens of UN staff, including the widely revered head of mission, Sergio Vieira de Mello. The organization was in shock, finally having to realize that the blue flag was not their ultimate protection any more, and staff and member state diplomats were calling for better threat assessments and security precautions in missions around the world. In this context, Patrick Cammaert, a Dutch Major-General who had recently started his job as the Military Adviser to the Secretary-General and head of DPKO's Military Division, became a champion of an idea that two colonels in his division, François Dureau and Bob Phillips, had been kicking around for a while already with the support of Guéhenno's office.[21] The officers built on their previous experience with UN and NATO forces in the Balkans, but for the organization their analysis and proposal only became relevant when they found the support of DPKO senior management. With Cammaert's forceful backing, the states' demand for better security provided an opportunity to introduce a new form of intelligence capability at the mission level.

When he advocated for the concept of a 'joint mission analysis cell' (later renamed to 'centre,' a label that invoked less ominous associations), Cammaert laid out the impact of the UN's intelligence challenge and the promise of their proposal in the starkest possible terms:

> The lessons of Rwanda have been clear – the failures there go back to the absence of a strong mandate. However, we can take this back one step. Had there been a more detailed intelligence assessment considering historical tendencies, the political will and military capability of the belligerents and looking at all escalation scenarios, we could have seen a stronger mandate. This together with a broader, multi-source and credible intelligence capability on the ground, could have prevented the genocide and atrocities which followed. (Cammaert 2003: 3)

In the modern peace operations environment marked by 'chaotic conflict' in with 'mercenaries fight alongside government forces, soldiers open their barracks to rebel gun-runners, veterans of insurrection in country A show up to assist rebels in country B' and so on, Cammaert argued, 'you need information. Accurate, in-time information. Specifically, the analyzed product we call intelligence' (Cammaert 2003: 2). Yes, blue helmets needed better military intelligence capabilities and modern surveillance technology, but much closer to home, they needed to harness sources that were already close at hand but had not been sufficiently exploited in the past:

> Of the types of [intelligence] needed for a mission, much is already available in the UN system between open source information and the various departments, organs and associated organizations in the UN that have the same ultimate humanitarian aim. You do not need to meet Mr. Bond at the hard rock café to receive a thick red

---

[21] Interviews, DPKO officials, May 2008. While no actual JMAC existed at the time, the concept was mentioned briefly as a tool of integrating the military and civilian branches of missions in DPKO's *Handbook on Multidimensional Peace Operations* (2003: 69).

dossier under the table in order to have an accurate intelligence product. The trick is to develop a system of 'data mining', and to have the expertise available for this info to [be] analyzed and assessed within the framework of military strategic political objectives to produce [an] intelligence product on which decisions can be made and an (sic) operational campaigns planned. (Cammaert 2003: 2)

At mission headquarters, the UN could build on existing strengths: 'those individuals in the system that have become regional experts on a theatre of operation or problem area,' who 'build up contacts across agencies and organizations and down to the tactical field worker level in order to be able to see the "bigger picture" and do their specific job better. They gather some of the puzzle pieces together, add a bit of open source information and "presto" – they are both the local expert and the holder of what some would refer to as "secret intelligence."' With just 'a few more specialists and the freedom to coordinate and data-mine the "information knowledge" of our many left and right hands,' which included humanitarian agencies and even NGOs, a vision of modern, low-cost, all-source analysis for peace operations would become reality. On the 'mission planning level, if we were able to "data mine" this resource, add some commercial or open source intelligence from Satellite imagery, [Geographic Information Systems], CNN and other resources, add in selective operational level and perhaps tactical intelligence from concerned member states with a vested interest in stability in their region – then we could have a very successful formula' (Cammaert 2003: 7).

The proponents of the JMAC concept wasted no time. In the fall of 2003, DPKO briefed the various relevant committees and had four missions – those in Sierra Leone, Timor-Leste, DRC, and the new one in Liberia – establish a pilot version out of existing military resources, because the civilian budget process would need almost a year to provide funding. By February 2004, the Secretary-General (2004b: para. 8) was able to report the 'successful establishment of Joint Mission Analysis Cells in four missions.' By late April, the Special Committee on Peacekeeping Operations (2004: para. 46) welcomed the concept as filling 'a major gap in threat and risk analysis and security assessment in the field.'

This was a gap filled only on paper, as the events in Bukavu barely four weeks later would show. However, in the middle of a running budget cycle there was no leeway to hire new civilian experts for whom no job descriptions existed, so the four new JMACs could only be 'created' by re-hatting or reorganizing the few military intelligence officers that each of the four force commanders had available to them. The result had little to do with anybody's idea of JMACs, and everything with the kind of military intelligence cell these UN missions had acquired already in the Congo in 1960–4, but it was a start.[22]

---

[22] Interviews with UN officials in Timor-Leste, Liberia, and Haiti. See also Malan (2005: 20) and UN reports by the ACABQ (2004: para. 31) and DPKO (UN DPKO/PBPU 2004: 8).

Without relying on a learning infrastructure that was still in its infancy in 2003, however, it required not just protection but an effective leadership coalition reaching into senior management to put a previously acquired lesson on the agenda and start an advocacy process.

* * *

By June 2004, the time of the Bukavu crisis, the initial enthusiasm about JMACs had already given way to a more sober reassessment of the speed of change in the UN peace operations bureaucracy. Cammaert, Dureau, and Phillips had initially built their advocacy around the demand from troop contributors and field commanders for better force protection. As Cammaert argued in December 2003, '[the] growing operational requirement for intelligence can be pulled through to the ground on basic Force Protection (*sic*) issues. The recent tragic loss of the special representative and the other UN personnel killed in the bomb attack on the UN HQ in Baghdad, brought home the lesson of the lack of intelligence structures in the UN and the resultant poor situational and threat awareness and failure to plan for the worst case scenario on both Force Protection (*sic*) and operational levels.' As a result of the attack, 'member states are ... recognizing that on an operational and tactical level, a Force Commander needs accurate information and intelligence on the armed groups and former warring factions in order to be pre-emptive and neutralize destabilizing influences and "spoilers"' (Cammaert 2003: 3).

The force protection rationale and the deliberate strategy to address force commanders' demands and their military constituencies in their home countries was the one that created the necessary momentum in the diplomatic realm (Shetler-Jones 2008: 523). At the same time, what the proponents of JMAC and DPKO's senior managers really wanted to establish was more than just an effective information-sharing mechanism to guard against potential security threats. It was also a way of drawing the various parts of the mission, military and civilian, closer together:

> On mission HQ level there has long been a challenge in coordinating the availability and analysis of available information from all role players. A mission is after all a complex mixture of political, military and humanitarian processes. Each with its own sources of information, analytical process and operational objectives with related intelligence requirements and planning cycles. What we need is the formation of a Joint Mission Analysis Cell (JMAC) as a central location for information to be received, analyzed, evaluated and appropriately disseminated. Contributing role-players would include military, political and humanitarian organizations. This structure enables a broader spectrum of information contributions and for information to be analyzed in terms of its impact across a much broader scope of the mission and enable analyses of the impact of different factors

on each other e.g. political developments on the military situation. (Cammaert 2003: 5)

For the idea of truly 'joint' JMACs acting not just as relabeled military intelligence sections but as fusion centers for civilian and military input, DPKO needed funding for civilian analysts. Long before the initiative had been coupled with the force protection issue in 2003, the department's own budget experts had resisted a proposal to ask member states for JMAC funding because they feared being turned down for deviating from the accepted budget template. Their concerns may have been well founded, given the initially frosty reaction of member states in 2000/1 to the JMAC idea in general.[23]

In addition to force protection and better integration, there was a third aim linked to the JMAC proposal. Senior officials in the field, mainly military commanders in vulnerable missions, had long demanded to be given greater authority and resources to gather information by recruiting and paying local informants, and to conduct similar 'open' intelligence gathering that did not violate the laws of the host country or involve UN personnel misrepresenting their identity. Such efforts could be conducted by military intelligence units, but they would be much more palatable in the UN context in an integrated, civilian-led group such as the JMAC – an argument that makes no appearance in official reports but served to rally the military and security elements of the peace operations bureaucracy behind the concept (Shetler-Jones 2008: 523).

The decision to 'sell' the JMAC to troop contributors as a force protection measure helped to enlist a large constituency of member states that were naturally closest to the Military Division and that dominated the Special Committee. They were keen to see their soldiers and police officers better protected if the JMACs worked as advertised, so they stressed their support and asked for adequate staffing and equipment to be provided. The UN's paymasters, on the other hand, are fewer in number and therefore not as influential in setting the agenda of the Special Committee. Instead, they control the powerful Advisory Committee on Administrative and Budgetary Questions (ACABQ), where they basically exercise a line-item veto over funding – which is precisely what they did in the spring 2004 budget cycle.

Even before the Secretariat's regular budget submissions for the 2004–5 fiscal year were due, three new missions were deployed in the spring of 2004, to Haiti, Burundi, and Côte d'Ivoire. In each of their start-up budgets, DPKO requested a few civilian positions for a JMAC and was turned down every time because the Advisory Committee felt that the proposed task of the cell was insufficiently delineated from that of the mission's security

---

[23] Interviews, senior DPKO official, May 2008; member state diplomat, October 2010.

section which is in charge of guarding mission premises and keeping abreast of direct, short-term threats to mission personnel and assets (UN ACABQ 2004: para. 32).

In effect, the framing of JMACs as an initiative for improving staff safety that the Secretariat had used successfully to win the support of troop contributors had the opposite effect with the financial contributors, blocking a process of advocacy and partial institutionalization that had been very swift up to this point.

* * *

Before they would withdraw their veto over funding, the budget advisors asked DPKO to better demonstrate the value-added of the JMAC concept vis-à-vis the established security sections in every mission[24] – and therefore, strengthen and develop the needs for intelligence and integration rather than force protection. Not least, it was the concept's supporters in the Special Committee on Peacekeeping Operations (2005: para. 16) that 'looked forward to the effective implementation of the joint mission analysis cells' and used the 2004 fall session to push for DPKO to 'better define the concept, structure and role of the cells and their linkages to United Nations Headquarters.'

At the same time, the Bukavu crisis created a new sense of urgency among member states that constrained the political space for the technical experts in ACABQ to demand a high standard of conceptual clarity before allocating funds. MONUC became the real test case, and both New York and the mission invested considerably into its success. Even before the end of 2004, the UN had created an actual integrated JMAC unit in Kinshasa. As its first chief, the mission recruited François Grignon, a widely respected area expert who had been the Central Africa director for the International Crisis Group and a prominent critic of MONUC. Supported by MONUC's military chief of staff and helped internally by a weak Political Affairs section whose leaders had little interest in deep analysis and therefore little turf to lose to JMAC, Grignon's team produced relevant analysis not just on national and regional but also on local developments, particularly in the volatile east of the country (Autesserre 2010: 128). At the same time, the JMAC under Grignon was also seen as excessively secretive and as directing too much attention to military

---

[24] A look into the UNOCI budget documents shows that the ACABQ's May 2004 reaction was not unreasonable. DPKO requested funding for a JMAC that should be responsible for the 'management (...) of information from civilian and military sources, analysis of risk and development of risk management advice and providing integrated mission-level security/risk management advice' while a few pages later, a Security Section was tasked to 'conduct threat assessments, risk analysis and investigations,' as well. No more detailed explanation is given in the budget document (UN Secretary-General 2004a: para. 29, 62).

affairs – perhaps a natural by-product of its institutional pedigree but also a fateful precedent for JMACs elsewhere.[25]

Elsewhere, progress came more slowly, if at all. By all accounts, the missions in Timor-Leste and Sierra Leone which were already drawing down in mid-2004 only assigned their chief military intelligence officers an additional job title as Chief JMAC and never sought or received the budgetary means to properly implement the concept.[26] Most JMACs were purely military organizations for several years, such as in Liberia where the unit was located '15 kilometers from Mission HQ, but only 10 meters from the force commander's office. The symbolism … is pervasive' (Malan 2005: 20). It was neither accepted by the mission as a joint unit nor was it able to establish some track record of getting there. In a telling moment, our UNMIL interlocutors in March 2008 informed us that the mission's JMAC had been established 'just before' November 2007, when the current chief had taken over. This person was still a military officer, and still struggling to build relationships with the civilian branches of the mission, although by 2008 there were a few civilians and police officers seconded to the unit.[27]

The lack of integration into the mission as a whole did not mean that these JMACs did not make an important and innovative contribution when they were able to make themselves useful to their mission leaderships. Without wide-ranging buy-in from the civilians, however, that contribution was necessarily limited to the military's own information sources and their genuine intelligence work. An example of how the latter could massively benefit the effectiveness of a robust peace operation is provided by the success of antigang operations in Haiti in 2006–7. A year earlier, the UN had lost significant credibility in a frontal assault against the stronghold of a notorious gang leader. The target, a number of gang members and several civilians were killed, providing further ammunition to the gangs' anti-UN propaganda, and residents of the slums poured into the streets protesting against the UN. Violent crime and gang killings increased. After a change in the Haitian government and internal changes within the mission, the UN began in December 2006 to conduct intelligence-led operations with the Haitian National Police to apprehend gang leaders and break their hold over certain parts of the slums in the capital, Port-au-Prince. JMAC ran paid and unpaid human intelligence sources and collected various other kinds of information that were critical in enabling

[25] Interviews, UN official, April 2009; member state diplomat, October 2010. Funding for the MONUC JMAC was regularized in the 2005–6 and 2006–7 budgets (UN Secretary-General 2005: para. 12; 2006a: para. 19).

[26] In the official budgets and reports on UNAMSIL (Sierra Leone) and UNMISET (Timor-Leste), there is no evidence for a JMAC being established before both missions were closed in 2005. ONUB in Burundi received a budget for two civilian positions only in its final year of operations (2005–6); whether those positions were ever filled remains equally unclear.

[27] Interviews, UNMIL officials, March 2008.

successful operations with minimal violence over a four month period (Dorn 2009).

The mounting complexity of threats in places such as the Congo and Darfur combined with a few examples of success such as the one from Haiti deflected most of the pressure from member states to invest in conceptual clarity and doctrine development for JMACs. The result was that in the short term, serious and potentially fatal obstacles for the learning process were overcome, but at the steep price of losing the envisaged 'jointness' or full-scale integration with the civilian mission components and UN agencies. In effect, JMACs delivered intelligence for tactical operations and mission protection while the lack of integration and management buy-in severely constrained their effect on strategic decision-making.

The opportunity to bypass a more in-depth conceptual development effort at the advocacy stage may have been the only way for this learning process to achieve anything at all, for a number of reasons. The JMAC idea as a genuine fusion center to create something new and 'joint' from relationships with every part of a mission, civilian, police, or military, even including agencies and NGOs in some way, was so new and innovative that the challenges of writing doctrine would probably have overwhelmed a learning infrastructure that was still weak at the time, at the price of losing crucial political momentum with member states. Unlike any other learning process studied in this book, DPKO had no existing institutional 'home' in the sense of an established unit whose staff already possessed the relevant expertise. As a result, it fell to an ad hoc group of interested officials from the Military Division, the Situation Centre, the Department of Safety and Security (DSS), and the Best Practices Section to write the first policy directive (formally issued on July 1, 2006) and guidance documents for JMACs. While some of these papers languished for years in discussions between various stakeholders within the peace operations bureaucracy, the delay also allowed for the participation of several JMAC managers in the field through a global retreat in 2007.[28]

At the same time, the rush to implementation had two consequences that significantly hampered the attempt to fully institutionalize the concept. The first was that even the temporary dominance of JMACs by the military created path dependencies in the organizational structures and the cultural construction of 'the JMAC' in many missions that proved extremely hard to overcome later. Deep-seated mistrust on the part of civilian mission components effectively cut JMACs off from some of the very information flows that had been expected to add the most value to their analysis, such as reporting from humanitarian agencies (Shetler-Jones 2008: 524).[29] The second consequence

---

[28] Interviews, UN officials, November 2007 and April 2009.
[29] Confirmed by interviews, UN officials, November 2007, March 2008, April 2009.

was that divergent expectations about the role of the JMAC at the headquarters level were glossed over in compromise language rather than clearly resolved. The Secretariat's security people expected medium-term threat analysis to support their field staff, much of the military wanted JMACs to support their military intelligence cells and the political affairs teams wanted analytic support in a subordinate role to themselves. As a result, recruitment for management positions often became a tug-of-war between various players, and the expectations and buy-in from senior managers in the field depended a lot on who had briefed them on the concept rather than how it actually operated in their mission.[30]

* * *

When member states accepted the JMAC as a regular element for a peace operation in a volatile security environment – which covers almost every mission – and the bureaucracy formally adopted a principal policy in 2006, the original learning process was completed. Starting from a group of mid-level managers tapping into their personal experiences from previous assignments, the organization had developed a new tool for information management and analysis, and overcame the usual budgetary obstacles to put at least a skeletal version of it into practice across the globe.

By April 2009, thirteen missions had a unit called 'Joint Mission Analysis Centre' but none of them came close to fulfilling the original aspirations to 'include military, political and humanitarian organizations [to enable] a broader spectrum of information contributions,' as Cammaert had defined the vision six years earlier. In fact, what at least some of its original proponents had envisaged as a fully integrated mechanism drawing on and working for the entire UN community in the field turned out to be purely a political-military asset owned by DPKO. This was DPKO's own assessment from a series of evaluation visits to JMACs in 2008 – an assessment so bleak, in particular in terms of the level of resistance or ignorance on the part of senior mission managers that it uncovered, that officials on the working level seriously considered to propose 'killing' the JMAC entirely. At this point, another learning cycle began, focused on defining a clearer role for JMACs, re-linking it to the strategic integration agenda and institutionalizing this next lesson more effectively.[31]

The evaluation effort was one of the first that was coordinated and partly implemented by the nascent two-person evaluation team that had just been created. As such, the JMAC case was also one of the first in which the learning cycle was completed from knowledge acquisition and advocacy to

---

[30] Interview, UN official, April 2009.
[31] Interviews, UN official, April 2009; member state diplomat, October 2010.

institutionalization and evaluation as a feedback mechanism to kick off a new iteration of learning.

Conclusion

In this chapter, we reviewed three attempts at learning to integrate better within the UN family. Two of these attempts were ultimately completed and sparked follow-up processes that may lead to further learning while the development of the IMPP failed to reach full implementation even eight years after the Brahimi report.

The failed IMPP, our second case, tried to tackle what is probably the hardest issue on the integration agenda: joint planning. Therefore, this is the case that may have required the strongest and most sustainable leadership support both within DPKO and its partner units and agencies, and among member states. In practice, the case is an example of how even solid general pressure from the diplomatic level has a hard time reaching down into the trenches of complex bureaucratic processes and conflicts. Within the apparatus, top-level bureaucratic pressure by Jean-Marie Guéhenno and some of his counterparts was not matched by an effective mid-level coalition to neutralize the resistance mounted on that level. Add to this the somewhat overbearing nature of the IMPP proposals and it is easy to see why this learning process did not succeed. At the same time, the field-driven evolution of alternative planning frameworks that fed into the subsequent development of the Integrated Strategic Framework offers an interesting example of how creative initiatives in the field can proceed even against the odds of a failed organization-wide learning process.

As we found across all our cases on integration, without very strong political support learning was doomed: the bureaucratic and political obstacles of fragmentation were too strong for a purely infrastructure-driven learning process to succeed – particularly existing learning infrastructures were fragmented and, for most of the time under review in this study, also weak. The required kind of political support existed for the two completed cases of learning, finding an integrated structure for senior field leadership and institutionalizing JMACs. While each case had its own obstacles and support requirements depending on the kinds of changes sought as a result of each learning process, both were significantly driven by political factors, and both emerged at headquarters at the middle- and senior-management level. In the first case, based on the successful 'prototype' established by the influential Lakhdar Brahimi in Haiti, two top managers got together and turned the Liberia crisis into an opportunity for change. At the diplomatic level, they rode on ancillary support from some member states that funded the 2005 report. Even more importantly, however, the integration agenda as such was sufficiently accepted across the membership that there was no specific political opposition to overcome.

In the third case, the weakness of DPKO's learning infrastructure well into the early 2000s made it more of a challenge to build an effective internal leadership coalition and generate the senior management support required to draw diplomatic support from troop contributors and take on the resistance of the budget division and financial stakeholders. The result was a partial lesson, fully institutionalized: DPKO succeeded in creating a basic analysis and intelligence unit for its mission, but failed to integrate with its UN partners in doing so. At least part of the reason was lesson's practical complexity: unlike many other innovations, JMACs had to be created from scratch as a new type of organization within mission for which there where neither blueprints nor experienced personnel available on the job market.

The overwhelming significance of political factors to make or break these three attempts at learning in the field of integration may be explained with reference to the fact that there was, and is still, no functional equivalent to a single department's learning infrastructure at the level of the entire UN system. A well-oiled network of individually effective and better endowed learning infrastructures within each agency or an interagency process like the recently created high-level Integration Steering Group at headquarters may change this situation in the future, but we will probably find what the UN painfully discovered to be true for integration is also true for learning about integration. Namely, it will only work in a way that respects the fundamental fragmentation of mandates among the different parts of the system. Particularly in the early part of the decade, the adverse incentives and cultural predispositions within each organization were shown to stifle self-organizing bottom-up collaboration, and the contrived appearance of hierarchy that was at the core of Kofi Annan's push for integration (UN Secretary-General 2000, 2006b) could not hide the fact that the emperor had in fact no clothes (Campbell 2008; Campbell and Kaspersen 2008).

8

Conclusion

> I sometimes wonder if those of us engaged in peacekeeping are the human equivalent of goldfish. These animals are said to have memories that last in the region of two seconds. Now, for them that means life swimming around and around in a bowl will not be interminably dull. When it applies to us, the impact is greater and far more serious.
>
> Sergio Vieira de Mello[1]

If Sergio Vieira de Mello had lived to see this past decade of expansion for peace operations and sat down again, more than ten years after penning his memo in Timor-Leste, what would he have to say on the UN's learning capacity in peace operations? Is the UN apparatus still, as he wrote in 2000, 'more adept at repeating mistakes, than at learning lessons' (Vieira de Mello 2000: 21)? Our analysis of twelve learning attempts, embedded in ten years of evolution in the peace operations bureaucracy as a whole, suggests some possible answers to this question. First, we summarize the findings from our twelve case studies in the previous chapters. Second, we draw conclusions as regards the learning capacity of the UN peace operations apparatus. Third, we outline an agenda for future research on learning. We conclude with final observations on learning and the limits of peace operations.

Empirical Findings from Case Studies

What do the twelve case studies tell us about the learning capacity of the UN peace operations apparatus? Given the number and complexity of causal factors and the widely divergent institutional and thematic contexts examined in our case studies, any conclusions drawn are limited in scope. With this

---

[1] Quoted by Samantha Power (2008: 527).

caveat in mind, it is worth considering a number of common findings from our empirical analysis.

More than half of our cases (seven out of twelve) ended up incomplete according to our definition of organizational learning as *a knowledge-based process of questioning and changing organizational rules to change organizational practice* (Chapter 3). Four of the seven incomplete cases fizzled out during the advocacy stage before they even reached the point of decision on the merits of the proposed lesson. The remaining three were officially adopted as lessons but never implemented – the change of rules did not translate into organizational practice.[2] The pattern of aborted learning during advocacy or institutionalization is also very common among other cases which we did not select as in-depth case studies. Taken together, the cases paint a mixed picture of the past decade's record on learning. The five completed cases demonstrate that organization-wide learning indeed takes place on crucial issues in the UN peace operations apparatus. The instances of aborted learning processes (especially in the institutionalization stage) point to serious persisting weaknesses in the learning capacity. So neither the doomsayers who hold that bureaucracies cannot learn save in situations of extreme crisis nor the management gurus who promise swift transformations into a "learning organization" have it right. To conduct a more fine-grained analysis of the factors that influence learning, we find our analytical distinction between two clusters of infrastructure and politics (Chapter 3) to be eminently useful. It allows us to examine two different mechanisms of affecting a learning process separately, and then to analyze their interactions. Since the infrastructure factors vary only with time and institutional context, they allow for comparisons between lessons within the same time and context – that is, two cases on reintegration in 2004–6. Political factors, in contrast, tie in with the lesson and its proponents and often evolve much more rapidly, even erratically, as actors' priorities change or realign according to some external issue, such as the post-Iraq drive to find consensus on anything at the UN that may have helped the Standing Police Capacity (SPC) to be established.

Given the diverse factors bundled in each cluster, it is unsurprising that only very rarely do the individual factors in each cluster neatly line up to support or obstruct a given case. Instead, we often find political factors to be in conflict, such as a supportive leadership coalition trying to overcome the obstacles of bureaucratic politics, or the various aspects of the learning infrastructure to be unevenly developed and therefore partly supporting and partly obstructing a learning process. The interaction between political factors and infrastructure

---

[2] In terms of our three-stage process model, the first step (successful knowledge acquisition at the small group level) was a given in all our cases by virtue of our selection method, since without an initial paper trail we could not have detected and examined any cases.

factors followed the expected logic in every case (see Chapter 3). Whenever they clashed, politics carried the day, whether to propel a lesson to success or to thwart it entirely.

On the one hand, despite a weak infrastructure, political factors can propel a lesson forward. Such was the case for the SPC, the doctrinal changes on police institution-building and gender concerns in reintegration, the new way of organizing senior management for integration, and a nascent intelligence capacity in field missions. They all succeeded at least to the decision point on the wings of political factors such as member state pressure and effective bureaucratic coalitions. What we find in these cases is basically a mechanism of substitution: with sufficient high-level diplomatic or senior bureaucratic leadership attention, resources to develop proposals will be found to make up for a weak infrastructure, supporting coalitions built and decisions made even in the absence of a regular process, particularly if there is little political opposition to the lesson. With only one exception, every case of successful learning in our small sample (four out of five) turns out to be driven by political factors.

On the other hand, when political factors intervene against the proposed change in rules, even a supportive infrastructure of dedicated staff capacity, procedures, and (most recently) a more learning-friendly culture fails to overcome the obstacles of bureaucratic politics. This was the case with the push for a community focus to reintegration programs and the application of fully integrated planning procedures.

Naturally, political factors are particularly salient with regard to lessons that have been politicized. A lesson is politicized either by being drawn into a conflict within the bureaucracy or as a result of external political pressure. Politicization occurs for many different reasons, and it may either support or obstruct the learning process. For example, the SPC was politicized almost exclusively for budgetary reasons (which allowed the duty station controversy to emerge), while almost everything in the realm of judicial reform got politicized because of the unresolved political debate about the UN's role in that field and its implications for the principle of sovereignty in global governance. Conversely, the introduction of gender concerns to reintegration is a case that profited significantly and may not have been successful without being politicized through member state pressure by means of Security Council resolution 1325 and the associated NGO campaign. Some lessons are therefore inescapably politicized and require skilful political management and diplomatic support to succeed. In other cases, it may be a conscious strategy on the part of some stakeholder to politicize a learning process, either to support or to obstruct it. Further research needs to investigate these dynamics in greater depth.

In the absence of strong political support, a weak infrastructure is often a major factor inhibiting a learning process. Among the seven incomplete learning attempts, in five cases we identified some aspect of a weak learning infrastructure to be a significant part of the explanation. One important aspect is the deficient sourcing of knowledge. In three of our cases (the two attempts to infuse the practice of building police and judicial institutions with a more political and less 'technical' approach, and the proposal to address traditional justice systems as part of judicial reform) the weak infrastructure failed to produce the essential fuel for the learning process to go forward: knowledge. As a long-time practitioner said, 'we have no idea what we are doing' in these areas.[3] His top boss, current Under-Secretary-General for Peacekeeping Operations, Alain Le Roy, concurs: 'our expertise is not very deep in critical peace-building areas. The UN does not retain in-house expertise on many aspects of statebuilding, yet we are mandated to assist in building national institutions' (Le Roy 2009: 16). This lack of in-house knowledge affects DPKO in particular because the tasks of institution-building are far removed from its traditional core of peacekeeping activities. Knowledge-sourcing partnerships with other UN agencies that have more expertise on these issues are often underdeveloped. "Boundary-spanning" activities where DPKO could draw on the expertise of academia and think tanks also remain far below their potential. Partly this is due to the lack of digestible research on many of the complex tasks of modern peace operations. Part of the explanation, however, is the weakness of the UN's infrastructure for sourcing and digesting knowledge.

This is a weakness that the Brahimi Report clearly identified and linked back to the unwillingness of member states to upgrade the bureaucracy's resources. Looking back ten years after presenting the report that bears his name, Lakhdar Brahimi (2010) recalled in front of the General Assembly how 'the Panel bluntly pointed out that the UN is often taking very serious decisions about how to respond to crises it does not know enough about. We stressed the importance of seriously upgrading the UN's regional expertise and its general analytical capacities. . . . The General Assembly . . . firmly refused to give the Secretary General the quality analytical capacity he needs.'

A weak infrastructure is also a factor for learning processes to stall at a later stage. This was particularly interesting to observe in the absence of political obstacles: in cases such as the lesson to include gender concerns into reintegration programs, nascent institutional support systems (supported by political advocacy) carried a learning process through the advocacy stage to the decision point before momentum was lost. This pattern points to an important observation as regards to the uneven development of the peace

---

[3] Interview, senior UN official, November 2007.

operations learning infrastructure in terms of its support for the different stages of learning. Its creators as well as member states prioritized guidance development and knowledge management – which mostly support the knowledge acquisition and advocacy stages of learning – over training and evaluation. However weak these early stages still are, the parts that would provide support mechanisms for 'rolling out' a formally 'learned' lesson (let alone evaluate its application in practice) fare much worse. This has contributed to many learning processes remaining incomplete.

Of course, a better developed training and evaluation infrastructure will not singlehandedly overcome resistance against the implementation of a particular lesson that might be politically motivated. But it would raise the stakes and the political cost considerably for those willing to obstruct a lesson. And what is more, the peace operations apparatus is still largely flying blind with regard to the utility and implementation of its guidance: without a successful follow-on advocacy effort putting the weaknesses of a previously adopted lesson on the agenda of decision-makers in New York, the system is often unable to know if and how changes in formal rules are implemented in the field. A strengthened evaluation capacity would allow the headquarters level to gather feedback and fine-tune its doctrine much more quickly and make it more useful to its field staff.

Evaluation and training are also critical to help the UN peace operations apparatus to guide its staff in adapting general principles and insights to the diverse local contexts of individual missions in the field. Given the weakness of local expertise and analytical capacity that Lakhdar Brahimi points out, this critical part of implementing lessons is likely to suffer from serious shortcomings. This is particularly salient for the slim body of experience and doctrine on deeply political mandates such as tinkering with another country's institutions.

Policy Conclusions

These empirical findings suggest a number of conclusions on the current state and future prospects of the learning infrastructure in the UN peace operations bureaucracy, and the choices before member state governments and the UN's senior management.

While political support is the 'trump card' for learning processes to succeed, the supportive power of political campaigning for a particular lesson is in very limited supply and thus not scalable. In the decade reviewed in this study, at no point in time did we see more than two or three major learning efforts that found effective political support at a similar level. To marshal a strong and sustained leadership effort and to organize a winning coalition of senior officials, diplomats, and member states requires a significant investment in time and attention on the part of many exceptionally busy people. Depending on the lesson proposed, the bottleneck is somewhere between a handful of senior Secretariat officials and an equally small number of key ambassadors, each of whom can only champion a couple of high-profile efforts at a time. In addition, these key players have learned to pick their fights carefully, as Jean-Marie Guéhenno did when he delayed the toxic issue of judicial institution-building, or simply find the urgent day-to-day demands of crisis management to crowd out the medium-term tasks of learning and organizational development. In addition, not every issue benefits from top-level political attention, as mentioned earlier, and for some lessons to be raised to the political level spells more trouble than their supporters may be able to overcome. For all of these reasons, political support for learning is extremely limited in bandwidth, that is, in the number and scope of learning processes that an organization may pursue at the same time. Governments, diplomats, and senior officials need to support the lessons they find important because their backing is the only effective way to overcome political obstacles, and may on occasion substitute for particular weaknesses of the learning infrastructure. At the same time, no bureaucracy will come close to becoming a learning organization based on political pressure and leadership coalitions alone.

Infrastructure is in a sense the mirror image of politics: while even the most effective infrastructure alone cannot overcome entrenched political resistance, unlike politics infrastructure is scalable. After 2005, when the gradual investment into a learning infrastructure for peace operations began to bear fruit, even in an incipient state, those systems managed to spark a basic flow of reflection that can lead to full-fledged learning processes. In order to further scale this up and make it sustainable, the organization needs to address the uneven development of the different elements of the learning infrastructure and the different parts of the learning cycle.

The progress made since 2000 started from a very low baseline: as the Brahimi report pointed out, there were effectively no institutional support systems for learning in place at that time. As described in detail in Chapter 2, the reformers consciously prioritized the knowledge acquisition and guidance development parts of the learning cycle, both of which they addressed from the beginning with the knowledge sharing and guidance projects run by the Peacekeeping Best Practices Section. Fueled by the imagination and determination of only a handful of junior officials who had the backing of the department's leadership, both efforts were arguably more successful than a dispassionate analysis of the political and cultural obstacles in the first half of the decade would have suggested. Procedures are now in place to encourage informal, horizontal sharing of knowledge between peers across missions (through an online document repository, discussion boards, and face-to-face conferences) and more formal knowledge capture through individual and collaborative tools for reflection and reporting to inform guidance development as well as headquarters decision-making at large, supported by full-time Best Practices Officers in the field helping their colleagues to find guidance and facilitating contributions to the knowledge base. During our field research, we found that the face-to-face workshops in which junior managers (from a diverse set of organizations involved in peacekeeping) get a chance to discuss their experiences and provide feedback on guidance are particularly effective, not just in knowledge sharing but also in giving participants a stake in the institution of peacekeeping.

The Best Practices Section has also become an effective supporter to the drafting of guidance materials, and shepherds them through the approval process. In the early years after the Peace Operations 2010 agenda started, Best Practices officials drafted most of the guidance materials themselves. In part, that was for lack of capacity and attention in other units. From the beginning, the reformers sought to have the functional divisions build their own capacity. They knew their unit could not realistically expect to grow to the dozens of staff that would be required to develop all the necessary guidance all by themselves, nor would that be healthy for the goal of changing organizational culture: only by engaging each part of the organization and every manager in the learning effort could the entire staff develop a stake in the agenda.

Since 2008, member states have gradually been asked to make the required investments and fund individual posts for policy development in the various parts of the rule of law and military affairs offices. So far, progress in this regard remains insufficient to scale up the guidance development capacity to a level that would allow the organization to cover at least the more pressing operational challenges in a timely and sustainable way, including the need for periodic revision of doctrine. Complex and knowledge-intensive tasks such as police and justice development, in particular, as well as the core functions of political analysis (which is still treated as a skill staff members need to have acquired elsewhere, despite its central role for the organization) and information (read: intelligence) assessment need more than a single officer to sustain a doctrine development program at the required scale.

Overall member states should help the Best Practices Section to focus on its unique role as a driver and facilitator of learning. This also means that the responsibilities for cross-cutting issues that do not have a dedicated home in the bureaucracy should gradually be farmed out. Historically, for cross-cutting issues such as raising awareness for gender concerns for which no bureaucratic focal point existed within DPKO, Best Practices secured some funding, often temporary, for a specialist that was then based within the section. In the future, crosscutting human security challenges such as civilian protection and gender mainstreaming that are currently attached to Best Practices for lack of a dedicated home in the department should be split into a new unit which may be called the Human Security Section. Such a step would create more transparency in resource allocation between the infrastructure for learning itself and the policy expertise for key human security challenges.

Even if the guidance development capacity would reach the scale required, much larger gaps remain in the systems supporting the latter parts of the learning cycle, to institutionalize a formally adopted lesson into practice by effective training and accountability systems, and to systematically feed observations from that experience back into the next iteration of learning by means of evaluation. As the cases discussed in this book document, all three of these elements of the learning infrastructure are still deficient.

The first gap is the lack of functional training and professional education. Training suffers mainly from structural challenges beyond the power of the Secretariat to change. That begins with the recognition that few jobs in peace operations have a close equivalent in the kinds of backgrounds that applicants bring with them. A police officer from Canada is not professionally prepared to be an effective mentor and change agent for the Haitian National Police, nor is a Ghanaian business lawyer in charge of setting up a rural court in Timor-Leste. Since the UN bureaucracy is forced by its member states to almost exclusively rely on temporary secondments and short-term hires, it has negligible means to shape the functional education of its staff.

Any further progress toward professionalization will require a two-pronged approach: to draw a critical mass of civilian officials (and ultimately also police and military officers) into a genuine career in UN peace operations, and to dramatically scale up existing national and regional pools of pretrained personnel for UN deployments. By creating an actual field-based workforce, the UN can shape the professional education and training of at least a core part of its peace operations staff in the long term. In 2006 and 2008, Secretaries-General Annan and Ban proposed to invite a select best 25–30 percent of civilian staff into such a 'civilian core cadre' (UN Secretary-General 2006, 2007a). They were repeatedly and forcefully rebuffed by member states.[4]

For the sharply fluctuating number of additional staff, the training gap can only be filled by governments and regional organizations investing in their own pools for deployment with the UN or other providers of peace operations.

---

[4] Various human resources reforms were also torpedoed from within the bureaucracy itself. In a telling moment, when asked at a recruiting event about the progress of the Secretary-General's reform program in April 2009, Assistant-Secretary-General for Human Resources, Catherine Pollard, responded that the 'core cadre' proposal that her boss had just put before the membership was entirely unnecessary. Pollard was tasked with spearheading advocacy among member states for the initiative.

So far, too few governments have even begun to make such an investment. Even those that did, like Germany and more recently the United States, have yet to internationalize their programs in a way that would give not just their own citizens access to state-of-the-art training for peace operations, guided by UN-coordinated training standards. These tailored opportunities for continuing education will only have a systemic impact on the quality of peace operations if they are extended to UN officials from developing countries whose governments cannot afford to make that offer to their own citizens.[5] Doing so would not just enrich the learning experience with more diverse cultural perspectives but also contribute to the effectiveness and efficiency of the bureaucracy as a whole – long a key goal of Western countries' UN policies. DPKO has already laid the groundwork for such a network of national and regional training providers with the 2008 relaunch of its own training role as a standard setter for such institutions.

The second gap that limits the institutionalization of lessons is the lack of effective accountability mechanisms for how managers in the field choose to implement their mandate. Most UN officials, traditionalists and reformers alike, rightly insist that effective peacebuilding requires decentralizing authority for how to implement the mandate to the lowest possible level, where field officers are in the best position to know local conditions. Given the glaring lack of training and experience of many mission staff, there is a need for accountability mechanisms to hold officials to the principles of what the organization has learned and codified as doctrine without being unnecessarily constraining. In the historically German tradition of *Auftragstaktik*, many military forces found a way to walk this fine line rather effectively. Because low-level field commanders are usually better informed about local battlefield conditions than their superiors, they are given latitude to choose the most effective way of implementing their higher commander's intent. To make sure they keep within the boundaries of law and doctrine, the military relies on years of training, real-time assessments (often in the form of physical visits by higher commanders) and after-action reviews backed up by the incentives of a rigid career structure. Well used, these tools ensure that commanders carefully walk a middle ground between excessively sticking to 'the book' and wildly exceeding their orders. The UN should work toward a tailored application of this approach to the specific challenges of authority, command and control in peace operations. The creation of a permanent workforce as originally suggested by Kofi Annan in 2006 would replicate a similar incentive structure

---

[5] Many Western countries regularly invite a few military officers or even civilians from developing countries to their training programs or fund installations such as the Kofi Annan International Peacekeeping Training Centre in Accra, Ghana. The scale of these laudable efforts is far below the requirement, however.

with the right carrots and sticks to back up doctrine, real-time remedial interventions and after-action reviews.

The third and related infrastructure gap is the lack of systematic evaluation. In 2007, the budgetary committees denied DPKO the establishment of a five-person team to drive a systematic program of mission evaluations that would inform remedial interventions, guidance, and training development, cutting the Secretary-General's budget request down to two posts. Since then, DPKO has continued to undertake the kinds of assessment visits that have been common in peacekeeping for decades: checking on the political situation in field operations and the basic soundness of their management. Rarely are functional activities such as police development programs systematically evaluated, and never using the state of the art in program evaluation methods. With few exceptions such as the JMAC concept (see Chapter 7), the same is true for the systematic evaluation of official guidance, a task that will become more urgent as the first pieces of doctrine from 2005–6 become outdated and overdue for revision. This is the one glaring capacity gap where the infrastructure of learning will need additional resources to define a strategy and develop a methodology that translates the best of program evaluation to the specific context of peace operations, and to systematically apply this strategy along the twin tracks of evaluating missions and doctrine. Here DPKO can and should also learn from other parts of the UN system and other organizations that have more advanced evaluation systems in place. One further non-conventional evaluation mechanism would be for the UN bureaucracy, chiefly DPKO, to open guidance to public scrutiny. This can be a good way to ensure to make guidance fully operational, effective and accountable. Furthermore, the results of different types of evaluations need to systematically inform the planning of new missions at both the Secretariat and Security Council levels. Only then would the learning cycle be completed.

In addition to addressing these gaps, the UN also needs to improve in other parts of the learning equation where initial progress has been achieved over the past decade. One area is the sourcing of knowledge. Here, the UN apparatus needs to become more effective in tapping outside sources such as academia and think tanks, as well as to invest in its own knowledge generation if key aspects of its mandated activities find insufficient interest in the academic community or if research findings are insufficiently accessible. Even closer relations inside the UN system can help, since some agencies occasionally do make such investments in critical knowledge in the form of research projects or commissioned studies – knowledge that should be allowed to inform substantive debate rather than being used only as bureaucratic ammunition. The interagency development of UN standards for disarmament, demobilization, and reintegration programs is a case in point. While a laudable effort was made to develop policy and guidance jointly, the debate as well as its product were often too shallow. Rather than debating contentious issues and perhaps resolving them supported by further research, conflicts were papered over with empty compromises that made everyone happy except those in the field who looked to the document for guidance (Chapter 6). Still, the inter-agency process was an example of joint-up reflection and learning across organizational borders that unfortunately is still the exception rather than the rule in the UN system. For some, the Peacebuilding Commission and the Peacebuilding Support Office that UN member states created as a result of the 2005 World Summit were meant to facilitate system-wide learning. But so far such a broad-ranging goal seems elusive for both organizations in their current set-up.

At the same time, it is important to acknowledge the progress that has been achieved so far. The overall rather modest investments in the UN's learning infrastructure over the past decade have paid off. The progress made with regard to the infrastructure supporting guidance development demonstrates this. After persistent lobbying by DPKO and its allies, the membership supported these steps with a limited amount of investment in dedicated resources. A few governments such as those of Norway, Sweden, Canada, Britain, and Germany voluntarily provided complementary funds for studies, conferences, and consultant positions. Even at this modest level, their investment made a significant difference in allowing the reformers to set up the very structures and procedures that began to support guidance development in dozens of fields, including the capstone doctrine released in 2008. The nascent cultural opening toward learning, reflection, and constructive self-criticism could hardly have been achieved without the clear signal from member states that they supported such a shift.

Continued and increased member state support for investments to close the training, accountability, and evaluation gaps and scale up support for knowledge acquisition and guidance development is critical, particularly as long as 'the average peacekeeper serves for less than two years, and the turnover and loss of institutional knowledge brings its own uncertainty' (Le Roy 2009: 15). It is an investment with guaranteed returns. This is even more critical, as many original members of the reform cohort at headquarters have since moved on. The reformers managed to spark the first steps of a self-transformation toward a learning organization with comparatively few resources because they put in the extra effort that a pioneering spirit brings with it. This pioneering spirit, however, wears off over time, and as the original drivers of this agenda move on to new tasks, sufficient resources are required to maintain the existing infrastructure and develop it further to take its proper place as a core part of the peace operations bureaucracy.

Without these additional resources, the nascent cultural transformation toward learning will not advance. Progress critically depends on the resources invested – both material and immaterial in terms of time and attention on the part of top officials as well as key member states. If the power of persuasion and the power of incentives align, the cultural shift will advance further. Persuasion critically depends on the attention invested by the leadership both at headquarters and on the ground as well as the demonstration effects through trainings, career incentives, staff development opportunities, and in critical situations in the field, when it becomes clear that through policies and guidance officials are able to address problems more effectively and efficiently. As long as that cultural change remains being undermined by senior field managers using their best practice officers as surplus staff to fill in for whatever position the weaknesses of UN recruitment leaves vacant, the organization has a long way to go.

The weakest link among these elements of the infrastructure is the incentive structure for individuals to invest in the organization and particularly its learning activities. Only if staff members identify with the organization, get rewarded and see a medium-term future, do they go the extra mile of contributing actively to the shared knowledge base of the organization. Right now, the UN apparatus does not have effective systems in place to recruit, develop and retain the best possible pool of civilian professionals for peace operations. This is to a large part due to member states not giving the bureaucracy the necessary tools. To a significant degree, however, it is also the story of bureaucracy not able to use existing leeway to move its personnel policy closer to the needs of the twenty-first century. Giving more people an opportunity to identify with the organization would also broaden the pool of future leaders that the lack of medium-term careers has made dangerously small at a time when it desperately needs 'outstanding personnel within the organization with the requisite experience, competence, stature and charisma to manage the UN's presence in situations where thousands if not millions of lives and livelihoods are at stake' (Hood 2004).

Research Agenda

Within the growing field of research on peacebuilding and international bureaucracies, our study represents a first cut at studying processes of organizational learning. As detailed above, based on a multidisciplinary framework and a dozen case studies we were able to draw preliminary conclusions on the factors influencing learning processes and the organization's learning capacity. We combined an analytical–explanatory focus with prescriptive and policy-oriented concerns of institutional development.

Further research is needed that is both more detailed and broader in scope:

- *Zooming in*: In order to get a more fine-grained understanding of the dynamics of learning we need studies that provide an even more detailed analysis of learning processes in particular units, both in the field and at headquarters. Ethnographic or sociological frameworks building on theories of practice present interesting methods for conducting this kind of micro-level analysis (see, e.g., Büger 2010). A particular focus of future studies should be the sources and politics of knowledge. More than a decade ago, in one of the first articles on the subject, Thant Myint-U and Elisabeth Sellwood, two former officials in UN peace operations, rightly stressed the need to ask a basic question: 'How did the UN "know" what it believed it "knew" about the countries in which it intervened, and how did this matter?' (Myint-U and Sellwood 1999: 1). A related question is that of the 'blind spots' in the perception of situations on the ground. In a ground-breaking study, Séverine Autesserre detailed why the peace operations community by and large chose to overlook the local dimensions of conflict and violence in parts of the Congo (Autesserre 2010). Michael Barnett points to the larger question at hand: 'The problem is more than the standard concern that outsiders do not know the lay of the land, that is, the local culture, language, networks, cleavages, and so on (though this is a concern). Instead, is that their already existing categories and models of the world will determine what knowledge is relevant and thus lead them to ignore essential information' (Barnett 2005: 5). To get to the heart of these questions presupposes the kind of long-term 'embedded' research in both the field and at headquarters that social scientists (especially in international relations) find hard to reconcile with their careers.[6] Another important concern relates to a study of training mechanisms. Do training programs simply convey standard operating procedures or do they sensitize officials to the needs for contextualization and adaptation of guidance and lessons to the particular conditions at hand? What effect does this have on officials?

Another little understood dimension is accountability and evaluation. As Kate Weaver argues, 'despite a rich body of work on organizational evaluation in sociological theory, public administration and business management, there is simply a dearth of knowledge in international relations scholarship regarding the role of evaluation in bigger questions regarding IO learning and change' (Weaver 2010). What kinds of evaluation mechanisms are best suited

---

[6] Autesserre's book is one example for this kind of detailed field research. Michael Barnett's book on the UN and Rwanda (based on his year working and researching at the US mission to the UN) is another example (Barnett 2002).

to supporting learning? Or does evaluation (especially if it includes transparency mechanisms) lead to a culture of fear and passivity?[7]

Research should also illuminate the politics of reform with regard to efforts to build learning organizations in peace operations – both within the bureaucracy and in terms of relations between the bureaucracy and its principals. For one, this means taking a closer look at leadership. The cases in this book (in line with the cursory evidence put forward by other researcher and practitioners alike) clearly demonstrate the importance of leadership at various levels. Yet, research has thus far shied away from taking a systematic look at the role of what IR theorists call the 'first image': the role of individuals. For another, research on the politics of reform should also analyze the workings of 'winning coalitions' composed of officials in the bureaucracy and member state representatives that according to our case studies play a major role in promoting institutional reform and learning.

- *Zooming out*: Research should also focus on comparative questions beyond the analysis of single organizations. In terms of 'learning to learn' (Haas/Haas 1995), this includes comparisons within the UN system (DPKO, UNDP, the Peacebuilding Commission/Peacebuilding Support Office, Department of Political Affairs, etc.), with other players outside the system (the international financial institutions, NATO, regional organizations such as the EU, the OSCE, as well as governments and bilateral players) as well as with nonprofit organizations. Further research should also undertake comparisons between learning with regard to different issue areas, for example, compare peace operations with a contested state of knowledge with questions where there is a clearer consensus in epistemic communities (which is the case with a number of environmental issues).

We hope that scholars from international relations, public administration, and organization studies push forward the research agenda on learning in international bureaucracies in a multidisciplinary fashion.

Outlook: Learning and the Limits of Peace Operations

The new learning infrastructure has already helped the peace operations bureaucracy to reflect on the challenges of coping with rapid growth, finding ways to confront a changing operational environment and developing the capacity required to build an institutional foundation for sustainable peace in

---

[7] We thank Michael Barnett for alerting us to this point.

the countries to which it deploys. UN Secretary-General Ban argued in early 2011 that the UN's success in meeting ambitious institution-building goals 'depends on whether we can deploy the right expertise and resources at the right time, how well we work with our national and international partners, and whether we actually apply the lessons we have learned.'[8] The UN apparatus has increasingly learned to stop camouflaging ambitious goals of institution-building in the police and justice sectors or in reintegration as 'technical' tasks. The UN more and more acknowledges the inherently political nature of the challenges in the case studies of the book. Yet, this has been a slow process – not just within the different parts of the bureaucracy but also among member states. Both have yet to confront the many dilemmas and contradictions of peacebuilding head on(Sisk/Paris 2009). It is safe to say that these dilemmas and contradictions have continued to outpace the newly created capacity of the UN to meet them – and despite several rounds of budget increases, this capacity remains a drop in the bucket compared to the military doctrine, training, and evaluation establishments or the policy-planning staffs and diplomatic academies of a foreign ministry in any country that deploys even a fraction of the UN's 130,000 people globally.[9] During the decade of expansion of peace operations from 2000 to 2010, meeting that growth had 'entailed redirecting efforts that would have otherwise been dedicated to strategic management, regular evaluation and review, building a risk management and doctrinal framework of policies, procedures, and training and other forms of guidance and preparing qualified, trained staff in all areas' (UN Secretary-General 2007b: 5).

What, then, does it mean that after a decade of expansion, as Alain Le Roy said in 2010 before the General Assembly, 'UN peacekeeping may now be headed toward a period of consolidation and perhaps even contraction'? The fact that for the first time in a long time the number of peacekeepers is going down should not be a pretext for mindlessly cutting resources across the board. Rather, the governments that are interested in improving effectiveness, efficiency, and professionalization at the UN should recognize this moment as

---

[8] http://www.un.org/News/Press/docs//2011/sgsm13358.doc.htm

[9] Despite the recent growth in the size of DPKO and DFS, however, the peace operations bureaucracy remains an exceptionally and, in many ways, dangerously lean organization at the headquarters level. While there are no perfectly comparable benchmarks available, a look at the second biggest player in the peace operations realm is instructive. With a ratio of headquarters staff to field personnel of nearly 1:100, every peacekeeping official supports about four or five times as many colleagues in the field as their NATO colleagues, with a ratio of about 1:18 in 2009 that has since slightly decreased with the deployment of a larger US contingent to ISAF in Afghanistan (NYU-CIC 2009: 2). While the NATO bureaucracy is widely regarded as bloated, even DPKO-led missions alone (without their humanitarian and development partners) cover a much wider range of tasks, particularly in the political and governance realms, and draw their troops from poorer countries that are able to provide much less by way of national support on training, equipment, and logistics than NATO members do.

an opportunity for consolidating reform efforts while strengthening the learning infrastructure. In particular, a time of decreasing deployment figures, if used wisely, would allow for better evaluation to be enforced and an overall policy review of what works and what does not to be conducted with regard to the major challenges of peace operations.

Such a review may well conclude that meeting the most daunting challenges, such as protecting civilians amid violence and building sustainable institutions where there are few local elites ready to assume 'responsible ownership,' in a way that brings battered societies closer to the bold ideals of peace, security and good governance laid out in Security Council mandates is beyond the capacity of the instrument of peace operations and the time frames as we know them now. The recent debate on moving from the goals of 'good governance' to 'good enough governance' (Grindle 2007) indicates the need to re-think means, ends, priorities and time frames. An improved learning capacity can inform these discussions and would also help to determine the limits of peace operations. In terms of expectations, for some peace operations have already become the victim of their relative success in what Richard Gowan calls the 'tragedy of peacekeeping:' 'while the UN has significantly improved the way it does business, this has raised false expectations about what its operations can achieve. Meanwhile, peacekeepers juggle bad options and make poisonous choices. Looking ahead, UN officials, Security Council diplomats and outside analysts have a shared responsibility to recognize the tragic, ambiguous and plain ugly realities of peacekeeping' (Gowan 2010). There is a growing chorus of analysts who conclude that 'despite a number of achievements, these stabs at state building by foreigners will not be foundational or transformative in any *intended* sense. In fact, they may turn out to be curiously transient moments in the history of the societies subjected to them.' (Mayall/Soares de Oliveira 2011). James Mayall and Ricardo Soares de Oliveira argue that future historians will likely look back at the ambitious institution-building agenda of the past two decades as 'minor utopias' (Jay Winter) – 'the often forgotten, decent and optimistic dreams of human improvement.' (Mayall/Soares de Oliveira 2011).

At the same time, in the world of here and now for millions of civilians in conflicts around the world UN peace operations remain the major hope for progress toward a more secure life. In light of these hopes and with a clear view to the UN's imperfections, it is therefore important to struggle to 'retain a space for genuinely emancipatory action in an otherwise deeply flawed and tragic world' (Barnett 2010: 210). Peace operations, if done in a responsible way with a level-headed view to their potential and limits, have this emancipatory potential. Investing in the learning capacity and thereby cultivating the 'spirit of epistemological uncertainty' that Michael Barnett has called for will help make us the most out of this potential while more clearly realizing the limits.

References

Ahmed, Salman, Paul Keating and Ugo Solinas (2007) 'Shaping the Future of UN Peace Operations: Is there a Doctrine in the House?'. *Cambridge Review of International Affairs* 20:1, 11–28.

Allison, Graham T. and Morton H. Halperin (1972) 'Bureaucratic Politics: A Paradigm and Some Policy Implications'. *World Politics* 24:Supplement, 40–79.

A Need for Protection, a Thirst for Justice. London, AI Document AFR 62/032/2003.

Anderson, James H., David S. Bernstein and Cheryl W. Gray (2005) *Judicial Systems in Transition Economies: Assessing the Past, Looking to the Future*. Washington, DC: The World Bank.

Annan, Kofi (1997*a*) 'The Two Sovereignties'. *The Economist*, September 18, 1999.

—— (1997*b*) *Renewing the United Nations. A Programme for Reform. Report of the Secretary-General*. UN Document A/51/950.

Ansell, Christopher K. and Steven Weber (1999) 'Organizing International Politics: Sovereignty and Open Systems'. *International Political Science Review* 20:1, 73–93.

Argyris, Chris (1986) 'Reinforcing Organizational Defense Routines: An Unintended Human Resources Activity'. *Human Resource Management* 25:4, 541–55.

—— Donald A. Schön (1978) *Organizational Learning: A Theory of Action Perspective*. Reading, MA: Addison-Wesley.

Associated Press (2007*a*) 'Investigation Finds Romanian Officers Responsible for Deaths in Kosovo Riots'. *International Herald Tribune*, April 17.

—— (2007*b*) 'U.N. Suspends Use of Rubber Bullets in Peacekeeping Missions'. *International Herald Tribune*, July 12.

Autesserre, Séverine (2010) *The Trouble with the Congo: Local Violence and the Failure of International Peacebuilding*. Cambridge: Cambridge University Press.

Ball, Nicole (2006) *DDR. Mapping Issues, Dilemmas and Guiding Principles*. The Hague: Netherlands Institute of International Relations.

—— Dylan Hendrickson (2005*a*) 'Review of International Financing Arrangements for Disarmament, Demobilization and Reintegration'. *Phase 1 Report to Working Group 2 of the Stockholm Initiative on Disarmament, Demobilization and Reintegration (SIDDR)*, May 16.

—— —— (2005*b*) 'Review of International Financing Arrangements for Disarmament, Demobilization and Reintegration'. *Phase 2 Report to Working Group 2 of the Stockholm Initiative on Disarmament, Demobilization and Reintegration (SIDDR)*, September 26.

Barnett, Michael (2002) *Eyewitness to a Genocide: The United Nations and Rwanda*. Ithaca, NY: Cornell University Press.

Barnett, Michael (2010) The International Humanitarian Order. New York: Routledge.

Barnett, Michael (2011) 'Humanitarianism, Paternalism, and the UNHCR'. In Alexander Betts and Gil Loescher (eds.), *Refugees in International Relations*. Oxford: Oxford University Press, 105–132.

—— (2005) 'Illiberal Peacebuilding and Liberal States'. Paper presented on February 8 at the Roundtable on Humanitarian Action, Social Science Research Council.

—— (2006) 'Building a Republican Peace: Stabilizing States after War'. *International Security* 30:4, 87–112.

—— Martha Finnemore (1999) 'The Politics, Power, and Pathologies of International Organizations'. *International Organization* 53:4, 699–732.

—— —— (2004) *Rules for the World: International Organizations in Global Politics*. Ithaca, NY: Cornell University Press.

—— Hunjoon Kim, Madalene O'Donnell, and Laura Sitea (2007) 'Peacebuilding: What Is in a Name?'. *Global Governance* 13:1, 35–58.

Barré, Anton (2004) 'An Analysis of Transitional economic Reintegration'. *Swedish Initiative for Disarmament, Demobilization and Reintegration (SIDDR)*, Working Group 3, input paper.

Benner, Thorsten and Philipp Rotmann (2008) 'Learning to Learn? UN Peacebuilding and the Challenges of Building a Learning Organization'. *Journal of Intervention and Statebuilding* 2:1, 43–62.

—— Andrea Binder, and Philipp Rotmann (2007) *Learning to Build Peace? United Nations Peacebuilding and Organizational Learning: Developing a Research Framework*. Forschung DSF Nr. 9. Osnabrück: Deutsche Stiftung Friedensforschung.

—— Stephan Mergenthaler, and Philipp Rotmann (2008) 'Doctrine Development in the UN Peacebuilding Apparatus: The Case of UN Constabulary Police, 1999–2006'. Paper presented on March 29 at the International Studies Association Annual Convention, San Francisco.

—— —— —— (2009) 'Internationale Bürokratien und Organisationslernen: Konturen einer Forschungsagenda'. *Zeitschrift für Internationale Beziehungen* 16:1, 203–36.

Berdal, Mats (2001) 'United Nations Peace Operations: The Brahimi Report in Context'. In Kurt R. Spillmann, Thomas Bernauer, Jürg M. Gabriel, and Andreas Wenger (eds.), *Peace Support Operations: Lessons Learned and Future Perspectives*. Bern: Peter Lang, 35–53.

—— (2009) Building Peace after War. London: International Institute for Strategic Studies.

Berman, Eric and Melissa Labonte (2006) 'Sierra Leone'. In William J. Durch (ed.), *Twenty-First Century Peace Operations*. Washington, DC: United States Institute for Peace and Henry L. Stimson Center, 141–228.

Biermann, Frank and Bernd Siebenhüner (eds.) (2009a) *Managers of Global Change. The Influence of International Environmental Bureaucracies*. Cambridge, MA: MIT Press.

—— —— (2009b) 'The Role and Relevance of International Bureaucracies'. In Frank Biermann and Bernd Siebenhüner (eds.), *Managers of Global Change. The Influence of International Environmental Bureaucracies*. Cambridge MA: MIT Press, 1–14.

Blume, Till (2004) Analyzing Organizational Change and Adaptation of Civilian Police Components in UN Peace Operations. M.A. thesis, submitted to the Fachbereich Politik- und Verwaltungswissenschaft. Konstanz: Universität Konstanz.

—— (2007) 'Security and Justice Institutions in Liberia. From State Collapse Towards Institutions? Research Note'. Paper presented on May 16 at the Research Seminar of the Crisis States Research Centre, Development Studies Institute, London School of Economics and Political Science.

—— (2008) 'Implementing the Rule of Law in Integrated Missions: Security and Justice in the UN Mission in Liberia'. *Journal of Security Sector Management* 6:3, 1–18.

Body, Tom (2005) *Reintegration of Ex-Combatants through Micro-Enterprise: An Operational Framework*. Toronto: Canadian Peacekeeping Press.

Böhling, Kathrin (2005) 'Boundary Spanning Activities, Organizing Processes, and Learning'. Paper presented on June 30–July 2 at the 21. EGOS Colloquium, Berlin.

—— (2007) *Opening up the Black Box: Organizational Learning in the European Commission*. Frankfurt am Main: Peter Lang.

Bouta, Tsjeard (2005) *Gender and Disarmament, Demobilization and Reintegration*. Amsterdam: Netherlands Institute of International Relations 'Clingendael'. March.

—— Georg Frerks and Ian Bannon (2005) *Gender, Conflict and Development*. Washington, DC: World Bank Publications.

Boutros-Ghali, Boutros (1992) *An Agenda for Peace. Preventive Diplomacy, Peacemaking and Peacekeeping*. Report of the Secretary-General Pursuant to the Statement Adopted by the Summit Meeting of the Security Council on January 31. UN Document A/47/277-S/24111.

—— (1995) *Supplement to an Agenda for Peace: Position Paper of the Secretary-General on the Occasion of the Fiftieth Anniversary of the United Nations*. UN Document A/50/60-S/1995/1.

Brahimi, Lakhdar (2010) *Contribution to the General Assembly Debate on Peace Keeping*. Speech. New York: United Nations (retrieved August 28, 2010 from http://www.un.org/ga/president/64/thematic/peace/Brahimi.pdf).

Breslauer, George W. and Philip E. Tetlock (1991) *Learning in U.S. and Soviet Foreign Policy*. Boulder, CO: Westview Press.

Breul, Rainer (2005) 'Organizational Learning in International Organizations. The Case of UN Peace Operations'. M.A. thesis submitted to the Fachbereich Politik- und Verwaltungswissenschaft.

Büger, Christian (2010) 'The New Spirit of Technocracy? Ordering Practices in United Nations Peacebuilding'. Ph.D. thesis, submitted to the Department of Political and Social Sciences. Florence: European University Institute.

Bull, Carolyn (2008) *No Entry Without Strategy: Building the Rule of Law under UN Transitional Administration*. New York: United Nations University Press.

Call, Charles T. (2007) 'Conclusion: Constructing Justice and Security After War'. In Charles T. Call (ed.), *Constructing Justice and Security After War*. Washington, DC: United States Institute of Peace, 375–409.

—— Elizabeth M. Cousens (2008) 'Ending Wars and Building Peace: International Responses to War-Torn Societies'. *International Studies Perspectives* 9:1, 1–21.

Cammaert, Patrick (2003) 'Conceptual, Organizational and Operational Issues Facing the United Nations in Providing Strategic Information and Peacekeeping Intelligence for its Peace Support Operations'. Paper presented on December 4–5 at the 2nd Annual Peacekeeping Intelligence Conference, Ottawa.

Campbell, Susanna P. (2007) 'Multidimensional and Integrated Peace Operations: Trends and Challenges'. Paper presented on April 26 at the Addis Ababa, Ethiopia.

—— (2008) '(Dis)integration, Incoherence and Complexity in UN Post-conflict Interventions'. *International Peacekeeping* 15:4, 556–69.

—— Anja T. Kaspersen (2008) 'The UN's Reforms: Confronting Integration Barriers'. *International Peacekeeping* 15:4, 470–85.

Caplan, Richard (2005) *International Governance of War-Torn Territories: Rule and Reconstruction*. Oxford: Oxford University Press.

Carlson, Scott N. (2006) *Legal and Judicial Rule of Law Work in Multidimensional Peace Operations: Lessons-Learned Study*. New York: UN Department of Peacekeeping Operations.

Carothers, Thomas (2003) *Promoting the Rule of Law Abroad: The Problem of Knowledge*. Washington, DC: Carnegie Endowment for International Peace.

—— (ed.) (2006) *Promoting the Rule of Law Abroad: In Search of Knowledge*. Washington, DC: Carnegie Endowment for International Peace.

Challenges Project (2006) *Concluding Report II: Coordination and Cooperation*. Stockholm: Folke Bernadotte Academy and The Challenges Project.

Chesterman, Simon (2004) *You, the People: The United Nations, Transitional Administration, and State-Building*. Oxford: Oxford University Press.

—— (2006) 'Does the UN Have Intelligence?'. *Survival* 48:3, 149–64.

Chopra, Jarat (1995) 'Facing the Truth at the U.N.'. *George Street Journal*, September 29.

COESPU (2005) 'Future Roles for Stability Police Units'. Proceedings of the Future Roles for Stability Police Units Conference, April 4–5, Washington, DC, Vicenza: Center of Excellence for Stability Police Units.

Cohen, Michael D. and Lee S. Sproull (eds.) (1991) *Organizational Learning. Special Issue of Organization Science*. London: Sage Publications.

Colletta, Nat J. and Robert Muggah (2009) 'Context Matters: Interim Stabilisation and Second Generation Approaches to Security Promotion'. *Conflict, Security & Development* 9:4, 425–53.

Cook, J. A., D. Staniforth, and J. Stewart (eds.) (1997) *The Learning Organization in the Public Services*. Brookfield, VT: Gower.

Crawley, Mike (2004) 'Fewer Guns, but Tensions Persist in Liberia'. *Christian Science Monitor*, October 28.

Crossan, Mary, Henry W. Lane and Roderick E. White (1999) 'An Organizational Learning Framework: From Intuition to Institution'. *Academy of Management Review* 24:3, 522–37.

Crozier, Michel (1964) *The Bureaucratic Phenomenon*. Chicago, IL: University of Chicago Press.

Crucini, Cristina (2002) 'Knowledge Management at the Country Level: A Large Consulting Firm in Italy'. In Lars Engwall and Matthias Kipping (eds.), *Management Consulting: Emergence and Dynamics of a Knowledge Industry*. Oxford: Oxford University Press, 109–28.

Dahrendorf, Nicola (2003) *A Review of Peace Operations: A Case for Change. Synthesis Report*. London: Conflict, Security and Development Group, King's College London.

229

—— Mark Dalton, Jose Luis Herrero, Tim Judah, Serge Rumin, and Mark Thompson (2003) *A Review of Peace Operations: A Case for Change. Kosovo Report.* London: Conflict, Security and Development Group, King's College London.

—— Anthony Goldstone, Alexander Mayer-Rieckh, Arezou Azad, Tanja Hohe, Antonia Potter, Caitlin Reiger, Edward Rees, and Craig Wilson (2003) *A Review of Peace Operations: A Case for Change. East Timor Report.* London: Conflict, Security and Development Group, King's College London.

Dekker, Sander and Dan Hansén (2004) 'Learning under Pressure: The Effects of Politicization on Organizational Learning in Public Bureaucracies'. *Journal of Public Administration Research and Theory* 14:2, 211–30.

Detzel, Julian (2008) 'Organizational Learning in International Bureaucracies: The Case of UN Peace Operations and the Development of the Concept "Integrated Missions"'. M.A. thesis, submitted to the Department for Politics and Public Management, University of Konstanz, Konstanz.

Dierkes, Meinolf, Ariane Berthoin Antal, John Child, and Ikujiro Nonaka (eds.) (2001) *Handbook of Organizational Learning and Knowledge.* Oxford: Oxford University Press.

Dodgson, Mark (1993) 'Organizational Learning: A Review of Some Literatures'. *Organization Studies* 14:3, 375–94.

Dorn, A. Walter (1999) 'The Cloak and the Blue Beret: Limitations on Intelligence in UN Peacekeeping'. *International Journal of Intelligence and Counterintelligence* 12:4, 414–47.

—— (2009) 'Intelligence-led Peacekeeping: The United Nations Stabilization Mission in Haiti (MINUSTAH), 2006–07'. *Intelligence and National Security* 24:6, 805–35.

—— David J. H. Bell (1995) 'Intelligence and Peacekeeping: The UN Operation in the Congo, 1960–64'. *International Peacekeeping* 2:1, 11–33.

Doss, Alan (2003) *Squaring the Circle – Can Coherence Work?* Freetown, Sierra Leone.

Durch, William J. (2004) *Building a Better Peace Operation: Lessons from the Brahimi Report Process.* Expert Policy Brief to the Secretary-General's High Level Panel on Threats, Challenges and Change. New York: United Nations Foundation.

—— (2010) 'United Nations Police Evolution, Present Capacity and Future Tasks'. Paper presented on January 27–28 at the GRIPS State-Building Workshop 2010. Tokyo: Organizing Police Forces in Post-Conflict Peace-Support Operations.

—— Victoria K. Holt, Caroline R. Earle and Moira K. Shanahan (2003) *The Brahimi Report and the Future of U.N. Peace Operations.* Washington, DC: The Henry L. Stimson Center.

Dwan, Renata (ed.) (2002) *Executive Policing: Enforcing the Law in Peace Operations.* Oxford: Oxford University Press.

Dziedzic, Michael J. (1998) *Introduction.* In Robert Oakley, Michael J. Dziedzic, and Eliot M. Goldberg (eds.), *Policing the New World Disorder: Peace Operations and Public Security.* Washington, DC: National Defense University, 3–18.

Easterby-Smith, Mark and Marjorie A. Lyles (eds.) (2005) *The Blackwell Handbook of Organizational Learning and Knowledge Management.* Oxford: Blackwell.

Eide, Espen B., Anja T. Kaspersen, Randolph Kent, and Karin von Hippel (2005) *Report on Integrated Missions. Independent Study for the Expanded UN ECHA Core Group.* Oslo, London: Norwegian Institute of International Affairs and King's College.

Engwall, Lars and Matthias Kipping (2002) 'Introduction: Management Consulting as a Knowledge Industry'. In Lars Engwall and Matthias Kipping (eds.), *Management Consulting: Emergence and Dynamics of a Knowledge Industry*. Oxford: Oxford University Press, 1–16.

Farrall, Jeremy (2007) 'United Nations Peacekeeping and the Rule of Law'. *Australian National University Centre for International Governance and Justice*, Issues Paper 1.

Farr, Vanessa (2002) 'Gendering Demilitarization as a Peacebuilding Tool'. *Paper 20*, Bonn International Center for Conversion.

Fortna, Virginia Page and Lise Morjé Howard (2008) 'Pitfalls and Prospects in the Peacekeeping Literature'. *Annual Review of Political Science* 11, 283–301.

Giddens, Anthony (1984) *The Constitution of Society: Outline of a Theory of Structuration*. Berkeley, CA: University of California Press.

Golub, Stephen (2003) 'Beyond Rule of Law Orthodoxy: The Legal Empowerment Alternative'. Carnegie Paper 41.

Goulding, Marrack (2002) *Peacemonger*. London: John Murray.

Gowan, Richard (2008) 'The Strategic Context: Peacekeeping in Crisis, 2006–08'. *International Peacekeeping* 15:4, 453–69.

—— (2010) 'The Tragedy of 21st Century U.N. Peacekeeping'. *World Politics Review*.

Graydon, Carolyn (2005) 'Local Justice Systems in Timor-Leste: Washed Up, or Watch This Space?'. *Development Bulletin* 68, 66–70.

Guéhenno, Jean-Marie (2004) *Remarks by Mr Jean-Marie Guéhenno, Under-Secretary-General for Peacekeeping Operations, to the Fourth Committee of the General Assembly, 24 October 2004*. New York: UN Department of Peacekeeping Operations.

Guéhenno, Jean-Marie (2009) 'Foreword'. In: Robert Muggah (ed.) *Security and Post-conflict Reconstruction: Dealing with Fighters in the Aftermath of War*. New York: Routledge, xvi–xvii[TBI].

—— (2005a) *Interoffice Memorandum by Mr Jean-Marie Guéhenno, Under-Secretary-General for Peacekeeping Operations, to all DPKO Headquarters and Mission Staff, Dated 30 November 2005*. New York: UN Department of Peacekeeping Operations.

—— (2005b) *Remarks of Mr Jean-Marie Guéhenno, Under-Secretary-General for Peacekeeping Operations, to the Fourth Committee of the General Assembly*. New York: UN Department of Peacekeeping Operations.

Grindle, Merilee S. (2007) 'Good Enough Governance Revisited', Development Policy Review 25 (5), 553–574.

Haas, Ernst B. (1990) *When Knowledge is Power: Three Models of Change in International Organizations*. Berkeley, CA: University of California Press.

Haas, Peter M. and Ernst B. Haas (1995) 'Learning to Learn: Improving International Governance'. *Global Governance* 1:3, 255–84.

Halperin, Morton H. and Priscilla Clapp (2006) *Bureaucratic Politics and Foreign Policy*. Washington, DC: Brookings Institution.

Hansen, Annika S. (2002) *From Congo to Kosovo: Civilian Police in Peace Operations*. Adelphi Paper 343. London: Oxford University Press.

Hartmann, Michael E. (2003) 'International Judges and Prosecutors in Kosovo: A New Model for Post-Conflict Peacekeeping'. Special Report 112, United States Institute of Peace.

Hermann, Charles F. (1963) 'Some Consequences of Crisis Which Limit the Viability of Organizations'. *Administrative Science Quarterly* 8:1, 61–82.

Herrhausen, Anna (2009) *Organizing Peacebuilding: An Investigation of Interorganizational Coordination in International Post-Conflict Reconstruction Efforts*. Frankfurt: Peter Lang.

Hill, Richard, Gwendolyn Taylor and Jonathan Temin (2008) 'Would You Fight Again? Understanding Liberian Ex-Combatant Reintegration'. Special Report 211, United States Institute of Peace.

Hills, Alice (1998) 'International Peace Support Operations and CIVPOL: Should there be a Permanent Gendarmerie?'. *International Peacekeeping* 5:3, 35.

—— (2001) 'The Inherent Limits of Military Forces in Policing Peace Operations'. *International Peacekeeping* 8:3, 79–98.

Hochschild, Fabrizio (2004) 'It is Better to Leave, We Can't Protect You': Flight in the First Months of United Nations Transitional Administration in Kosovo and East Timor'. *Journal of Refugee Studies* 17:3, 286–300.

Hood, Ludovic (2004) 'The UN must Let Talent Rise: Remembering de Mello'. *International Herald Tribune* August 13, 6.

—— (2006) 'Security Sector Reform in East Timor, 1999–2004'. *International Peacekeeping* 13:1, 60–77.

Howard, Lise Morjé (2008) *UN Peacekeeping in Civil Wars*. Cambridge: Cambridge University Press.

—— (2009) 'Organizational Learning: Managing Knowledge'. In Caty Clement and Adam C. Smith (eds.), *Managing Complexity: Political and Managerial Challenges in United Nations Peace Operations*. New York: International Peace Institute, 32–5.

Huber, George P. (1991) 'Organizational Learning: The Contributing Processes and the Literatures'. *Organization Science* 2:1, 88–115.

Hurwitz, Agnès (2008) 'Conclusion: The Rule of Law and Peacebuilding Processes'. In Agnès Hurwitz and Reyko Huang (eds.), *Civil War and the Rule of Law*. Boulder, CO: Lynne Rienner.

—— Kaysie Studdard (2005) *Rule of Law Programs in Peace Operations*. Policy Paper. New York: International Peace Academy.

ICG (2003) *Tackling Liberia: The Eye of the Regional Storm*. Freetown/Brussels: International Crisis Group.

—— (2004) *Pulling Back from the Brink in Congo*. Kinshasa/Nairobi, Brussels: International Crisis Group.

—— (2006) *Liberia: Resurrecting the Justice System*. Liberia/Brussels: International Crisis Group.

—— (2006) *Resolving Timor-Leste's Crisis*. Jakarta/Brussels: International Crisis Group.

ICG (2007) *Haiti: Justice Reform and the Security Crisis*. Port-au-Prince/Brussels: International Crisis Group.

Janowitz, Morris (1959) *Sociology and the Military Establishment*. New York: Russell Sage Foundation.

Jennings, Kathleen M. (2007) 'The Struggle to Satisfy: DDR Through the Eyes of Ex-combatants in Liberia'. *International Peacekeeping* 14:2, 204–18.

—— (2008a) *Seeing DDR from Below. Challenges and Dilemmas Raised by the Experiences of Ex-combatants in Liberia*. New Security Programme.

—— (2008b) 'Unclear Ends, Unclear Means: Reintegration in Postwar Societies – The Case of Liberia'. *Global Governance* 14, 327–45.

—— (2009) 'The Political Economy of DDR in Liberia: A Gendered Critique'. *Conflict, Security & Development* 9:4, 475–94.

Jensen, Erik G. (2008) 'Justice and the Rule of Law'. In Charles T. Call and Vanessa Wyeth (eds.), *Building States to Build Peace*. Boulder, CO, London: Lynne Rienner.

Jones, Bruce D. (2001) 'Challenges of Strategic Coordination: Containing Opposition and Sustaining Implementation of Peace Agreements in Civil Wars'. IPA Policy Paper Series on Peace Implementation. New York: International Peace Academy.

—— (2007) *Rwanda*. In Mats Berdal and Spyros Economides (eds.), *United Nations Interventionism, 1991–2004*. Cambridge: Cambridge University Press, 139–67.

King, Iain and Whit Mason (2006) *Peace At Any Price: How the World Failed Kosovo. Crises in World Politics*. London: Hurst.

Kingma, Kees and Robert Muggah (2009) 'Critical Issues in DDR: Context, Indicators, Targeting, and Challenges'. *Congreso Internacional de Desarme Desmovilizacion y Reintegracion*.

Kraja, Garentina (2007) 'Kosovo Police Chief Fired Over Clashes'. *International Herald Tribune*, February 14.

Kühne, Winrich (1999) 'Peace Support Operations: How to Make them Succeed?'. *Internationale Politik und Gesellschaft* 1999:4, 358–67.

LaPalombara, Joseph (2001) 'The Underappreciated Contributions of Political Science to Organizational Learning'. In M. Dierkes, A. Berthoin Antal, J. Child, and I. Nonaka (eds.), *Handbook of Organizational Learning and Knowledge*. Oxford: Oxford University Press, 137–61.

Le Roy, Alain (2009) 'Keynote address: Managing 'Complexity''. In Caty Clement and Adam C. Smith (eds.), *Managing Complexity: Political and Managerial Challenges in United Nations Peace Operations*. New York: International Peace Institute, 14–18.

—— (2009) *Statement by Under-Secretary-General for Peacekeeping Operations, Mr. Alain Le Roy, to the Fourth Committee*. October 23.

Levy, Jack S. (1994) 'Learning and Foreign Policy: Sweeping a Conceptual Minefield'. *International Organization* 48:2, 279–312.

Lewis, William, Edward Marks and Robert Perito (2002) *Enhancing International Civilian Police Operations*. Washington, DC: US Institute for Peace.

Lipshitz, Raanan, Micha Popper, and Victor J. Friedman (2002) 'A Multifacet Model of Organizational Learning'. *Journal of Applied Behavioral Science* 38:1.

Lipson, Michael (2007) 'A "Garbage Can Model" of UN Peacekeeping'. *Global Governance* 13:1, 79–97.

—— (2010) 'Performance under Ambiguity: International Organization Performance in UN Peacekeeping'. *The Review of International Organizations* 5:3, 249–84.

Lovell, John P. (1984) '"Lessons" of U.S. military involvement: Preliminary Conceptualization'. In Donald A. Sylvan and Steve Chan (eds.), *Foreign Policy Decision Making: Perception, Cognition, and Artificial Intelligence*. New York, NY: Praeger, 129–57.

Maguire, Robert (1996) *Haiti Held Hostage: International Responses to the Quest for Nationhood*. Providence, RI: The Thomas J. Watson Jr. Institute for International Studies, Brown University.

Malan, Mark (2005) *Intelligence in African Peace Operations: Addressing the Deficit.* KAIPTC Paper No. 7. Accra: Kofi Annan International Peacekeeping Training Centre.

Malone, David M. and Ramesh Thakur (2001) 'UN Peacekeeping: Lessons Learned?' *Global Governance* 7:1.

Mani, Rama (2002) *Beyond Retribution: Seeking Justice in the Shadows of War.* New York: Polity Press.

March, James G. and Johan P. Olsen (1976) *Ambiguity and Choice in Organizations.* Bergen: Universitetsforlaget.

Mayall, James/Ricardo Soares de Oliveira (2011) Introduction in James Mayall/Ricardo Soares de Oliveira (eds) The New Protectorates. International Tutelage and the Making of Liberal States (New York: Columbia University Press).

Mayntz, Renate (ed.) (1968) *Bürokratische Organisation.* Köln: Kiepenheuer & Witsch.

Mazurana, Dyan and Khristopher Carlson (2004) *From Combat to Community: Women and Girls of Sierra Leone.* Cambridge, MA: Hunt Alternatives Fund.

McKay, Susan and Dyan Mazurana (2004) *Where are the Girls? Girls Fighting Forces Northern Uganda, Sierra Leone and Mozambique, their Lives after the War.* Toronto: Canada International Center for Human Rights and Democratic Development.

Meisler, Stanley (2007) *Kofi Annan. A Man of Peace in a World of War.* Hoboken, NJ: John Wiley & Sons.

Mobekk, Eirin (2005) *Identifying Lessons in United Nations International Policing Missions.* Geneva: Geneva Centre for the Democratic Control of Armed Forces (DCAF).

Muggah, Robert (2005) 'No Magic Bullet: A Critical Perspective on Disarmament, Demobilization and Reintegration (DDR) and Weapons Reduction in Post-conflict Contexts'. *The Round Table* 94:379, 239–52.

—— (2006) *Reflections on Disarmament, Demobilization and Reintegration in Sudan.* London: Overseas Development Institute.

—— (2007) *Great Expectations: (Dis)integrated DDR in Sudan and Haiti.* London: Overseas Development Institute.

—— (ed.) (2009) *Security and Post-conflict Reconstruction: Dealing with Fighters in the Aftermath of War.* New York: Routledge.

Myint-U, Thant and Elizabeth Sellwood (1999) *Knowledge and Multilateral Interventions: The UN's Experiences in Bosnia and Cambodia.* Working Paper, 33pp. London: Centre for History and Economics, King's College London.

Nagl, John A. (2005) *Learning to Eat Soup with a Knife. Counterinsurgency Lessons from Malaya and Vietnam.* Chicago, IL: University of Chicago Press.

Nichols, Ryan (2005) 'Disarming Liberia: Progress and Pitfalls'. In Eric G. Berman and Nicolas Florquin (eds.), *Armed and Aimless: Armed Groups, Guns, and Human Security in the ECOWAS Region.* Geneva: Small Arms Survey.

Nonaka, Ikujiro (1994) 'A Dynamic Theory of Organizational Knowledge Creation'. *Organization Science* 5:1, 14–37.

NUPI (2006) *A Fork in the Road or a Roundabout? A Narrative of UN Reform Process 2003–2005.* NUPI's UN Programme. Oslo: Norwegian Institute of International Affairs.

NYU-CIC (2004) *New Thinking on State Formation and Peacebuilding.* New York, NY: Center for International Cooperation, New York University.

—— (2009) *Peacekeeping Overstretch: Symptoms, Causes, and Consequences*. Background Paper for the thematic series 'Building more effective peace operations'. New York: Center for International Cooperation, New York University.

Oakley, Robert B. and Michael J. Dziedzic (1998) 'Conclusions'. In Robert Oakley, Michael J. Dziedzic, and Eliot M. Goldberg (eds.), *Policing the New World Disorder: Peace Operations and Public Security*. Washington, DC: National Defense University, 509–36.

O'Connor, Vivienne (2005) 'Traversing the Rocky Road of Law Reform in Conflict and Post Conflict States: Model Codes for Post Conflict Criminal Justice as a Tool of Assistance'. *Criminal Law Forum* 16, 231–55.

—— (2006) 'Rule of Law and Human Rights Protections through Criminal Law Reform: Model Codes for Post-conflict Criminal Justice'. *International Peacekeeping* 13:4, 517–30.

O'Neill, William G. (2008) 'UN Peacekeeping Operations and Rule of Law Programs'. In Agnès Hurwitz and Reyko Huang (eds.), *Civil War and the Rule of Law*. Boulder, CO: Lynne Rienner.

Oswald, Bruce (2005) *Addressing the Institutional Law and Order Vacuum: Key Issues and Dilemmas for Peacekeeping*. New York: UN DPKO, Peacekeeping Best Practices Unit.

Paes, Wolf-Christian (2005) 'The Challenges of Disarmament, Demobilization and Reintegration in Liberia'. *International Peacekeeping* 12:2, 253–61.

Paris, Roland (2004) *At War's End: Building Peace after Civil Conflict*. Cambridge: Cambridge University Press.

—— Timothy D. Sisk (eds.) (2009) *The Dilemmas of Statebuilding: Confronting the Contradictions of Postwar Peace Operations*. London, New York: Routledge.

Perito, Robert M. (2004) *Where Is the Lone Ranger When We Need Him? America's Search for a Post-Conflict Stability Force*. Washington, DC: United States Institute of Peace.

Perlez, Jane (2006) 'East Timor's Capital Spirals Into Violence, Despite U.N. Peacekeepers'. *New York Times*, May 28.

Peterson, Jenny H. (2009) "'Rule of Law' Initiatives and the Liberal Peace: The Impact of Politicised Reform in Post-conflict States'. *Disasters* 34:S1, S15–39.

Porter, Toby (2003) *The Interaction between Political and Humanitarian Action in Sierra Leone, 1995 to 2002*. Geneva: Centre for Humanitarian Dialogue.

Pouligny, Béatrice (2003) 'UN Peace Operations, INGOs, NGOs, and Promoting the Rule of Law: Exploring the Intersection of International and Local Norms in Different Postwar Contexts'. *Journal of Human Rights* 2:3, 359–77.

Power, Samantha (2008) *Chasing the Flame. Sergio Vieira de Mello and the Fight to Save the World*. New York: Penguin.

Pulver, Robert (2009) 'Rule of Law Programming by the United Nations: A Practitioner's Perspective'. Paper presented at the ISA's 50th Annual Convention, New York, February 15.

—— (2011) 'Rule of Law, Peacekeeping and the United Nations'. In Chandra Lekha Sriram, Olga Martin-Ortega, and Johanna Herman (eds.), *Peacebuilding and Rule of Law in Africa: Just Peace?* New York: Routledge, 60–87.

Rausch, Colette and Vivienne O'Connor (2007) 'Laying the Foundations of the Rule of Law in Post Conflict States: The Relevance and Applicability of Model Codes'. In

Agnes Hurwitz and Rekyo Huang (eds.), *Civil War and the Rule of Law: Security, Development, Human Rights*. Boulder, CO: Lynne Rienner.

Rees, Edward (2004) *Under Pressure: FALINTIL – Forcas de Defensa de Timor Leste. Three Decades of Defense Force Development in Timor-Leste (1975–2004)*. Geneva: Geneva Centre for the Democratic Control of Armed Forces (DCAF).

—— (2005) 'Public Security Management and Peace Operations. Kosovo and UNMIK: Never Land'. In Anja H. Ebnöther and Philipp H. Fluri (eds.), *After Intervention: Public Security Management in Post-Conflict Societies. From Intervention to Sustainable Local Ownership*. Geneva: Geneva Centre for the Democratic Control of Armed Forces (DCAF).

—— (2006) *External Study: Security Sector Reform (SSR) and Peace Operations: 'Improvisation and Confusion' from the Field*. New York: Peacekeeping Best Practices Section, UN Department of Peacekeeping Operations.

Reno, William (2001) 'The Failure of Peacekeeping in Sierra Leone'. *Current History* May 2001, 201–25.

Rice, Susan E. (2010) *Statement by Ambassador Susan E. Rice, Permanent Representative of the U.S. to the United Nations at the Special Committee on Peacekeeping Operations*. February 22, 2010.

Rid, Thomas (2007) *War and Media Operations: The US Military and the Press from Vietnam to Iraq*. Cass Military Studies. London: Routledge.

Rotmann, Philipp (2009) *First Steps Toward a Police Doctrine for UN Peace Operations (2001–2006)*. Geneva: International Police Executive Symposium, Geneva Centre for the Democratic Control of Armed Forces.

Roy, Alain Le (2009) 'Managing Complexity'. In Caty Clement and Adam C. Smith (eds.), *Managing Complexity: Political and Managerial Challenges in United Nations Peace Operations*. New York: International Peace Institute, 14–18.

Ryan, Jordan (2009) 'Speech by Jordan Ryan, Assistant Administrator and Director, Bureau for Crisis Prevention and Recovery'. *International Disarmament, Demobilization and Reintegration Congress (ICIDDR)*. 6 May 2009, Cartagena, Colombia.

Samuels, Kirsti (2006) 'Rule of Law Reform in Post-Conflict Countries, Operational Initiatives and Lessons Learnt'. World Bank Social Development Papers 37.

Sannerholm, Richard (2006) 'Beyond Criminal Justice: Promoting Rule of Law in Post-conflict Societies'. Paper presented at the Conference on Globalization and Peace-building, Uppsala, 6–9 November.

Seibel, Wolfgang (2009) 'UN-Friedensmissionen: Zwischen politischer und bürokratischer Logik'. *Universitas* 44:4, 346–71.

Senge, Peter (1990) *The Fifth Discipline: The Art and Practice of the Learning Organization*. New York: Doubleday Currency.

Senghaas-Knobloch, Eva, Jan Dirks and Andrea Liese (2003) *Internationale Arbeitsregulierung in Zeiten der Globalisierung. Politisch-organisatorisches Lernen in der Internationalen Arbeitsorganisation (IAO)*. Münster: LIT.

Serafino, Nina H. (2004) *Policing in Peacekeeping and Related Stability Operations: Problems and Proposed Solutions*. Washington, DC: Congressional Research Service.

Shetler-Jones, Philip (2008) 'Intelligence in Integrated UN Peacekeeping Missions: The Joint Mission Analysis Centre'. *International Peacekeeping* 15:4, 517–27.

Siebenhüner, Bernd (2008) 'Learning in International Organizations in Global Environmental Governance'. *Global Environmental Politics* 8:4, 92–116.

Smith, Joshua G., Victoria K. Holt and William J. Durch (2007) *Enhancing United Nations Capacity for Post-Conflict Policing and Rule of Law.* Report from the Project on Rule of Law in Post-Conflict Settings, Future of Peace Operations Program. Washington, DC: The Henry L. Stimson Center.

Specker, Leontine (2008) *The R-Phase of DDR processes: An Overview of Key Lessons Learned and Practical Experiences.* The Hague: Netherlands Institute of International Relations 'Clingendael'.

Stanley, William and Robert Loosle (1998) 'El Salvador: The Civilian Police Component of Peace Operations'. In Robert Oakley, Michael J. Dziedzic and Eliot M. Goldberg (eds.), *Policing the New World Disorder: Peace Operations and Public Security.* Washington, DC: National Defense University.

Stern, Eric (1997) 'Crisis and Learning: A Conceptual Balance Sheet'. *Journal of Contingencies and Crisis Management* 5:2, 69–86.

Strohmeyer, Hansjörg (2001a) 'Making Multilateral Interventions Work: The U.N. and the Creation of Transitional Justice Systems in Kosovo and East Timor'. *Fletcher Forum of World Affairs* 25:2.

—— (2001b) 'Policing the Peace: Post-Conflict Judicial System Reconstruction in East Timor'. *UNSW Law Journal* 24:1, 171–83.

Stromseth, Jane, David Wippman and Rosa Brooks (2006) *Can Might Make Rights? Building the Rule of Law after Military Interventions.* New York: Cambridge University Press.

Taylor, Mark and Rick Hooper (1999) *Command from the Saddle: Managing United Nations Peace-building Missions.* Oslo: Fafo Institute for Applied Social Science.

Thompson, James D. (1967) 'Boundary Spanning in Different Types of Organizations'. In James D. Thompson (ed.), *Organizations in Action. Social Science Bases of Administrative Theory.* New York: McGraw-Hill, 66–73.

Torjesen, Stina (2009) 'New Avenues for Research in the Study of DDR'. *Conflict, Security & Development* 9:4, 411–23.

Traub, James (2006) *The Best Intentions: Kofi Annan and the UN in the Era of American World Power.* New York: Farrar, Straus and Giroux.

UN ACABQ (2004) *Proposed budget for the period from 4 April 2004 to 30 June 2005 for the United Nations Operation in Côte d'Ivoire. Report of the Advisory Committee on Administrative and Budgetary Questions.* UN Document A/58/806.

—— (2005) *Second to Thirty-third Reports on the Proposed Programme Budget for the Biennium 2006–07 and Thirty-fourth to Forty-third Reports on the Programme Budget for the Biennium 2006–07.* UN Document A/60/7/Add.1-42.

UN CEB (2003) *Organizational Learning Framework Overview. Note presented by the UN System Learning Managers.* UN Document CEB/2003/HLCM/17.

UN DFS (2008a) *Opening Remarks of Ms. Jane Holl Lute, Fifth Committee, Tuesday, 4 March 2008. Agenda Item 133: Human Resource Management.* New York: United Nations (retrieved 2008-08-20 from http://www.un.org/Depts/dpko/dpko/articles/article040308.htm).

—— (2008b) *Statement of ASG Ms. Jane Holl Lute, Officer-in-Charge of the Department of Field Support, to the Special Committee on Peacekeeping Operations, 10 March 2008.* New

York: United Nations (retrieved 2008-08-20 from http://www.un.org/Depts/dpko/dpko/articles/JHLarticle100308.htm).

UNDP (2005) *Practice Note Disarmament, Demobilization and Reintegration of Ex-combatants.* New York: UN Development Programme.

—— (2007a) *Afghanistan Human Development Report.* United Nations Development Programme.

—— (2007b) *Strengthening the Rule of Law in Conflict- and Post-Conflict Situations: A Global UNDP Programme for Justice and Security 2008–2011.* Geneva: Bureau for Crisis Prevention and Recovery.

—— (2009) *The Rule of Law in Fragile and Post-Conflict Situations.* Geneva: Bureau for Crisis Prevention and Recovery.

UN DPI (1998) *Transcript of the Press Conference by Mr Bernard Miyet, Under-Secretary-General for Peacekeeping Operations, United Nations Headquarters, 29 May 1998.* New York United Nations Department of Public Information.

—— (2005) *UN Peacekeeping Mission in Timor-Leste Comes to an End.* UN News Centre, 2005-05-19.

—— (2006) *Annan Sends Seasoned Envoy to Timor-Leste Following Mob Violence.* UN News Centre, 2006-05-25.

—— (2007) *Electoral Unrest Continues in Timor-Leste as UN Police, Partners Deploy.* UN News Centre, 2007-08-08.

UN DPKO (1999) *Disarmament, Demobilization and Reintegration of ex-combatants in a Peacekeeping Environment – Principles and Guidelines.* New York: Lessons Learned Unit.

—— (2000) *United Nations Civilian Police Principles and Guidelines.* General Guidelines for Peacekeeping Operations. New York: United Nations Department of Peacekeeping Operations.

—— (2001) *Note by the Military Advisor, Major General Tim Ford (Australian Army), to Andrew Grene, Policy Analysis Unit, 2001-07-02,* 1pp. United Nations Department of Peacekeeping Operations.

—— (2003) *Handbook on Multidimensional Peace Operations.* New York: United Nations.

—— (2004) *Guidelines for Formed Police Unit in United Nations Mission in Liberia (UNMIL).* New York: Civilian Police Division, Department of Peacekeeping Operations.

—— (2005) *Gender Mainstreaming in Peacekeeping Operations Progress Report.* New York: UN Department of Peacekeeping Operations.

—— (2005) *Integrated Mission Planning Process.* New York: Training and Evaluation Service, UN Department of Peacekeeping Operations.

—— (2005) *Standard Operating Procedure: Development of DPKO Guidance Materials.* UN Document SOP/6400/ADM/05/01.

—— (2005a) *Guidelines for Formed Police Units on Assignment With Peacekeeping Operations.* UN Document DPKO/CPD/2005/00983.

—— (2005b) *Handbook on Policing in UN Peacekeeping Operations.* New York: Police Division, UN Department of Peacekeeping Operations.

—— (2005c) *Informal Paper on the Standing Police Capacity, 2005-08-22.* New York: UN Department of Peacekeeping Operations.

—— (2006) *DPKO Policy Directive: Gender Equality in UN Peace Operations.* New York: UN DPKO.

—— (2006) *Primer for Justice Components in Multidimensional Peace Operations: Strengthening the Rule of Law*. New York: Department of Peacekeeping Operations.

—— (2006a) *Capstone Doctrine for United Nations Peacekeeping Operations – Draft 2, 2006-07-08*, 44pp. United Nations Department of Peacekeeping Operations.

—— (2006a) *Establishment, Functions and Organization of the United Nations Standing Police Capacity (SPC). Policy Directive*. UN Document.

—— (2006b) *Functions and Organization of Formed Police Units in United Nations Peacekeeping Operations*. UN Document DPKO/PD/2006/00060.

—— (2006b) *United Nations Peace Operations: Improving Peace Operations Toward 2010. Tools for Professional Peacekeeping*. Presentation, dated February 2006. New York: UN Department of Peacekeeping Operations.

—— (2006c) *Guidelines for Formed Police Units on Assignment With Peacekeeping Operations*. UN Document DPKO/PD/2006/00015.

—— (2006d) *Support for the Reform, Restructuring and Rebuilding of Police and Law Enforcement Agencies*. UN Document DPKO/PD/2006/00070.

—— (2007) *Capstone Doctrine for United Nations Peacekeeping Operations – Draft 3, 2007-29-06*, 54pp. United Nations Department of Peacekeeping Operations.

—— (2009) *Methodology for Review of Justice and Corrections Components in United Nations Peace Operations*. UN Document 2009. 27.

—— (2010) *Justice Update*. UN Document April 2010.

—— (2010) *Second Generation Disarmament, Demobilization and Reintegration (DDR) Practices in Peace Operations*. UN Document.

—— (2010a) *Monthly Summary of Contributions (Police, Military Observers and Troops) as of 31 July 2010*. New York: United Nations Department of Peacekeeping Operations (retrieved 2010-08-19 from http://www.un.org/en/peacekeeping/contributors/2010/july10_1.pdf).

—— (2010b) *UN Missions Summary of Military and Police, 31-Jul-2010*. New York: United Nations Department of Peacekeeping Operations (retrieved 2010-08-19 from http://www.un.org/en/peacekeeping/contributors/2010/july10_4.pdf).

—— (not dated) *Monthly Summary of Military and Civilian Police Contribution to United Nations Operations, 1995–2004*. New York: United Nations Department of Peacekeeping Operations (retrieved 2010-08-19 from http://www.un.org/en/peacekeeping/contributors/documents/Yearly_Summary.pdf).

UN DPKO/DFS (2008) *United Nations Peacekeeping Operations: Principles and Guidelines*. New York, NY: United Nations Department of Peacekeeping Operations and Department of Field Support.

—— (2009) *Policy on Justice Components in United Nations Peace Operations*. UN Document.

UN DPKO/PBPU (2003) *Lessons Learned from United Nations Peacekeeping Experiences in Sierra Leone*. New York: Peacekeeping Best Practice Unit, DPKO.

—— (2004) *Lessons Learned Study on the Start-Up Phase of the United Nations Mission in Liberia*. New York, NY: UN DPKO, Peacekeeping Best Practices Unit.

—— (2005) *MONUC and the Bukavu Crisis 2004*. New York, NY: UN DPKO, Peacekeeping Best Practices Unit.

UN ECPS (2002) *Final Report: ECPS Task Force for Development of Comprehensive Rule of Law Strategies for Peace Operations*. Executive Committee on Peace and Security, 15.08.2002.

UN General Assembly (1998) *The Situation in Bosnia and Herzegovina*. UN Document A/RES/53/35.

—— (2005) *2005 World Summit Outcome*. UN Document A/RES/60/1.

—— (2005) *Administrative and Budgetary Aspects of the Financing of the United Nations Peacekeeping Operations: Cross-cutting Issues*. UN Document A/RES/59/296.

—— (2010) *Administrative and Budgetary Aspects of the Financing of the United Nations Peacekeeping Operations. Report of the Fifth Committee*. UN Document A/64/820.

UNIFEM (2004) *Getting it Right, Doing it Right: Gender and Disarmament, Demobilization and Reintegration*. New York: United Nations Development Fund for Women.

United Nations (2000) *Report of the Panel on United Nations Peace Operations*. UN Document A/55/305-S/2000/809.

—— (2004) *A More Secure World: Our Shared Responsibility. Report of the High-Level Panel on Threats, Challenges and Change*. New York: United Nations.

—— (2006) *Report of the United Nations Independent Special Commission of Inquiry for Timor-Leste*. Geneva: United Nations.

—— (2006) *The Integrated Disarmament, Demobilization and Reintegration Standards (IDDRS)*. New York: United Nations.

UN JIU (2005) *Evaluation of Results-Based Budgeting in Peacekeeping Operations*. UN Document JIU/REP/2005.

UNMIK (2008) *End-of-Mission Report of the Seventh Police Commissioner of the United Nations' International Police in Kosovo and the Kosovo Police Service, March 2007-February 2008*. Pristina: United Nations Mission in Kosovo.

UNMISET (2003) *Report of the Joint Assessment Mission carried out by The Government of Timor-Leste, UNMISET, UNDP and Development Partner Countries for the Timor-Leste Police Service*. Dili: United Nations Mission of Support in Timor-Leste.

UNMIT Transition Team (2006) *Mandate Implementation Plan*. Dili: United Nations Integrated Mission in Timor-Leste.

UNODC (2006) *Criminal Justice Assessment Toolkit*. Vienna: UN Office on Drugs and Crime.

UN OHCHR (2006a) *Rule of Law Tools for Post-conflict States: Mapping the Justice Sector*. New York and Geneva: Office of the United Nations High Commissioner for Human Rights.

—— (2006b) *Rule of Law Tools for Post-conflict States: Monitoring Legal Systems*. New York and Geneva: Office of the United Nations High Commissioner for Human Rights.

—— (2006c) *Rule of Law Tools for Post-conflict States: Prosecution Initiatives*. New York and Geneva: Office of the United Nations High Commissioner for Human Rights.

—— (2006d) *Rule of Law Tools for Post-conflict States: Truth Commissions*. New York and Geneva: Office of the United Nations High Commissioner for Human Rights.

—— (2006e) *Rule of Law Tools for Post-conflict States: Vetting, an Operational Framework*. New York and Geneva: Office of the United Nations High Commissioner for Human Rights.

—— (2008a) *Rule of Law Tools for Post-conflict States: Maximizing the Legacy of Hybrid Courts*. New York and Geneva: Office of the United Nations High Commissioner for Human Rights.

—— (2008b) *Rule of Law Tools for Post-conflict States: Reparations Programmes*. New York and Geneva: Office of the United Nations High Commissioner for Human Rights.

UN OIOS (2006) *Report of the Office of Internal Oversight Services on the Comprehensive Management Audit of the Department of Peacekeeping Operations*. UN Document A/60/717.

—— (2007) *Report of the Office of Internal Oversight Services on the Audit of the Management Structures of the Department of Peacekeeping Operations*. UN Document A/61/743.

UN Secretary-General (1998) *Report of the Secretary-General pursuant to General Assembly Resolution 53/35: The Fall of Srebrenica*. UN Document A/54/549.

—— (1999) *Report of the Secretary-General on the Situation in East Timor*. UN Document S/1999/1024.

—— (2000) *Fourth Report of the Secretary-General on the United Nations Mission in Sierra Leone*. UN Document S/2000/455.

—— (2000) *Note of Guidance on Relations between Representatives of the Secretary-General, Resident Coordinators and Humanitarian Coordinators*. UN Document.

—— (2000) *Report of the Secretary-General on the Implementation of the Report of the Panel on United Nations Peace Operations*. UN Document A/55/502.

—— (2000) *The Role of United Nations Peacekeeping in Disarmament, Demobilization and Reintegration*. UN Document S/2000/101.

—— (2001) *No Exit without Strategy: Security Council Decision-making and the Closure or Transition of United Nations Peacekeeping Operations. Report of the Secretary-General*. UN Document S/2001/394.

—— (2001a) *Implementation of the Recommendations of the Special Committee on Peacekeeping Operations and the Panel on United Nations Peace Operations. Report of the Secretary-General*. UN Document A/55/977.

—— (2001b) *Comprehensive Review of the Whole Question of Peacekeeping Operations in all their Aspects; Programme Budget Implications of Draft Resolution A/C.4/55/L.23*. UN Document A/C.5/55/46/Add.1.

—— (2002) *Women, Peace and Security*. Study submitted by the Secretary-General pursuant to Security Council resolution 1325 (2000), United Nations.

—— (2003) *Budget for the United Nations Mission in Liberia for the period from 1 August 2003 to 30 June 2004. Report of the Secretary-General*. UN Document A/58/539.

—— (2003) *Implementation of the Recommendations of the Special Committee on Peacekeeping Operations: Report of the Secretary-General*. UN Document A/57/711.

—— (2003) *Report of the Secretary-General to the Security Council on Liberia*. UN Document S/2003/875.

—— (2003a) *Budget for the Support Account for Peacekeeping Operations for the Period from 1 July 2003 to 30 June 2004*. UN Document A/57/732.

—— (2003b) *Report of the Secretary-General to the Security Council on Liberia*. UN Document S/2003/875.

—— (2004) *Report of the Office of Internal Oversight Services on the Evaluation of the Impact of the Recent Restructuring of the Department of Peacekeeping Operations*. UN Document A/58/746.

—— (2004) *The Rule of Law and Transitional Justice in Conflict and Post-conflict Societies*. UN Document S/2004/616.

—— (2004a) *Budget for the Support Account for Peacekeeping Operations for the Period from 1 July 2004 to 30 June 2005*. UN Document A/58/715.

—— (2004a) *Budget for the United Nations Operation in Côte d'Ivoire for the period from 4 April 2004 to 30 June 2005. Report of the Secretary-General*. UN Document A/58/788.

—— (2004b) *Implementation of the Recommendations of the Special Committee on Peacekeeping Operations: Report of the Secretary-General*. UN Document A/59/608.

—— (2004b) *Implementation of the Recommendations of the Special Committee on Peacekeeping Operations: Report of the Secretary-General*. UN Document A/58/694.

—— (2004c) *Report of the Secretary-General on Haiti*. UN Document S/2004/300.

—— (2004c) *Third Special Report of the Secretary-General on the United Nations Organization Mission in the Democratic Republic of the Congo* UN Document S/2004/650.

—— (2005) *Budget for the United Nations Organization Mission in the Democratic Republic of the Congo for the period from 1 July 2005 to 30 June 2006. Report of the Secretary-General*. UN Document A/60/389.

—— (2005a) *Administrative and Budgetary Aspects of Financing of the United Nations Peacekeeping Operations*. UN Document A/C.5/59/31.

—— (2005a) *Implementation of the Recommendations of the Special Committee on Peacekeeping Operations: Report of the Secretary-General*. UN Document A/60/640.

—— (2005b) *In Larger Freedom: Towards Development, Security and Human Rights for All*. New York: United Nations.

—— (2005b) *Report of the Secretary-General on Women and Peace and Security*. UN Document S/2005/636.

—— (2005c) *Sixth Progress Report of the Secretary-General on the United Nations Mission in Liberia*. UN Document S/2005/177.

—— (2006) *Investing in People. Report of the Secretary-General, Addendum: Reforming the Field Service Category: Investing in Meeting the Human Resources Requirements of United Nations Peace Operations in the Twenty-first Century*. UN Document A/61/255/Add.1.

—— (2006a) *Budget for the Support Account for Peacekeeping Operations for the Period from 1 July 2006 to 30 June 2007*. UN Document A/60/727.

—— (2006a) *Budget for the United Nations Organization Mission in the Democratic Republic of the Congo for the period from 1 July 2006 to 30 June 2007. Report of the Secretary-General*. UN Document A/60/840.

—— (2006a) *Report of the Secretary-General on Darfur*. UN Document S/2006/591.

—— (2006b) *Note of Guidance on Integrated Missions*. UN Document.

—— (2006b) *Report of the Secretary-General on the Sudan*. UN Document S/2006/160.

—— (2006b) *Tenth Progress Report of the Secretary-General on the United Nations Mission in Liberia*. UN Document S/2006/159.

—— (2006c) *Report of the Secretary-General on Timor-Leste Pursuant to Security Council Resolution 1690 (2006)*. UN Document S/2006/628.

—— (2006d) *Second Report of the Secretary-General on the United Nations Integrated Office in Sierra Leone.* UN Document 695.

—— (2006e) *Thirteenth Progress Report of the Secretary-General on the United Nations Mission in Liberia.* UN Document S/2006/958.

—— (2006f) *Uniting our Strengths: Enhancing United Nations Support for the Rule of Law.* UN Document A/61/636-S/2006/980.

—— (2007) *Peacekeeping Best Practices. Report of the Secretary-General.* New York: United Nations.

—— (2007a) *Civilian Career Peacekeepers. Report of the Secretary-General.* UN Document A/61/850.

—— (2007a) *Fifteenth Progress Report of the Secretary-General on the United Nations Mission in Liberia.* UN Document S/2007/479.

—— (2007b) *Comprehensive Report on Strengthening the Capacity of the United Nations to Manage and Sustain Peace Operations: Report of the Secretary-General.* UN Document A/61/858.

—— (2007b) *Fourteenth Progress Report of the Secretary-General on the United Nations Mission in Liberia.* UN Document S/2007/151.

—— (2008a) *Guidance Note of the Secretary-General: United Nations Approach to Rule of Law Assistance.* UN Document 28-03987, 14 April 2008.

—— (2008a) *Report of the Expert Mission to Timor-Leste on Policing, 17 to 27 March 2008.* UN Document S/2008/329 (annex).

—— (2008b) *Report of the Panel of Experts on the Standing Police Capacity's First Year of Operation. Note by the Secretary-General.* UN Document A/63/630.

—— (2008b) *Strengthening and Coordinating United Nations Rule of Law Activities.* UN Document A/63/226.

—— (2009) *Budget for the Support Account for Peacekeeping Operations for the Period from 1 July 2009 to 30 June 2010.* UN Document A/63/767.

—— (2010a) *Budget for the Support Account for Peacekeeping Operations for the Period from 1 July 2010 to 30 June 2011.* UN Document A/64/697.

—— (2010b) *Budget for the United Nations Logistics Base at Brindisi, Italy, for the Period from 1 July 2010 to 30 June 2011. Report of the Secretary-General.* UN Document A/64/698.

UN Security Council (1999) *Presidential Statement.* UN Document S/PRST/1999/21.

—— (1999) *Report of the Independent Inquiry into the Actions of the United Nations during the 1994 Genocide in Rwanda.* UN Document S/1999/1257, annex.

—— (1999) *Security Council Resolution 1272.* UN Document S/RES/1272 (1999).

—— (2000) *Security Council Resolution 1325.* UN Document S/RES/1325 (2000).

—— (2003) *Security Council Resolution 1509.* UN Document S/RES/1509 (2003).

—— (2003a) *4835th Meeting, Justice and the Rule of Law: the United Nations Role.* UN Document S/PV.4835.

—— (2003b) *Security Council Resolution 1509.* UN Document S/RES/1509 (2003).

—— (2008) *5895th Meeting: Post-conflict Peacebuilding.* UN Document S/PV.5895.

UN Special Committee on Peacekeeping Operations (2004) *Report of the Special Committee on Peacekeeping Operations and its Working Group at the 2004 Substantive Session.* UN Document A/58/19.

—— (2005) *Report of the Special Committee on Peacekeeping Operations and its Working Group at the 2005 Substantive Session*. UN Document A/59/19.

—— (2006) *Report of the Special Committee on Peacekeeping Operations and its Working Group at the 2006 Substantive Session*. UN Document A/60/19.

Urquhart, Brian (1998 [1993]) *Ralph Bunche. An American Odyssey*. New York: W. W. Norton.

Vieira de Mello, Sergio (2000) *How Not to Run a Country: Lessons for the UN from Kosovo and East Timor*, Dili: n/a (retrieved 2010-08-29 from http://www.jsmp.minihub.org/Resources/2000/INTERFET%20DETAINEE%20MANAGEMENT%20UNIT%20(e).pdf).

Villeneuve, Daniel and Marc-André Lefebvre (1996) 'Intelligence and the UN: Lessons from Bosnia - A Canadian Experience'. *Military Intelligence* 1996:4.

Watteville, Nathalie de (2002) 'Addressing Gender Issues in Demobilization and Reintegration Programs' *Africa Region Working Paper Series*. World Bank, May.

Weaver, Catherine (2008) *Hypocrisy Trap: The World Bank and the Poverty of Reform*. Princeton: Princeton University Press.

—— (2010) 'The Politics of Performance Evaluation: Independent Evaluation at the International Monetary Fund'. *The Review of International Organizations* 5, 365–85.

Weber, Max (1980 [1921]) *Wirtschaft und Gesellschaft. Grundriß der verstehenden Soziologie*. Tübingen: Mohr.

Weinlich, Silke (2010) *The UN Secretariat and Peace Operations: The Internationalization of Security Politics*. New York: Palgrave Macmillan.

Willibald, Sigrid (2006) 'Does Money Work? Cash Transfers to Ex-combatants in Disarmament, Demobilisation and Reintegration Processes'. *Disasters* 30:3, 316–39.

Wilson, Bu V.E. (2008) 'Smoke and Mirrors: Institutionalizing Fragility in the Polícia Nacional Timor-Leste'. In David Mearns (ed.), *Democratic Governance in Timor-Leste: Reconciling the Local and the National*. Darwin: Charles Darwin University Press.

Zeebroek, Xavier (2006) *Humanitarian Agenda 2015: Burundi and Liberia Country Studies*. Medford, MD: Feinstein International Center, Tufts University.

Index